Slovak Republic

Living Standards, Employment, and Labor Market Study

The World Bank
Washington, D.C.

CONTENTS

List of Tables

vi

List of Figures

List of Boxes

ABSTRACT

The Slovak Republic has achieved a high level of human and social development. The UNDP's *Human Development Report 2000* ranked the country 40th among all countries in its level of human development—the third highest among all the transition economies, and ahead of some countries with higher levels of income per capita.

Despite the country's high living standards and overall level of development, there are families in the Slovak Republic whose living conditions are below what is considered to be socially acceptable. By societal standards, these families and individuals are poor. Some may lack jobs, or not earn enough to adequately support their families; others may not have a sufficient level of skills or education; or they may suffer from ill-health; some may face discrimination, or simply lack the opportunities to improve their situation. To one degree or another, all these families are economically and socially deprived of the same freedoms of action and choice enjoyed by those who are better off.

The objective of this study is to analyze the phenomenon of poverty in the Slovak Republic and its relationship with labor market outcomes, so as to help design actions and policies to reduce poverty and improve the welfare of the Slovak population.

ACKNOWLEDGMENTS

This report was prepared by a team led by Ana Revenga and Carlos Silva-Jauregui and comprising Lucia Haulikova, Thesia Garner, Anton Marcincin, Dena Ringold, Manuel de la Rocha, Carolina Sanchez-Paramo, Helen Shahriari, Diane Steele, Katherine Terrell, and Ruslan Yemtsov. The work on the Roma benefited from the crucial inputs of a team of Slovak sociologists led by Iveta Radicova, and from the extensive knowledge and comments of Michal Vasecka. Duilio Pighi and Erlinda Inglis provided invaluable assistance with the production of the report.

The report also benefited from the constructive inputs of the peer reviewers—Alexandre Marc, Michelle Riboud and Radwan Shaban—and from comments by Emily Andrews, Mary Canning, Carlos Cavalcanti, Christine Jones, Bernard Funck, Kyle Peters, Helena Ribe and the Slovak Republic Country Team. Daniela Gressani, Maureen Lewis, and Pradeep Mitra all provided guidance to the report team at various stages. The work was carried out under the general direction of Roger Grawe, Country Director for the Slovak Republic.

The team would like to thank the Government of the Slovak Republic, and especially senior government officials from the Statistical Office, the Ministry of Labor and Social Affairs, the National Labor Office, the Ministry of Finance, and the National Bank of Slovak Republic, for the excellent cooperation received. The team also wishes to thank the many academics, researchers, NGO members, and representatives of the trade unions who met with the report team, for their productive discussions and inputs.

ACRONYMS AND ABBREVIATIONS

AFDC	Aid to Families with Dependent Children
CIS	Commonwealth of Independent States
EBRD	European Bank of Reconstruction and Development
ECA	Europe and Central Asia
EPL	Employment Protection Legislation
FDI	Foreign Direct Investment
FIAS	Foreign Investment Advisory Service
GDP	Gross Domestic Product
HEI	Higher Education Institutions
HZDS	Movement for a Democratic Slovak Republic
ILO	International Labor Organization
LFS	Labor Force Survey
MFIP	Minnesota Family Investment Program
MLS	Minimum Living Standard
MSL	Minimum Subsistence Level
NADSME	National Agency for the Development of Small and Medium Enterprises
NLO	National Labor Office
NPF	National Property Fund
OECD	Organization for Economic Co-operation and Development
PPP	Per Capita per Day
ROI	Roma Civic Initiative
SME	Small-Medium Enterprises
SNS	Nationalist Party
SOE	State Owned Enterprise
SSP	Self-Sufficient Program
TANF	Temporary Assistance to Needy Families
TI	Total Income
UR	Unemployment Registry

CURRENCY AND EQUIVALENT UNITS

Currency Unit = Slovak Koruna
US$1.0 = SKK 48.99
(As of August 9, 2001)

EXECUTIVE SUMMARY

LIVING STANDARDS, POVERTY AND INEQUALITY

By most indicators the Slovak Republic has achieved a high level of human and social development. The UNDP's *Human Development Report 2000* ranked the country 40th among all countries in its level of human development—the third highest among all the transition economies, and ahead of some countries with higher levels of income per capita. However, despite the country's generally high living standards and overall level of development, there are families in Slovak Republic whose living conditions are below what is considered to be socially acceptable. By societal standards, these families and individuals are poor. The objective of this study is to analyze this poverty, so as to help design measures and policies to reduce it. The study also seeks to understand the phenomenon of unemployment—the main cause of poverty—and propose actions to alleviate it.

Measuring Poverty

Poverty is multidimensional and goes well-beyond a narrow lack of material consumption or resources. It encompasses many other aspects, including the psychological pain of being poor, a sense of vulnerability to external events, and a sense of powerlessness vis-à-vis the institutions of the state and society. Unfortunately, measuring these non-material dimensions of poverty is extremely difficult as, often, the information needed to do so simply does not exist. In this study, as in most quantitative analyses of poverty, we focus mainly on a narrow definition of welfare that identifies poverty with a lack of material consumption or income.

As our main measure of household welfare, we use annual household monetary income, adjusted for household composition and thus, implicitly, for households' varying needs. The main data for our poverty analysis come from the 1996 Microcensus, which was administered in March 1997. These data describe annual household incomes and selected demographic variables for the previous year. A critical drawback of the 1996 Microcensus data is that they do not capture the impact of recent economic events in the country and hence may give an out-of-date picture of poverty. However, the absence of more recent nationally representative surveys prevent us from carrying out a more timely analysis. **This lack of adequate data represents a serious impediment to accurate poverty monitoring in the Slovak Republic; and makes it more difficult to design policies suited to combating poverty**.

The Slovak Republic stands out among the countries of Central and Eastern Europe as the only one lacking a recent nationally representative household budget survey measuring incomes and expenditures. The existing Household Budget Survey, which was last carried out in 1999, is unfortunately not nationally representative as it excludes many vulnerable groups—most notably, the unemployed. The lack of a timely and nationally representative household budget survey goes hand in hand with the absence of a well-defined strategy for monitoring and evaluating poverty. Building an adequate strategy for monitoring poverty and living standards should be Government priority, as it is impossible to measure the impact of economic policies and reforms—and hence difficult too make fully-informed policy choices- without such a system in place.

Launching a household budget survey that is nationally representative – based, for example, on the Census sampling frame- is an urgent and critical first step in developing an adequate poverty monitoring strategy. And it is an essential step in developing a system to monitor more broadly the evolution of living standards and the impact of economic policies and reforms. Such a survey needs to be carried out periodically and on a comparable basis. One such a survey is in place, moreover, it needs to be completed by instruments to measure (i) the dynamics of poverty (whether it is transient or permanent, for example); (ii) the impact of programs aimed at alleviating poverty or achieving other social goals; and (iii) the situation of particularly vulnerable groups such as the unemployed, or the Roma.

How Many Poor?

In this report we use several poverty lines. The first is the minimum subsistence level (as set by the government of the Slovak Republic) below which a family will find itself in a condition of material distress. The minimum subsistence level is not an internationally comparable measure, but is the most relevant from a policy perspective since it reflects the Government's implicit definition of poverty. A second poverty line is a common-use relative line, equal to 50 percent of median per equivalent adult income. We also use two absolute poverty based on purchasing power parity: US$2.15 purchasing power parity (PPP) per capita per day; and US$4.30 PPP per capita per day.

Using the MSL line, we find that in 1996 some 10.1 percent of individuals (7.9 percent of households) were poor (Table 1). However, poverty is very sensitive to the exact definition of the line. Increasing the poverty line by 10 percent, raises poverty at both the household and individual levels by approximately 30 percent. Decreasing the poverty line by 10 percent lowers poverty at both the household and individual levels by about 20 percent. This suggests that even small economic shocks can have potentially large effects on poverty. A positive shock (those associated with growth and good policies, for example) is associated with more-than-proportional declines in poverty; a negative shock (e.g., a recession) with more-than-proportional increases in poverty.

Table 1 Poverty Measures in the Slovak Republic, 1996 (% of households and individuals)

Poverty Line	Headcount		Depth		Severity	
	HH	Indiv.	HH	Indiv.	HH	Indiv.
Minimum subsistence level	7.9	10.1	2.8	3.4	1.6	2.0
50 percent median equivalent income	5.9	5.8	2.1	2.3	1.3	1.5
US$2.15 PPP per person per day	2.1	2.6	1.0	1.2	0.6	0.8
US$4.30 PPP per person per day	6.3	8.6	2.4	3.0	1.4	1.8

Notes: Poverty measure based on total income, including social transfers. Poverty depth measures how far the poor are, on average, below the poverty line. Poverty severity captures differences in the severity of poverty among the poor. *Source: 1996 Microcensus*

International Comparisons of Poverty

In terms of poverty, the Slovak Republic compares very favorably to other countries of the region (Table 2). Despite high unemployment, at US$4.30 PPP per person per day the incidence of poverty in 1996 was only 6.3 percent among households and 8.6 percent among individuals—one of the lowest poverty rates in the Europe and Central Asia region. However, although Slovakia has a much lower proportion of its population living under the US$4.30 PPP per person per day mark than do successful reformers such as Poland or Hungary, it has twice the population living under US$2.15 PPP per person per day than do those neighboring countries. In other words, there is a larger group of people at the very bottom of the income distribution in the Slovak Republic who are truly deprived in an absolute sense. Thus, **the Slovak Republic seems to have some deep pockets of poverty in the midst of a relatively well-off population**.

Who Are the Poor?

By examining the poverty risk for different groups of the population, one can gain useful insights into which factors are associated with poverty. This can then help us design potential policy responses. Because some of these risk factors may affect only a small share of the population, a group with high poverty risk need not necessarily account for a large fraction of the poor.

Table 2 Absolute Poverty Rates[a], Selected Transition Economies (percent of individuals)

Country	Year	At US$2.15 ppp/person/day	At US$4.30 ppp/person/day	GNP per capita[b]
Slovenia	1998	0.0	0.7	14,399
Czech Republic	1996	0.0	0.8	12,197
Hungary	1997	1.3	15.4	9,832
Slovak Republic	*1996*	*2.6*	*8.6*	*9,624*
Estonia	1998	2.1	19.3	7,563
Poland	1998	1.2	18.4	7,543
Croatia	1998	0.2	4.0	6,698
Lithuania	1999	3.1	22.5	6,283
Russian Federation	1998	18.8	50.3	6,186
Latvia	1998	6.6	34.8	5,777

Notes: [a] Headcount Index. Data for the Czech Republic and the Slovak Republic based on income measures, all other countries are consumption measures. [b] GNP per capita is from 1998 and is measured at purchasing power parity (PPP) using World Bank methodology. *Source: Table 1.1, World Bank (2000a) and Microcensus.*

We find three variables that are most strongly related to poverty: these are the *education* of the household head; the *employment status* of the household head; and the *location* of the household. Other aspects, such as demographic characteristics of the household including number of children and family size, are also very important determinants of poverty risk. Finally, ethnicity is very important, but hard to measure because of the difficulties of accurately identifying minority groups.

The group with the highest risk of poverty are households headed by a person who is unemployed. Nearly 45 percent of such households are poor; as compared to only 9 percent of those where the head is employed (Table 3). The risk of poverty a family headed by someone who is unemployed is thus four and a half times than that of the average family; and five times that of a household headed by someone who is employed. Households where the head has only an elementary education or less are also at a high risk of poverty, and approximately 14.3 percent of them are poor.

Table 3 Poverty Profile, 1996 (less than the minimum subsistence level)

	With all social transfers	Without transfers, with pensions	Without transfers, without pensions
Economic Activity of Household Head:			
Employed	9.0	17.3	20.5
Unemployed	44.7	79.7	82.9
Pensioner	6.0	10.5	78.8
Education of Household Head			
Elementary	14.3	24.5	64.1
Apprenticeship	8.8	20.5	42.0
Middle vocational	10.1	21.8	36.2
Completed middle vocational	8.2	14.7	28.1
Completed middle general	12.8	22.5	38.3
Higher vocational	11.1	16.7	42.2
University	7.9	9.9	22.0
Total	*10.1*	*18.7*	*38.3*

Notes: Individuals. Regions defined using old classification for comparability with Table 1.16 below.
Source: 1996, Microcensus

There are important differences in poverty risks both across regions, and between urban and rural households within the same region. Overall, the highest poverty rates are found for Kosice and Trencin (Table 4).

The demographic composition of the household also has a significant impact on the risk of poverty. Families with children appear to have a much higher risk of poverty than families without children, and the risk tends to increase significantly with the

Table 4 Poverty Risk by Region (%), 1996

	Urban	Rural	Total
Bratislava	9.0	20.8	9.4
Trnava	7.0	8.6	7.6
Trencin	13.0	8.6	12.2
Nitra	11.6	7.1	9.9
Zilina	7.9	10.5	8.6
Banska Bystrica	8.5	10.4	8.9
Presov	10.1	7.6	9.7
Kosice	13.5	16.4	14.3
Total	*10.1*	*10.1*	*10.1*

Notes: The unit of observation is the individual. Poverty measured as HH income less than the minimum subsistence level. *Source: 1996 Microcensus.*

number of dependents. Families with three children or more, for example, represent only 6.3 percent of the population, but account for 18.1 percent of the poor. By age groups, children faced the highest risk of poverty, while the elderly faced a much lower risk of poverty than other groups (Figure 1), reflecting the impact of the pension system.

The Role of the Safety Net

Poverty in the Slovak Republic would be much higher if households were not helped by very substantial social transfers. The overall incidence of poverty would jump from 10.1 percent of individuals to 18.7 percent in the absence of all transfers except for pensions—a huge

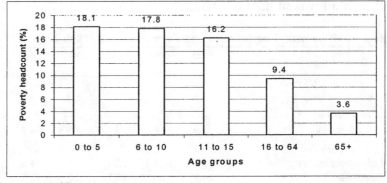

Figure 1 Poverty by Age Group, 1996

Source: Table 1.13.

increase. The increase in poverty would be even more marked for certain vulnerable groups. Among households where the head is unemployed, for example, poverty would increase from 44.7 percent to nearly 80 percent. Poverty among households with little education would increase by over 10 percentage points, as would poverty in certain regions. Poverty among children would also increase sharply.

Changes in Poverty Between 1992 and 1996

By most measures, poverty increased between 1992 and 1996. During this period, the profile of poverty remained fairly constant—with the same groups facing the greatest risk. However, some of the differentiation between groups has blurred, suggesting that poverty is spreading beyond easily defined groups. The lack of nationally representative data prevents us from examining what has happened to poverty since 1996. However, most indicators—such as the number of people requesting social assistance—would suggest that it has increased further since 1996. Given the strong correlation between poverty and the employment status of the household head, the fact that unemployment among the latter is growing is a reason for special concern.

THE CHALLENGE OF GENERATING EMPLOYMENT

Rising Unemployment and Inactivity

High unemployment is the Achilles heel of Slovak Republic's economic performance to date, and the country's most pressing social problem. Despite maintaining fairly robust growth rates since 1994, the number of unemployed in Slovak Republic has steadily mounted, reaching some 498,000 in the second quarter of 2000 (according to the LFS).[1] This represents about 18.7 percent of the labor force (Table 5)—the highest rate of unemployment in all of the OECD. Unemployment has

---

[1] Figures on *registered* unemployment, which are available on a more timely basis, are significantly higher. As of February 2001, some 558,726 were registered as unemployed, equivalent to 20.7 percent of the labor force.

risen in every region of the country—although much more in some regions than others—and among all groups of workers. Workers with only primary or secondary education have been more affected by unemployment than university graduates, but even among the latter unemployment has been rising.

Table 5 GDP Growth, Employment and Unemployment, 1993-2000

	1993	1994	1995	1996	1997	1998	1999	2000	Avg. 93-00
GDP, constant 1995 prices, *Annual % change*	1.9	4.9	6.7	6.2	6.2	4.1	1.9	1.8	4.2
Total employment, *Annual % change*	-2.6	-1.0	2.4	-1.4	-2.3	-1.0	-1.8	-1.4	-1.1
Unemployment rate									
Labor force survey	13.7	14.1	12.4	10.9	11.8	12.5	17.1	18.7	13.9
Registered	14.4	14.6	13.1	12.8	12.5	15.6	19.2	17.9	15.0
Labor force participation rate	--	70.8	70.9	70.7	67.6	66.8	66.3	66.6	68.5
Average wage, constant 1995 prices *Annual % change*	-3.9	3.0	4.3	10.6	6.6	1.7	-2.8	-3.1	2.1
Inflation, annual % change *CPI*	23.2	13.4	9.9	5.8	6.1	6.7	10.6	12.0	10.9

Source: Statistical Office of the Slovak Republic; National Labor Office, IMF.

As the rate of unemployment has increased so has the average duration of unemployment. At present more than 50 percent of all unemployed individuals have been so for more than a year. The share of long-term unemployment in total unemployment has remained stable over time, and has not really responded to either business cycle fluctuations nor to reforms in the unemployment insurance system—pointing towards deep structural causes of unemployment. Overall, flows in and out of unemployment are low, leading to little turnover among the stock of unemployed.

Unemployment developments reflect only a part of the underlying negative employment trends, as many unemployed workers have become discouraged and left the labor force. As a result of the combined rise in unemployment and fall in labor force participation, employment as a share of working age population—a good measure of the extent to which Slovak Republic is employing its *potential* labor resources—has dropped to 50.3 percent. This is significantly below the EU average of 61.1 percent and much below the OECD average of 65.1 percent (Figure 2). It suggests that a large (and rising) share of the potential Slovak workforce is idle.

Activity rates among Slovak men are strikingly low: employment to working age population ratios for men average 71 percent for the EU and 76 for the OECD as a whole; as compared to only 55 percent for Slovak Republic (Figure 2). The only other countries with relatively low activity rates for men are Hungary and Poland, suggesting that there may be some common elements due to transition. Nevertheless, both Hungary and Poland have male employment to population rates above 60 percent. Regardless of the cause, the fact that roughly only one-half of Slovak Republic's potential labor resources are employed means that the country is not fully exploiting its growth possibilities.

In the Fall of 1998 a new coalition Government took office and immediately announced its intentions to reverse the policies that threatened Slovak Republic's economic and political stability. Difficult but necessary measures have been introduced to cope with the fundamental imbalances and to reinvigorate the structural reform agenda. Since coming to power, the new government has successfully stabilized the economy and has launched an ambitious program of structural reforms. The Government's efforts have been recognized by the international community as indicated by the resumption of accession negotiations with the EU in November 1999, Slovak Republic's entry into the OECD in May 2000, the continuous improvement in the country's credit ratings, and the sharp decline in borrowing spreads. There will be lags before these measures have a positive impact on growth and employment, and indeed they may have contributed to increase the unemployment levels in the short term, but the medium- and long-term gains from these measures far outweigh the costs, and should reinvigorate the labor market.

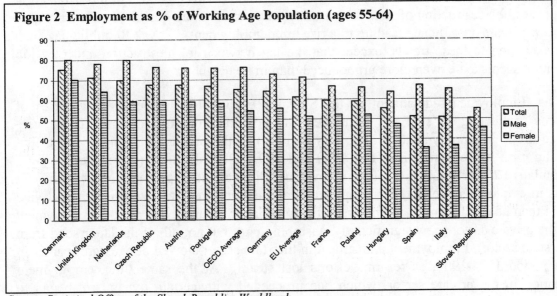

Figure 2 Employment as % of Working Age Population (ages 55-64)

Source: Statistical Office of the Slovak Republic; Worldbank

What Lies Behind the Sharp Rise in Unemployment and Inactivity?

Three main factors lie behind the spectacular rise in unemployment and inactivity in the Slovak Republic:

- The first factor is widespread *job reallocation* associated with transition, which has resulted so far in a net loss of jobs. A lag between the destruction of old, non-viable jobs and the creation of new ones is to be expected, but in the case of Slovak Republic this lag may have been accentuated by the reluctance of the previous administration to undertake widespread structural reforms, and by fundamental macroeconomic imbalances during 1996-1998;

- The second factor is the existence of severe mismatches between existing stock of labor resources and what is demanded in the new market economy. This mismatch has an important skills component—new jobs being created require skills that are very different from those offered by available workers—but also a location component as most of the emerging job opportunities are not located in the same geographical areas as the large pools of unemployed; and

- The third factor results from the interaction of demographic changes, labor supply decisions and job search behavior patterns. Large cohorts entering the labor market have put upward pressure on unemployment, while job search behavior has been negatively affected by the existence of unemployment and social assistance benefits which are very generous relative to the minimum wage.

Job Creation and Job Destruction

One of the main features of the transition process everywhere has been the massive reallocation of labor: first, from the state sector to the new private sector, comprising both new and privatized firms; and second, from the initially predominant industrial sectors to new activities in services and trade (EBRD, 2000). In most transition countries, the destruction of state jobs has happened much more quickly than the creation of new private ones, hence leading to a rise in unemployment. Slovak Republic has been no exception to these trends, except that the lag between job destruction and new job creation seems to be even more pronounced than in its neighbors.

Employment adjustment in the Slovak Republic has happened in a series of "steps", reflecting the stop and go nature of support for economic reforms. There were large drops in employment coming very early on in the process, accompanying a first strong push on reforms. Between 1989 and 1993, GDP declined (in real terms) by a cumulative 25 percent, while total employment fell by about 15 percent. Most of this net loss in employment reflected widespread labor shedding in state enterprises, which had until then hoarded significant amounts of surplus labor. During this period, employment in the private sector grew significantly, absorbing part, but not all, of the labor shed from the state sector. Employment adjustment in the state sector slowed down significantly in the period 1994-1998, as reforms efforts lost steam. At the same time, employment creation in the private sector, which had proceeded with certain dynamism, began to stagnate as more and more financial and investment resources began to be absorbed by the state, particularly in 1997-1998. When the macroeconomic crisis hit in 1998, the country suffered from a renewed round of layoffs, but this time coming from both state and private sectors. Although between 1994-2000, GDP has grown by an average annual rate of 4.7 percent, total employment has remained largely unchanged.

All in all, the data suggest that there is little net employment creation in the Slovak labor market. At the same time, economic restructuring appears to have slowed down significantly between 1994-1998. This points to a relatively sluggish labor market in which there are relatively few movements across labor market states (from employment into unemployment, and vice-versa). These trends are confirmed by evidence from firm-level data on job creation and job destruction. Job creation in Slovak Republic is low, and below that seen in neighboring countries. Gross job turnover in Slovak Republic is much lower than in Poland or other OECD economies: 5.59 percent on average for 1994-1998, as compared to 17.5 percent for Poland, or 15.3 percent for the

United Kingdom. This is mainly due to differences in gross job creation, as gross job destruction rates are closer to those seen elsewhere, albeit if still low (Figure 3).

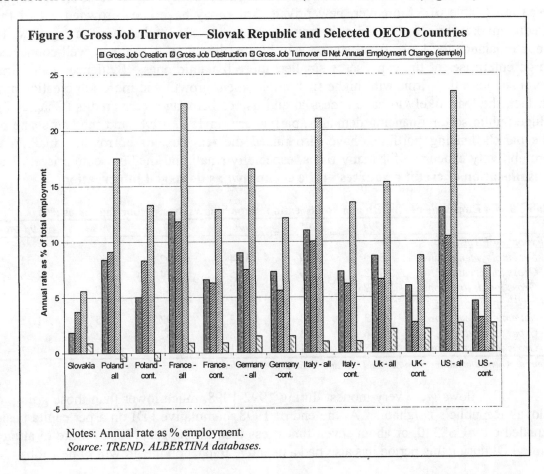

Figure 3 Gross Job Turnover—Slovak Republic and Selected OECD Countries

Notes: Annual rate as % employment.
Source: TREND, ALBERTINA databases.

Most of the new jobs are being created in services and in a few manufacturing industries such as metal products; transport equipment; leather, wood and paper. What is interesting is that several of these industries also have the highest rates of job destruction. The fact that **most job destruction takes place in the same industries that are creating most new jobs** indicates that a large share of job reallocation occurs within industries, as the result of labor moving from declining firms to expanding ones. This feature is not unique to Slovak Republic, but has been found for Poland (World Bank, 2001) and other countries as well (Haltiwanger, 2000). It indicates that **economic restructuring and job creation often go hand-in-hand—i.e., that you need to allow job destruction in order to create new jobs**. It also suggests that factors leading to job creation act primarily at the firm level, and not at the level of an industry. Thus policies aiming at creating (or saving) jobs at the industry level may be completely misdirected. What matters is ensuring that there is a favorable operating and investment environment at the firm-level.

Why is Job Creation so Low?

Our analysis suggests that a reluctance to allow more widespread restructuring during good part of the mid-1990s—while it may have postponed the inevitable job destruction—may have also affected the ability of the Slovak economy to create new, better jobs. **A pattern of growth biased against exports has not helped either, as it has stifled the most dynamic part of the Slovak economy—at least in terms of job creation** (Table 6). Moreover, new private firms may have been crowded out of the credit market by huge public borrowing requirements, tight monetary policy to counterbalance the loose fiscal stance, and by the directing of credit to well-connected large enterprises at the expense of smaller, more dynamic ones. Evidence at the firm level suggests that firms with higher net employment growth and more job creation are, in fact, the least likely to have access to and use of banking sector credits (Chapter 2). Huge public sector financing demands, particularly in 1997-1998, and the bad shape of the bank's lending portfolio, have also raised the real cost of borrowing, making it prohibitively expensive for many firms, especially small and medium enterprises. The **misallocation of credit resources in the economy has damaged job creation**.

Table 6 Net Employment Growth and Job Creation, Exporting vs. Non-Exporting Firms (%)

	1994	1995	1996	1997	1998	Avg 94-98
Exporting Firms						
Net employment growth	-5.19	3.89	6.84	4.92	3.57	4.31
Gross job creation	0.13	2.59	3.75	2.74	2.95	2.29
Gross job destruction	-1.67	-2.51	-1.53	-2.85	-4.98	-2.56
Non-Exporting Firms						
Net employment growth	-5.73	-4.03	1.88	-0.92	-2.95	-1.71
Gross job creation	0.06	2.03	1.48	2.52	1.42	1.67
Gross job destruction	-1.68	-7.71	-1.21	-4.26	-8.14	-4.83

Source: Own calculations from ALBERTINA and TREND firm databases.

FDI flows were very modest during 1992-1998, much lower than those going to Slovak Republic's neighbors. At the end of 1998, cumulative FDI on a per capita basis equaled only US$340, or about seven times less than in Hungary. The failure to attract more FDI during this period has also had a negative impact on the growth of new jobs.

Significant efforts have been made by the current administration to change the international perception about Slovak Republic. This effort has been successful. In combination with the recent OECD membership and a renewed and transparent privatization effort, particularly in the financial sector, these efforts have underpinned a steady increase in FDI flows. By 2000 FDI flows to Slovak Republic were estimated to have reached 8 percent of GDP, over four times the level attained in 1998 and almost seven times the average reached during 1994-1998.

Small and medium enterprises—elsewhere the engine of job creation—appear to face some serious obstacles in their development and expansion. In a recent survey of firms, high borrowing costs, were deemed to be a **critical** problem by 56.6 percent of small firms surveyed. A high level of taxes, the complexity of tax regulations, and restrictive entry procedures were also identified as additional barriers.

High rates of taxation of labor have also worked against job creation. In addition to high corporate income tax rates, Slovak firms face very high rates of social security payroll contributions. While this problem is common to many countries, it may be particularly acute in Slovak Republic. High payroll taxes increase the cost of labor, and create a wedge between labor costs and wages that both burdens employers and discourages labor supply. The problem of payroll taxes may be particularly acute for

SMEs, for whom the costs of complying with payroll taxes and with the necessary administrative procedures are likely to be higher than for big firms.

High payroll taxes may introduce a bias against unskilled labor since the wedge is more burdensome at lower incomes. For higher-skill workers, business can more easily separate compensation into a wage and non-wage component; in addition it is also easier to understate true incomes for workers at the top of the scale. Moreover, **data at the regional level suggest that high payroll taxes and non-wage costs are more burdensome in proportional terms in poorer regions. Adding this to the existence of large labor productivity differentials between rich and poor regions suggests that payroll taxes may be making labor in the lagging areas actually more expensive in relative terms**.

In this context, reducing social security contributions could help boost job creation and reduce employment in the gray economy. Such reductions would diminish the wedge between gross and net salaries, increasing both labor demand and incentives to work. However, these cuts need to be very carefully designed to avoid further straining the government budget and the large deficits that plagued Slovak Republic in the past. Preferably, they should be carried out only within the context of a general reform of social security benefits and unemployment insurance, in order to eliminate the perverse incentives and unemployment traps that the current system is generating (see Chapter 3).

The Importance of Regional and Skill Mismatches

Labor demand factors can yield only a part of the overall employment picture. An equally important determinant of employment and unemployment outcomes is the process by which labor demand and labor supply get matched: or in other words, how the labor market and its institutions mediate the process of transiting from old jobs (or no jobs) to new jobs. In this regard, **all indicators give evidence of serious matching problems in the Slovak labor market**.

A first indicator of mismatch is the existence of wide disparities in unemployment outcomes across regions and localities. Although the Slovak Republic is not a large country, the differences in unemployment rates between prospering areas and disadvantaged areas are huge. The district with highest unemployment is Rimavská Sobota, with a rate of 37.6 percent; the district with the lowest rate of unemployment is Bratislava IV, with only 4.8 percent unemployment—nearly eight times less. Moreover, the variability of unemployment rates across and within regions has been increasing over time, both in absolute and relative terms. Even in regions with low overall unemployment there is very high variability across districts. This indicates that there are districts with high unemployment in close proximity to districts with low unemployment.

A second, commonly-used, indicator of mismatch is the ratio of job seekers to job postings—that is the number of unemployed per vacancy. Figure 4 plots these ratios for the Slovak Republic as a whole, and by region. The figure shows that for country as a whole the number of unemployed per vacancy has increased more than fourfold, from 18 at end-1997 to 84 at end-2000. For certain depressed regions, the increase has been even sharper: for example, by end-2000 in the Kosice region there were 266 unemployed (or potential job seekers) per posted vacancy. Clearly, the expectations of getting a job for an unemployed individual in Kosice are very low.

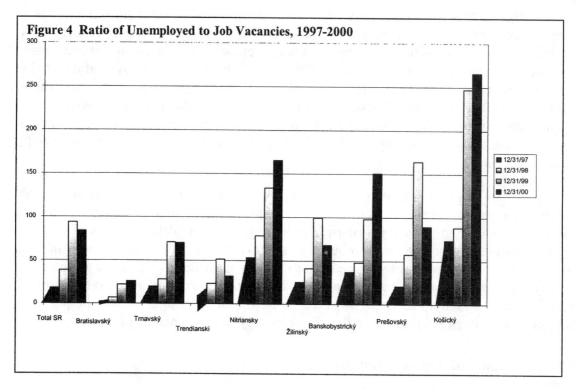

Figure 4 Ratio of Unemployed to Job Vacancies, 1997-2000

In addition to a geographical dimension, mismatch in the labor market also seems to have a skill component. A big fraction of the stock of the unemployed are workers with basic or less than basic education (including those who have not completed any formal schooling). Yet all evidence suggests that new jobs are demanding a higher level of skills. Workers with basic or less than basic education represent almost a third of the total unemployed, and nearly 40 percent of the long-term unemployed (those unemployed for over a year). Unemployment rates for workers with completed basic education are hovering around 30 percent; while those for the small group of workers with no completed formal education at all (mainly Roma) reach an outstanding 90 percent.

Barriers to Labor Mobility

The existence of large and persistence differences in unemployment rates across regions and districts suggests that there are significant barriers to labor mobility. Indeed, by most measures the extent of internal mobility has declined by almost 25 percent since the 1980s. The biggest problem to mobility seems to be the housing market. A first deterrent is the high cost of home purchase in better off regions, such as Bratislava. A second barrier is a narrow and expensive rental market, especially in the Bratislava region. And a third barrier is the continued existence of complex administrative regulations and requirements governing a change of permanent address.

Another reason why families may be reluctant to move away from depressed regions is because of social networks and the importance of family and friends as a means of support—especially when someone is unemployed. The amount of aid Slovak households receive from family and friends is very significant, and higher than in other CEEC countries. These networks are also very important to finding jobs. To the extent that moving residences may imply moving away from these support networks, it could have a large dampening effect on mobility. A similar phenomenon, for example, has been documented in Spain, where family support networks and changes have proved critical to the unemployed. The role of family support has been one factor explaining the persistence of regional unemployment differentials there.

UNEMPLOYMENT, INCENTIVES AND THE SOCIAL SAFETY NET

An Extensive System

The Slovak Republic provides cash benefits and support services to many jobless individuals and families through a web of programs. The scope of these programs as well as their coverage are broad, even for European standards, with total cash payments (including pensions) exceeding SK95 billion, or 14 percent of GDP, in 1999 (Table 7). Like other safety nets, the role of the Slovak system is twofold. It provides income for those who are not employed and whose income falls below the poverty level, and it aims to stimulate these individuals to find a job and obtain their own means of subsistence. **The safety net has been tremendously effective in achieving the first goal. Poverty in Slovak Republic would be significantly higher if its social assistance/support and unemployment insurance programs were to disappear.**

Table 7 Expenditure on Social Assistance and Labor Market Policies (in millions SK)

	Social Assistance		Labor Market Policies		Benefits to registered unemployed (Total)
	Total	To registered Unemployed	Passive (UI[A] benefits)	Active	
1991	NA	NA	NA	NA	NA
1992	2,218	1,526	1,711	3,812	3,237
1993	3,120	2,200	1,859	1,107	4,059
1994	5,134	3,824	1,710	1,896	5,534
1995	5,517	4,058	2,181	3,899	6,239
1996	5,510	3,850	3,063	4,290	6,913
1997	5,891	4,154	3,989	3,098	8,143
1998	7,978	5,813	5,484	2,289	11,297
1999	11,599	8,790	7,292	474	16,082

[A] Unemployment Insurance.
Source: Social Policy. Ministry of Labor, Social Affairs and Family.

However, while effective in fighting poverty, such a generous social safety net can also have negative effects—specifically it can alter the incentives of workers and individuals to look for a job and pull themselves out of poverty. And it can, if poorly designed, create a "poverty trap" for certain groups—for example, by excessively penalizing those who do manage to find a job and pull themselves just above the "cut-off" level for benefit recipiency. These types of phenomena have been extensively documented in many OECD economies. Simulations of replacement ratios for different types of families suggest that similar perverse incentives may hold in the Slovak case. Specifically, the simulations suggest that:

- Individuals who expect to be re-employed at the minimum wage level have few incentives to look for a job. The disincentive effects of unemployment insurance and social assistance/support should be strongest for workers with low levels of education;

- Disincentives are stronger when receiving unemployment insurance than when receiving social assistance/support because the payments are larger under the former (i.e., replacement ratios are higher). However, the unlimited duration of social assistance, together with its conditionality on income, can also have pervasive effects, especially at the household level;

- The smaller the worker's potential contribution to total household income, the more important the opportunity cost of working and the weaker the incentives for job search and further employment. This mechanism is specially relevant in the case of secondary earners;

- Disincentive effects are aggravated by the presence of children and the payment of child (or parental) allowances, since these bring the replacement ratio of actual income to potential income closer to one, or even above one in the case of families with low levels of education/low income; and

- Finally, all this implies that it is possible for certain households to be worse off when both adults are employed than when only one of them is because the potential net contribution to total household income of the secondary earner is very small, or even negative.

Impact on Behavior and Incentives

Our analysis suggests that, at least on theoretical grounds, there are likely to be some serious disincentive effects for families with low earning potential. However, there is still a large gap between what theory may predict and what may actually happen. For this reason, we try to go beyond simple simulations and carry out an actual empirical analysis of the behavior of unemployed individuals, both for those who are receiving support and those who are not; and for those who received support at some point in time and have since exhausted it. For this purpose, we use very detailed data on benefit recipiency from the Unemployment Registry (1990-2000) and the Labor Force Survey (1996, 1999 and 2000).

Based on our empirical analysis, we find that workers who receive UI benefits, social assistance, or social support tend to spend more time

Table 8 Unemployment Duration by Unemployment Insurance (UI) Recipiency

Duration of spell (in months)	% of all spells with UI	% of all spells without UI
Less than 3	21.40	48.35
4 to 6	21.02	16.19
6 to 12	25.90	14.38
12 to 24	19.92	11.17
More than 24	11.77	9.92

Source: Unemployment Registry, 1990-2000.

unemployed than workers who are not entitled to these benefits (Table 8 and Figure 5). In particular, the average spell for recipients is about 2 months longer than the average spell for non-recipients, and benefit entitlement explains most of this difference. This signals the existence of disincentive effects associated with these programs.

However, workers who receive unemployment insurance and/or social assistance/support also look for employment more actively than their counterparts, and have more demanding preferences regarding their future jobs. This seems to suggest that benefit payments, by reducing the opportunity cost of unemployment, act as a subsidy for these workers' search time and allow them to be 'choosier'. In addition, and maybe as a consequence of the above, **benefit**

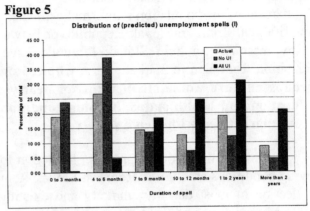

Figure 5

Source: Unemployment Registry.

recipients find jobs in the private sector more often, and these jobs turn out to be better matches than the ones obtained by non-recipients (where match quality is measured as duration of the match)—the average employment spell for those who received unemployment insurance/social assistance/support is almost 11 months long, compared to 9 months for workers with no benefits.

These results have to be interpreted with caution. Given the demographic differences that exist between recipients and non-recipients, it is difficult to draw any causal conclusions from the analysis. In particular, we cannot dismiss completely the idea that benefit recipients constitute a pool of better workers, younger and more educated, who search more actively and find jobs more often anyway, regardless of their entitlement status. However, when we use these workers as their own control group, examining their own behavior while they are receiving benefits and when the stop receiving them, we *do* find strong evidence that both unemployment insurance and social assistance/support have important disincentive effects, not only on unemployment duration, but also on search behavior and on exit-to-employment.

Specifically, we find that the behavior of recipients varies tremendously depending on whether they are currently receiving benefits or not. Their probability of exit from unemployment is very low while receiving benefits, and very high once the benefits are over. Similarly, although recipients have a much high probability of finding a job in the private sector than non-recipients, this probability is very small while receiving benefits, and very large afterwards. Recipients also search more than non-recipients (active search), but they search less when they are receiving benefits than when they stop receiving them.

POVERTY AND THE ROMA

Poverty and Living Conditions

The Slovak Republic has one of the largest Roma populations in Europe. Although the 1991 census identified only 75,802 individuals as Roma—or just 1.4 percent of the population—informal estimates suggest that there are between 420,000 and 500,000 Roma in Slovak Republic, or between 8-10 percent of the population. For many reasons, Roma in Slovak Republic have been hardest hit by the process of transition from plan to market. **As a whole, Roma are poorer than other population groups and are worse off in terms of nearly all basic social indicators, including education and health status, housing conditions and access to opportunities in the labor market and within civil society.**

Despite these developments, limited information is available on poverty and living conditions among the Roma in Slovak Republic. Privacy legislation prohibits the collection of most data by ethnicity and existing quantitative surveys – including the 1996 Microcensus and the 1991 census—have been found to significantly underestimate the Roma population, due to problems with self-reporting of ethnicity and under sampling of areas where Roma are likely to live. To address these information gaps, this study included a qualitative survey specifically focused on documenting conditions in Roma settlements.[2]

In contrast with the situation of Roma living in other countries in Central and Eastern Europe, more Roma in Slovak Republic live in settlements, on the outskirts of villages and towns. An estimated one-fourth of Roma in Slovak Republic live in settlements, many of which are in the poorer eastern regions of the country. Settlements vary significantly based upon geographic location and the level of ethnic segregation. Some settlements have their roots in policies adopted during the Second World War and early socialist period, which required Roma to move outside of towns. The population of Roma in settlements has been growing in the past decade, as many Roma have returned to settlements because of the availability of cheaper housing.

Poverty in Roma settlements is closely linked to three factors: (i) regional economic conditions; (ii) the proximity of the settlement to a neighboring town or village; and (iii) the degree of ethnic integration or segregation of the settlement. The situation of Roma in more economically developed regions is generally more favorable than that of Roma in poorer areas. Within regions, the level of poverty in a Roma settlement seems to be closely connected to the level of ethnic integration and segregation. Conditions in settlements which consisted only of Roma were significantly worse off than more integrated communities. The most segregated and geographically isolated settlements are the most economically and socially disadvantaged. In almost all of the completely segregated settlements formal unemployment was close to 100 percent.

---

[2] The study is a non-representative sociological study of settlements in the districts of Malacky, Stará Lubovna, and Rimavská Sobota.

Poor Roma identify several common elements of poverty, including: inadequate nutrition, poor housing conditions and ill health. Ability to provide a good education for their children and lead a better life are also identified as important, but take second place to more immediate issues of hunger and living conditions. Roma also view exclusion and discrimination as important dimensions of poverty.

Nutrition. In the poorest settlements, child nutrition was observed to be a frequent problem. Researchers observed evidence of stunting among some children. Some teachers reported that Roma children do not attend school lunches because their parents are unable to pay.

Housing. Housing conditions are the worst in the most isolated and segregated settlements Access to utilities and public services is nonexistent, or limited, in many of the more marginalized settlements. The most serious problems include lack of access to electricity, water, sewage and garbage collection. Most Roma in settlements do not own their homes or land. Lack of clarity regarding property ownership prevents the improvement of housing conditions—as individuals and local governments are unable to maintain or invest in buildings, or local infrastructure when ownership is unclear.

Health Status. The health status of Roma is generally worse than that of non-Roma. The prevalence of communicable diseases associated with poor living conditions such as hepatitis, trachoma, tuberculosis meningitis, and skin diseases is particularly high in isolated and segregated settlements. Doctors reported epidemics of these conditions in settlements, which have been eliminated in the majority population. These developments are likely linked to problems of overcrowding, unsafe water, lack of waste disposal and proximity to environmentally contaminated areas.

Educational Attainment. There are significant gaps in the education levels of Roma and non-Roma. Very few Roma in Slovak Republic continue on to secondary education. According to the 1991 census, 77 percent of Roma had completed primary education, 8 percent had completed vocational training, and less than two percent had completed academic secondary education or university. An earlier survey from 1990 found that 56 percent of Roma men and 59 percent of Roma women had not completed basic education (grades 1-8). Such low levels of education put the Roma at a huge disadvantage in the labor market and contribute to other correlates of poverty including poor health status.

Unemployment and Informality

The labor market status of Roma has changed dramatically during the transition period, with huge increases in unemployment and inactivity. The Roma were often among those first laid off in the early transition period, because they commonly held low or unskilled jobs. Because of low education levels and discrimination, Roma have faced substantial barriers to reentering the labor force.

While official unemployment data by ethnicity are lacking, a 1997 survey by the Ministry of Labor, Social Affairs and Family, estimated that Roma comprised between 17 to18 percent of the total unemployed in 1996, with this figure as high as 40 to 42 percent in eastern districts with large Roma populations. Similarly, the registries from the National Labor Office (which contained information on ethnicity until 1997) suggest that, for the country as a whole, the Roma represented between 15 and 20 percent of all the registered unemployed in the Slovak Republic up through 1997 (Table 9).

Table 9 Share of Roma in Total Registered Unemployment, 1990-97

	1991	1992	1993	1994	1995	1996	1997	1998
Number of registered unemployed and share of Roma:								
Total	301,951	260,274	368,095	371,481	333,291	329,749	347,753	428,209
Roma (%)	15.5	15.5	14.0	13.5	16.6	19.0	19.2	--
Eligibility for unemployment benefits:								
Total (%)	82.0	33.6	33.4	22.9	27.0	28.4	26.7	28.0
Roma (%)	--	15.2	10.7	4.7	5.3	--	--	--

Source: National Labor Office, as reported in Lubyova (2000). "--" = not available

Long-term unemployment among Roma is particularly high. Many of the Roma interviewed in the qualitative work had been unemployed for many years. Employment opportunities for Roma in marginalized areas are limited to temporary jobs in agriculture and construction, and public works. Social assistance benefits are the only source of income for some Roma families. Many Roma identified on-going unemployment and insecurity as the most demoralizing aspect of their lives.

Because of limited availability of formal sector jobs, many Roma work in the informal sector. Common activities include salvaging and selling scrap metal, petty trade and playing music. Informal sector activities are fueled by incentives for employers to hire labor while evading taxes and insurance contributions. Roma in geographically isolated and segregated areas have fewer opportunities for involvement in the informal sector, because communities are more closed and have limited connections outside of the settlement to find work.

Many Roma cited ethnic discrimination as a significant barrier to employment, and as a rationale for not searching for work outside of their communities and villages. Although Slovak Republic has legislation prohibiting discrimination in employment in place, Roma describe experiences of discrimination. A number of Roma in the study noted that they had applied for a job, and although they were accepted over the phone, they were subsequently rejected as soon as the employer realized that they were Roma.

Access to Public Services

Education. Roma children often face stiffer challenges in accessing education than other ethnic groups. In addition to issues common to other poor households, such as economic constraints, limited access to quality education and parents' education levels, Roma children face additional barriers including low demand for education, geographic isolation, discrimination and low Slovak language proficiency. Roma children are also more likely to end up in special schools for the mentally and physically disabled which limit their future education and labor market prospects. Children from the most segregated and isolated settlements face the greatest challenges in accessing education.

Health Services. Access to health care among Roma in the settlements was influenced negatively by the geographic distance of settlements from urban areas, by poor communication between Roma and health providers, and discrimination.

Social Assistance. Because of high levels of unemployment and poverty, social assistance benefits provide an important source of income for many Roma households. Nearly all of the long-term unemployed Roma interviewed for this study, and especially those living in poorer segregated settlements, are dependent upon social assistance benefits for income support. The dependency of Roma families on social assistance reinforces negative stereotypes about Roma among the non-Roma population. However, such dependency may be encouraged by the very the design of the social assistance and support mechanisms, which penalize those who can find only low-paying work.

Social Exclusion

A prevailing characteristic of Roma poverty is its relationship to social exclusion. Social exclusion and discrimination of Roma within civil society severely affects access to employment opportunities, education, and public services. Limited communication between Roma and non-Roma, and negative stereotypes on both sides, can lead to poor relations between Roma and local government officials and social service providers.

There are indications that negative perceptions of Roma are worsening for a number of reasons, including their declining social status, growing unemployment, and increasing dependency on social benefits. Negative stereotypes are also reinforced by geographic separation, and the limited contact between Roma and non-Roma. Contacts between Roma and non-Roma are extremely limited in segregated settlements. In integrated communities, the level of contacts and interactions between Roma and non-Roma was higher and relationships were reportedly smoother.

REGIONAL DISPARITIES

A Country of Wide Disparities

Slovak Republic is a country with **large and persistent regional disparities**. These disparities are most clearly reflected in large differences in poverty rates, unemployment and average incomes across regions. In 1996, the poorest region, Kosice, had 14.3 percent of its population living in poverty, as compared to 9.4 percent in richer Bratislava and 10.1 percent for the country as a whole. At the time, unemployment in Kosice was five times higher than in Bratislava. Since then, these disparities have only increased (Table 10). In 1999, Bratislava region had a GDP per capita equal to the EU average. In contrast, Eastern Slovakia's per capita income was only 39 percent the EU average.

Table 10 Slovak Republic: Selected Economic Indicators by Region, 1999-2000

	% of total population	% of business entities (2000)	% of economically active population	Unemployment rate (%)	% of foreign capital	% of inflow of FDI[1]	% of gross output	% of value added
Bratislava	11.5	31.2	13.1	6.80	51.9	60.5	22.9	23.6
Trnava	10.2	7.2	10.2	15.70	8.0	10	10.1	10.4
Trencin	11.3	9.6	11.6	13.51	8.3	6.4	10.2	9.7
Nitra	13.3	8.7	13.0	22.70	6.3	3.8	10.5	11.5
Zilina	12.8	10.0	13.0	17.75	7.5	3.1	10.8	10.7
Banska Bys.	12.3	11.2	12.2	22.84	6.6	4.9	11.8	10.9
Presov	14.5	9.5	13.5	23.18	3.6	3.6	9.7	9.1
Kosice	14.2	12.7	13.4	25.53	7.9	7.7	13.9	14.1

[1] Accumulated as of March 2000

Source: Statistical Office of the Slovak Republic

What Lies Behind These Differences?

One can divide the determinants of regional disparities intro three broad groupings: (i) endowments, comprising the stock of human and physical capital (including supporting infrastructure); (ii) the business and economic environment, which is affected by the inherited production structure but also by economic policies; and (iii) the institutional and political frameworks, which condition both policies and their outcomes.   In poor, lagging regions, worse initial conditions combine with a concentration of negative factors to reduce their economic and income potential.

- The poorer regions (mainly Eastern and Southern Slovakia) have overall less favorable endowments: younger populations (which could, however, be an asset if all were gainfully employed); lower levels of education of their work forces (lower human capital stock); worse health status; and lower-quality infrastructure (esp. roads) which makes production in these regions relatively less attractive and more expensive;

- Poorer regions have also inherited a less favorable structure of production, with a heavier reliance on agriculture and heavy manufacturing, both of which have gone through massive adjustment. Transition has required greater restructuring in these regions and been more costly in social terms than in the Western parts of the country;

- The poorer regions of Eastern and Southern Slovakia suffer much higher unemployment than the better-off regions, and especially face much more long-term unemployment. Vacancy to unemployment ratios are worse, job creation is lower, and individuals exhibit much lower probability of escaping from unemployment into jobs. Partly as a result, these regions show much greater dependency on social assistance and support payments, and may face a greater problem of disincentives to finding work and welfare dependency; and

- Poorer regions also have benefited less from FDI, which has worked to accentuate productivity differentials between west and east parts of Slovak Republic. In addition, they seem to have overall less attractive business environments and less dynamic private sectors. The attitude of the population in some of the poorer regions (e.g., Presov) is more suspicious and less supportive of markets and economic reform, possibly less open to foreign investors, and politically more supportive of anti-reform parties.

POLICY RECOMMENDATIONS

Reducing Poverty Requires, Above All, Reducing Unemployment

Reducing unemployment and generating new employment opportunities lies at the core of any long-term strategy for eliminating poverty and improving the incomes and living conditions for the more disadvantaged parts of Slovak society. Our analysis has shown that unemployment is the main risk factor for poverty, and that it strikes those with low education and those living in poorer regions the hardest.

This Report finds that fighting unemployment requires actions on three separate fronts: (i) measures to increase the demand for labor; (ii) measures to improve the matching of between new jobs and those searching for jobs; and (iii) measures to increase labor supply and reduce the disincentives created by the design of the social safety net system (e.g. ease the "welfare-to-work" transition).

Measures to Increase the Demand for Labor

- Maintain macroeconomic and political stability, and continue the current Government's efforts to build credibility of policy vis a vis both domestic and foreign investors. Support financial sector reform to improve access to credit by private borrowers, especially for small and medium firms, and to reduce the high cost of borrowing. Support to export growth and to the development of SMEs. Reduce existing high non-wage costs of labor (as part of a comprehensive package aimed also at curtailing expenditures financed through these revenues), which bias labor demand away from the low skill and from poorer regions. The changes in economic policy introduced since 1999 are steps in the right direction and in time will help to reinvigorate the labor market and improve the economy and business conditions so that the private sector can create more jobs to reduce the large unemployment rates. Sustaining this reform process and deepening the agenda are thus necessary steps.

Measures to Improve the Matching of New Jobs and Workers

- For young and future workers: a comprehensive reform of the education and vocational training system to ensure that they enter the labor market have the skills that the market demands. For older workers and those already in the labor force: a focus on fostering retraining and adult education, by encouraging firms to do training themselves or by allowing unemployed workers to use part of their unemployment benefits to invest in (privately-provided) training; and

- Measures to facilitate labor mobility including better flow of information on job vacancies and opportunities across regions and districts; liberalizing and encouraging the emergence of private job placement and temporary agencies, which can help mediate the supply of and demand for jobs; and housing sector reform.

Measures to Facilitate the Transition from Welfare to Work

- Adopt a benefit phasing-out scheme with a softer profile than the one currently in place, so that employed workers earning low wages would still be entitled to a (smaller) fraction of their benefits. This would improve work incentives for those at the margin and would also increase income among low-income working families; and

- Re-emphasize the role of social assistance offices as re-employment facilitators. Shift portion of existing expenditures on cash benefits to **work-related** programs, such as support for child care and transportation subsidies for employed individuals in low-income families. Support training in coordination with private sector firms as a way of getting unemployed workers in contact with potential employers. To keep costs in check, improve efficiency of expenditures through greater harmonization and coordination across different agencies and programs to improve targeting, reduce administrative costs, and prevent fraud.

But Some Groups—Most Notably the Roma—May Require Additional Support

Successful efforts to bring down unemployment and increase job creation in the Slovak economy should benefit all parts of the population, and should go a long way in terms of reducing poverty. But it is critical that employment opportunities be widely shared, and that the poorest have the means to take advantage of these jobs. Without this, a core group of poor will continue to exist. In the case of the Roma minority, the challenges are steeper than for other groups due to their lower educational status, more unfavorable demographic characteristics and location, and to discrimination.

Special policy measures to aid the Roma population, reduce poverty among Roma families and improve their living conditions (in addition to the measures discussed above) could include:

- Measures to improve housing conditions, expand coverage of utilities and of public services in the most isolated and disadvantaged Roma settlements. Measures would include clarifying property rights, and introducing incentives for local governments and communities to provide services in settlements;

- Measures to expand income generating opportunities for Roma workers: enforcing anti-discrimination legislation; reducing non-wage costs and other biases working against hiring of unskilled labor; and improving training/re-training opportunities;

- Measures to increase the educational attainment of Roma: reducing barriers that keep children from starting school; addressing the language constraint; training of teachers (including Roma teachers and teacher's assistants); increasing preschool attendance; and facilitating secondary school attendance;

- Improving access to health care in remote areas (improved local infrastructure, e.g. roads and telecommunications); increased outreach activities; and improved public health awareness, particularly reproductive health and contraception; and

- Addressing exclusion through anti-discrimination legislation; public education and information campaigns; multi-cultural education; and training for public officials such as mayors, health practitioners and other public servants.

Lagging Regions May Also Need Special Measures

Most of the measures aimed at reducing unemployment will benefit poor regions even more than richer ones. But redressing regional disparities over the long term will require also improving productivity growth, and dealing with essential human and physical capital constraints. Poorer regions clearly face a problem with low labor productivity relative to labor costs. Efforts to increase labor productivity should thus receive a high priority. These would include:

- Broad-based investments in education in poorer regions;

- Efforts to attract foreign investment flows to those regions, that can bring in new production and management tecniques, as well as technology and know-how can prove crucial in this regard;

- Improving the roads and transport network; ameliorating communications networks; strengthening and improving the provision of public services more generally;

- Building credibility and uniformity in the application and enforcement of business legislation, regulations and corporate taxation across regions; and

- Special programs of assistance to SMEs and new private firms in the poor regions, focusing on improving productivity and efficiency at the firm level.

Over time, investments in education, FDI and technology will all work to raise productivity, and help lagging regions catch up. However, improving labor productivity will take time. In the short term, measures have to focus on bringing down the cost of labor in the lagging regions to entice firms and investors to locate here. Two things can help:

- Reducing non-wage labor costs, which seem to hurt poor regions more than rich ones; and

- Allowing labor costs to differ more significantly across the country so as to reflect productivity differentials.

Continuation of Reforms Initiated in 1999 is Key

The employment challenge facing the Slovak Republic is daunting: with the highest unemployment rate in Europe, the country urgently needs to reinvigorate its labor market and create jobs. Such job creation, as we have seen, lies at the heart not only of fighting unemployment, but also of reducing the pockets of poverty that do exist throughout the country. Yet, as the experience of other transition and EU economies illustrates, generating employment can be extremely difficult, even in the face of strong growth. The experiences of Hungary and Poland during the 1990s, or of France and Spain during the 1980s and early 1990s are poignant reminders of such trials. Yet, their experience has also shown that a strong turnaround in employment is very possible, but that the engine of employment generation must to be the private sector, with the state playing a fundamental supporting role in terms of providing an adequate enabling environment and a sustainable macroeconomic framework. The policies introduced in Slovak Republic since 1999 (namely macroeconomic sustainability and a reinvigorated structural reform agenda) go in the right direction. But further efforts are still needed to allow the private sector to become truly an engine of job creation. The ongoing reforms need to be deepened and, most importantly, sustained on a continued basis. Only by following such a path will Slovak Republic be able to offer its citizens a future of new jobs and opportunities.

REFERENCES

Haltiwanger, John (2000). "Aggregate Growth: What Have We Learned from Microeconomic Evidence?". University of Maryland, processed.

Lubyova, M. 2000. "Labor Market", Chapter 7 in A. Marcincin and M. Beblavy, eds., *Economic Policy in Slovak Republic 1990-1999*. Bratislava: Center for Social and Media Analysis; Research Center of the Slovak Foreign Policy Association, and Institute for Economic and Social Reforms.

World Bank 2000a and Microcensus

World Bank 2001

POVERTY AND INEQUALITY IN THE SLOVAK REPUBLIC[3]

POVERTY IN THE SLOVAK REPUBLIC

By most indicators the Slovak Republic has achieved a high level of human and social development (Table 1.1). The *Human Development Report (*UNDP *2001)* ranked the country 40th among all countries in its level of human development—the third highest among all the transition economies, and ahead of some countries with higher levels of income per capita. However, despite the country's generally high living standards and overall level of development, there are families in Slovak Republic whose living conditions are below what is considered to be socially acceptable. By societal standards, these families and individuals are poor. Some may lack jobs, or not earn enough to adequately support their families; others may not have a sufficient level of skills or education; or they may suffer from ill-health; some may face discrimination, or simply lack the opportunities to improve their situation. To one degree or another, all these families are economically and socially deprived of the same freedoms of action and choice enjoyed by those who are better off. The objective of this study is to analyze the phenomenon of poverty in the Slovak Republic: its magnitude and severity, its characteristics and its causes, so as to help design actions and policy to reduce it.

Table 1.1 Indicators of Human and Social Development, 1993-99

Indicator	1993	1994	1995	1996	1997	1998	1999
Life expectancy							
Male	68.35	68.34	68.40	68.88	68.9	68.62	68.95
Female	76.66	76.48	76.33	76.81	76.72	76.71	77.03
Maternal mortality rate (per 100,000)	12	6	8	5	3	9	11
Child mortality (under 5)	--	--	2.2	2.1	11.9	2.1	1.9
Population per doctor	279	290	315	320	294	286	283
Crimes (per 1,000 inhabitants)	27.4	25.7	21.3	18.1	17.1	17.4	17.4
Tertiary enrollment (%)	17.7	18.0	19.4	20.8	22.5	23.6	21.7
Expenditure on education (% of GDP)	5.26	4.43	5.10	4.97	4.53	4.28	4.35
Expenditure on health (% of GDP)	5.25	5.69	6.17	6.58	6.70	6.40	6.65
Unemployment rate							
LFS	13.7	14.1	12.4	10.9	11.8	12.5	17.1
Registered	14.4	14.6	13.1	12.8	12.5	15.6	19.2

Source: UNDP, 2001.

---

[3] This chapter draws heavily on the work presented in Steele (2001), and Garner and Terrel (2001), included in Volume II of this study. Both papers contain a wealth of analysis not covered in this synthesis chapter.

Measuring Poverty

Poverty is multidimensional and goes well-beyond a narrow lack of material consumption or resources. It encompasses many other aspects, including the psychological pain of being poor, a sense of vulnerability to external events, and a sense of powerlessness vis-à-vis the institutions of the state and society (World Bank 2000a and 2000b). The Council of Europe (1995) has defined poverty as affecting those "persons, families or groups of persons whose resources (material, cultural and social) are limited to the extent that they exclude them from the minimally accepted lifestyle of the countries where they live." Unfortunately, measuring these non-material dimensions of poverty is extremely difficult as, often, the information needed to do so simply does not exist. In this Chapter, as in most quantitative analyses of poverty, we focus mainly on a narrow definition of welfare that identifies poverty with a lack of material consumption or income. Not because this dimension is the most important, but because it is the only one we can objectively measure with the data at hand. To the extent possible we then complement this information with sociological and subjective studies.

As our main measure of household welfare, we use annual household monetary income, adjusted for household composition and thus, implicitly, for households' varying needs.[4] The main data for our poverty analysis come from the 1996 Microcensus, which was administered in March 1997. These data describe annual household incomes and selected demographic variables (age, gender, highest education level, profession, social activity, relationship to household head) for the previous year. The sample is nationally representative and includes approximately 1 percent of all households in the Slovak Republic. A more detailed description of the data is given in Background Paper 1, Volume II (Steele, 2001).

A critical drawback of the 1996 Microcensus data is that they do not capture the impact of recent economic events in the country and hence may give an out-of-date picture of poverty. However, the absence of more recent nationally representative surveys prevents us from carrying out a more timely analysis. This lack of adequate data represents a serious impediment to accurate poverty monitoring in Slovak Republic and makes it more difficult to design policies suited to combating poverty (Box 1.1).

---

[4] Using household income as the sole indicator of household welfare presents several problems. Household income can vary substantially as individuals change jobs, harvest crops and realize other time specific activities. Income is difficult to measure as the number of income generating activities can be quite high and varied. In addition, inputs and revenues from small or informal business activities are often not separable from household accounts, and hence true income is not possible to calculate. Survey respondents may be unwilling to fully disclose illegal or semi-legal income sources. Moreover, worldwide households tend to under-report income (World Bank, 2000a). For all these reasons, it would have been preferable to use household expenditures or consumption as the welfare indicator. However, the only source of expenditure or consumption information in Slovakia is the Household Budget Survey (HBS) which, unfortunately, does not have a nationally representative sample. The HBS sample includes only households where the head is either employed or a pensioner. The unemployed, and those at the very top of the distribution (entrepreneurs, etc.) are excluded.

Box 1.1: Monitoring Poverty in The Slovak Republic

The Slovak Republic does not have an explicit strategy for monitoring and measuring poverty. Although for the purposes of delivering social assistance, the Government has defined a Minimum Living Standard—in essence, a poverty line—there is no official poverty line in the country, and no agency charged with regularly analyzing the evolution of poverty. Several Government or Government-supported agencies and organizations periodically publish reports and analysis that aims to capture social conditions in the country. The National Labor Office, for example, regularly publishes information on major unemployment trends and characteristics. Similarly, the Research Institute of Labour, Social Affairs and the Family, publishes studies documenting the evolution of incomes and living conditions among Slovak families. Many of these studies are based on detail survey data and use advanced poverty measurement techniques. Nevertheless, while the capacity exists, there has been no attempt to systematize the efforts to monitor poverty and social conditions. The absence of systematic poverty monitoring presents a major problem for the design of social and economic policies designed to combat poverty and improve living standards.

What would be required to build a systematic poverty monitoring strategy? The first critical element has to be the preparation and implementation of a regular, periodic and nationally representative household budget survey, which collects information on household expenditures and incomes. The existing household budget survey, while carried out periodically, is not nationally representative as it excludes critical vulnerable groups and most importantly the unemployed. This survey needs to be urgently revised, so as to be made nationally representative. Other existing sources of data which can be used to study poverty have their own drawbacks. For example, the lists of individuals requesting social assistance (which has been used as a proxy for individuals in poverty by the UNDP among others) is clearly inadequate as a measure of poverty since, as shown in the analysis here, it clearly misses an important fraction of the poor. Similarly, the Microcensus while nationally representative covers only incomes and not expenditures, which from a poverty-monitoring point of view is sub-optimal. Most importantly, the Microcensus is not carried out with sufficient frequency, as the last one was implemented in March 1997, and refers only to 1996. In addition, all signs suggest that it clearly under-samples the Roma population living in settlements and hence misses an important fraction of the most vulnerable Slovak households. If the Microcensus is to be useful for monitoring living conditions, these sampling problems need to be addressed and the survey carried out more frequently. However, from a strictly poverty monitoring point of view, improving and developing the Household Budget Survey is probably of higher priority.

A second critical element of developing a poverty monitoring strategy is defining an official poverty line, and charging an agency (not necessarily a Government one) with regular and periodic analysis of the existing data. Such analysis should be publicly disseminated and discussed on a regular basis. And the data used for the analysis should be made publicly available so that researchers and academics can do their own investigation of poverty and hence aid Government efforts.

A third critical element of a poverty monitoring strategy is to develop alternative instruments to the Household Budget Survey to study particular aspects of poverty and its causes and characteristics. Of primary importance is this regard is developing an instrument that allows analysts to determine whether poverty is mainly a transitory or permanent phenomenon, as the policy implications are very different for both. Such an instrument must follow households over time (e.g. have a panel dimension). One option is to start such a panel survey. A less-desirable but often less costly alternative is to design the sample for the Household Budget Survey so as to be a rotating one which follows households over a certain number of quarters (as in the Labor Force Survey). These instruments can also be complemented with periodic special modules aimed at capturing issues such as health and education status, access to public services etc. By building on the same sample as the regular HBS, these modules allow for more in depth exploration of issues than independent surveys.

A final important element of any poverty monitoring strategy is to build mechanisms to monitor and evaluate the impact of programs aimed to alleviate poverty or improve living conditions more generally. Two clear example of such programs in the Slovak republic are (i) social assistance and child allowances; and (ii) public works programs. In first instance, the revised HBS should be designed in a way that captures sufficient data about recipiency of such benefits and about participation in public works so as to allow evaluation of their impact and incidence. More sophisticated instruments for evaluation and monitoring of programs can be developed in a second phase.

Source: World bank, 2001

Poverty Rates and Poverty Lines

To measure poverty, we first need to choose a poverty line. In this report we use several. The first is the minimum subsistence level (MSL) as defined for each household (see Steele, 2001). This corresponds to the minimum income level (as set by the government of the Slovak Republic) below which a family will find itself in a condition of material distress. It includes amounts considered necessary to cover food, clothing, housing and energy, and other needs, and is calculated at the household level based on the composition of the family. Households whose income falls below the MSL calculated for that family are considered to be poor. The minimum subsistence level is not an internationally comparable measure, but is the most relevant from a policy perspective since it reflects the Government's implicit definition of poverty.

A second poverty line is a common-use relative line, equal to 50 percent of median per equivalent adult income. The equivalent number of people in the household was calculated according to the methodology used by the Luxembourg Income Study (to allow for comparisons with OECD countries). Households whose per equivalent income was less than 50 percent of the median per equivalent household were classified as poor. This line is useful for measuring poverty on a national standard, and for international comparisons of the characteristics of the most deprived individuals in any country.

Finally, we use two absolute poverty lines based on purchasing power parity: US$2.15 purchasing power parity (PPP) per capita per day; and US$4.30 PPP per capita per day. These are standard poverty lines that allow comparisons of real values between countries. These two lines were used in the recent World Bank study on poverty and inequality in the Europe and Central Asia (ECA) Region. The US$2.15 per capita per day line can be interpreted as a standard of absolute deprivation; while the US$4.30 per capita per day line can be considered a more appropriate poverty line for a middle-income country such as Slovak Republic (see World Bank 2000a). For a family of two adults and two children, the US$4.30 per capita line is approximately equal to the corresponding level of the MSL.

The values of all four lines in Slovak koruna are presented in Table 1.2. All lines depend on the composition of the household, but not in the same fashion: per person or per equivalent lines are adjusted for household size by simply multiplying the line per person times the number of people (or adult equivalents) in the household; in contrast the MSL changes in a more complex way (see Paper 1,

Table 1.2 Value of the Different Poverty Lines, 1996

Poverty Line	Value (SKK/year)
Below US$2.15 PPP per person per day (annualized)	9,619.77
Below US$4.30 PPP per person per day (annualized)	19,239.54
Below 50 percent median equivalent annual income	32,020.43
Below the minimum subsistence annual income	
Household with one adult	26,160.00
Household with one adult and one child 0-5	42,120.00
Household with two adults and one child 0-5	62,280.00
Household with two adults and one child 6-10	63,840.00
Household with two adults and one child 11-15	66,360.00
Household with two adults and two children 6-10	78,960.00

Notes: All amounts reported in annual terms.
Source: 1996 Microcensus; Ministry of Social Affairs.

Volume II, Appendix B). As we will see in the next section, the choice of the poverty line and the decision on how to adjust for composition of the household have a large impact on the measured level of poverty.

Table 1.3 reports the poverty rate and other often-used poverty statistics for these four poverty lines. The table reveals that, under the MSL line, in 1996 some 10.1 percent of individuals (7.9 percent of households) were poor. By this we mean that 10.1 percent of all individuals lived in households whose income was below the MSL calculated for that particular household. Our estimate of poverty is slightly lower when we use the US$4.30 PPP per person per day line, and much lower when we use the relative line or the US$2.15 PPP per capita per day.

Table 1.3 Poverty Measures in the Slovak Republic, 1996 (% of households and individuals)

	Headcount		Depth		Severity	
Poverty Line	*HH*	*Indiv.*	*HH*	*Indiv.*	*HH*	*Indiv.*
Minimum subsistence level	7.9	10.1	2.8	3.4	1.6	2.0
50 percent median equivalent income	5.9	5.8	2.1	2.3	1.3	1.5
US$2.15 PPP per person per day	2.1	2.6	1.0	1.2	0.6	0.8
US$4.30 PPP per person per day	6.3	8.6	2.4	3.0	1.4	1.8

Notes: Poverty measure based on total income, including social transfers. Poverty depth measures how far the poor are, on average, below the poverty line. Poverty severity captures differences in the severity of poverty among the poor. *Source: 1996 Microcensus*

In addition to these headcounts (percent of people below the poverty line), the table also presents measures of the poverty gap (or poverty depth) and of the severity of poverty. As we can see, the poverty gap when using the MSL is 3.4. This means that if the country could mobilize resources equivalent to 3.4 percent of the MSL poverty line for every family (both poor and non-poor), and if these resources were given solely to the poor, all the poor could in theory be lifted out of poverty.[5]

Sensitivity of Poverty Measures to the Poverty Line

A poverty line helps focus the attention of governments and civil society on the living conditions of the poor. It can show what the minimum level of living is before a person is no longer considered to be poor. It can also give the ability to make interpersonal comparisons (Ravallion, 1998). Using a specific line, however, can mask the ability of the analyst to know how many households are close to the poverty line and, therefore, how many households would be able to work their way out of poverty with relative ease; or alternatively, how many may fall into poverty in response to relatively small income shocks.

One way in which to show the sensitivity of poverty to the exact location of the poverty line is to increase and decrease the poverty line by a small amount, and then examine what share of the population moves in or out of poverty as a result. This simple exercise is carried out in Table 1.4. The results suggest that numerous households are clustered around the poverty line. By increasing the poverty line by 10 percent, poverty at both the household and individual levels increases approximately by 30 percent

---

[5] In practice, it would require more resources because individuals would likely change their behavior (lower their income) in order to obtain government transfers.

(for every line except the very low US$2.15 PPP line). Similarly, decreasing the poverty line by 10 percent lowers poverty at both the household and individual levels by about 20 percent (again, for all lines except the US$2.15 PPP line). Thus, there are very large movements in the poverty measure in response to small shifts in the line.

Table 1.4 also tells us something about the potential short-term impact of both negative economic shocks to the distribution of income (for example, those associated with recessions) and positive shocks (those associated with growth and good policies). As can be seen from the table, a small rightward shift of the distribution (e.g. a positive shock, equivalent to lowering the poverty line while keeping the distribution constant) is associated with more-than-proportional declines in poverty; a leftward shift (e.g. a negative shock) with more-than-proportional increases in poverty.

Table 1.4 Poverty Headcounts in 1996 and their Sensitivity to the Poverty Line (%)

	Poverty		Increased 10%		Decreased 10%	
	HH	Indiv.	HH	Indiv.	HH	Indiv.
Minimum subsistence level	7.9	10.1	10.3	12.9	6.0	7.5
50 percent median equivalent	5.9	5.8	8.1	7.5	4.6	4.8
US$2.15 per person per day	2.1	2.6	2.3	2.8	1.8	2.3
US$4.30 per person per day	6.3	8.6	8.0	10.8	5.0	6.8

Source: 1996 Microcensus.

Box 1.2 Characteristics of Top and Bottom Income Deciles

Whether a household is rich or poor usually reflects the influence of its own characteristics and those of the location where it lives. For this reason, it is often useful to divide the total population into deciles based on their <u>per capita income</u>, and then examine how households in the lowest income decile and those in the highest decile differ at first sight. Table B1.1.1 summarizes some of these differences.

Table B1.1.1 Household Characteristics by Income Decile, 1996

Lowest Decile	Characteristic	Highest Decile
20%	Headed by a female	17%
23%	Headed by an individual with only elementary education	8%
13%	Headed by pensioner	10%
19%	Headed by an unemployed individual	1%
36%	Headed by an individual with an unclassified occupation	12%
4.6	Average household size	2.8
54%	Percentage of total income from social transfers	9%
13%	Percentage of total income from pensions	8%
10%	Percentage of total income from unemployment benefits	0.2%

Income deciles based on total household income (e.g. unadjusted for the composition of household).
Source: 1996 Microcensus

Households headed by females, the unemployed, individuals with no more than elementary education, and individuals with unclassified occupations are the most likely to be at the bottom of the income distribution. Households in the lowest decile receive, on average, 54 percent of their total household income through social transfers, 13 percent through pension transfers, and 10 percent through unemployment benefits. In contrast, transfers account for only some 9 percent of the income of the richest households, most of it coming from pensions.

Source: Steele (2001), in Paper 1, Volume II of this study.

Poverty Among Those not Covered by the Survey

In principle, the 1996 Microcensus sample covers the whole Slovak population. However, there are some questions as to whether the sampling frame may adequately capture the Roma population, especially those living in isolated settlements.[6] This settlement population has mushroomed during the 1990s as many Roma moved out of towns and cities in response to the collapse of job opportunities for the unskilled. They live in visibly less favorable conditions than other population groups, and present all the characteristics that would put them at a high risk of poverty. Their exclusion from the sample is thus likely to bias our poverty estimates downwards.

How big is this population? This question is hard to answer as estimates of the size of the overall Roma population in Slovak Republic vary greatly. Data from the latest census identified only 1.6 percent of the Slovak population as Roma, but it is widely believed that these data—based on self-identification—grossly underestimate their true numbers. Other estimates suggest that some 10 percent of the population, or about 500,000 people, are Roma. According to Slovak experts, about a quarter of this Roma population in Slovak Republic would be found in settlements. An upper bound estimate for poverty would assume that all of the households living in settlements are poor. Adding these individuals to the estimates derived from the Microcensus would bring the overall poverty rate (under the MSL) from 10.1 percent up to about 12.5 percent of the population.

The living conditions of the Roma are very difficult to measure quantitatively. None of the existing household surveys capture ethnicity, since privacy legislation prohibits such gathering of data. So there is little objective basis on which to build an estimate of their poverty. However, the Roma do have a higher incidence of all the correlates of poverty, which suggests that poverty among this ethnic group is likely to be very high and probably deeper than among other groups of the population. In order to better understand the nature and characteristics of poverty among the Roma population, this study relies on qualitative data, collected specifically for this purpose. These data are presented and analyzed in Chapter 4, and in the corresponding background paper in Volume II of this Report.

International Comparisons of Poverty

International comparisons of poverty are difficult because they require that both equivalent consumption and the poverty line be calculated in the same way across countries. Recently, the World Bank study *Making the Transition Work for Everyone: Poverty and Inequality in Europe and Central Asia*, (World Bank 2000a) undertook the task of creating comparable poverty statistics for all the countries of this Region for which adequate household survey data were available. Using similar poverty lines and methodologies (the US$2.15 PPP and US$4.30 PPP per person per day lines) we can compare poverty in the Slovak Republic to that in other countries of the region. This is shown in Table 1.5.

---

[6] One indicator that the sample may not adequately cover the Roma is household size and the number of children. Very few families in the sample report having more than three children; yet we know that the average number of children for a Roma family is 4.2.

Table 1.5 Absolute Poverty Rates[a], Selected Transition Economies (% of individuals)

Country	Year	At US$2.15 ppp/person/day	At US$4.30 ppp/person/day	GNP per capita[b]
Slovenia	1998	0.0	0.7	14,399
Czech Republic	1996	0.0	0.8	12,197
Hungary	1997	1.3	15.4	9,832
Slovak Republic	*1996*	*2.6*	*8.6*	*9,624*
Estonia	1998	2.1	19.3	7,563
Poland	1998	1.2	18.4	7,543
Croatia	1998	0.2	4.0	6,698
Lithuania	1999	3.1	22.5	6,283
Russian Federation	1998	18.8	50.3	6,186
Latvia	1998	6.6	34.8	5,777
Ukraine	1999	2.7	24.6	3,130

Notes: [a] Headcount Index. Data for the Czech Republic and the Slovak Republic based on income measures, all other countries are consumption measures. [b] GNP per capita is from 1998 and is measured at purchasing power parity (PPP). using World Bank methodology.
Source: Table 1.1, World Bank (2000a) and 1996 Microcensus.

As can be seen in this table, when measured in an international context, absolute poverty in the Slovak Republic is low. Despite high unemployment, at US$4.30 PPP per person per day the incidence of poverty in 1996 was only 6.3 percent among households and 8.6 percent among individuals—one of the lowest poverty rates in the Europe and Central Asia region. However, although Slovak Republic has a much lower proportion of its population living under the US$4.30 PPP per person per day mark than do successful reformers such as Poland or Hungary, it has twice the population living under US$2.15 PPP per person per day than do those neighboring countries. In other words, there is a larger group of people at the very bottom of the income distribution in the Slovak Republic who are truly deprived in an absolute sense. Thus, the Slovak Republic seems to have some deep pockets of poverty in the midst of a relatively well-off population.

Box 1.3 Income versus Consumption

The lack of a nationally representative household budget survey makes it impossible to use consumption as the poverty indicator. We are thus forced to use income measures, with all the problems that may bring. In this context, it is useful to look at measures of consumption and income within the budget survey, and examine the differences between reported household incomes and consumption. This can be interpreted as a check on the robustness of using income as the poverty metric.

Table B1.2.1 Difference in Income and Expenditures by Decile, 1996 (koruna)

	Overall	Lowest	Highest
Quarter 1	628.9	67.8	1202.6
Quarter 2	267.4	9.1	1503.5
Quarter 3	343.7	278.5	533.9
Quarter 4	156.5	-432.9	2006.2

Note: Total quarterly income minus total quarterly expenditures.
Source: Household Budget Survey, 1996

As shown in Table B1.2.1, incomes are consistently higher than expenditures for all deciles, with the differences being the largest for those at the top. This indicates that most households have some savings, and that these are much larger for richer households. Poorer households, in fact, appear to have to save during some parts of the year to "smooth" out dis-savings during the fourth quarter. These findings also suggests that, unlike in other countries of the region, income may be an accurate indicator of well-being. At the very least, it does not appear to underestimate actual consumption (as is the case in much of the CIS, Bulgaria and Romania, for example).

By examining the poverty risk for different groups of the population, one can gain useful insights into which factors are associated with poverty. This can then help us design potential policy responses. Because some of these risk factors may affect only a small share of the population, a group with high poverty risk need not necessarily account for a large fraction of the poor.

We find three variables that are most strongly related to poverty: these are the *education* of the household head; the *employment status* of the household head; and the *location* of the household. Other aspects, such as demographic characteristics of the household including number of children and family size, are also very important determinants of poverty risk. Another important correlate of poverty is ethnicity but, as explained above, this dimension is hard to measure because of the difficulties of accurately identifying minority groups in our data. One thing that comes out clearly, however, is that ethnic minorities—especially the Roma minority—disproportionately reflect many of the correlates of poverty: low education, high unemployment, living in depressed or disadvantaged regions, and having many children.

Education

Table 1.6 shows the poverty risk by the *educational attainment* of the household head. The table shows that households with a less educated head (elementary education or less) face a higher poverty risk. This is true regardless of the poverty line used, although here for the sake of simplicity we show only the results using the MSL. According to Table 1.6, the poverty headcount for individuals living in households where the head has only an elementary education is 14.3 percent; their risk of poverty is thus 41 percent higher than the average (e.g., 14.3 divided by the national poverty rate of 10.1, expressed in percent). Households where the head has completed middle general education also have a relatively high poverty risk (26 percent above the average). In contrast, households where the head has a university education have a relative risk of poverty that is 22 percent lower than the average.[7] Households headed by an individual with a vocational education have an average or lower-than-average risk of poverty. In general, these patterns match those found for other countries of the ECA region (World Bank, 2000a). In these other countries, as in the Slovak Republic, one tends to find that lower education is associated with a higher poverty risk; and that university education is associated with a much lower risk of poverty. The findings for vocational/secondary education, on the other hand, are more mixed, and depend on the specifics of each educational system involved. In Bulgaria, for example, those with vocational education have a slightly lower risk of poverty than those with middle or general secondary. In Poland, it is the reverse.

---

[7] We also examine poverty risks by education of each individual. This yields very similar findings (see Paper 1, Volume II, for details).

Table 1.6 Poverty Risk by Education Level (%), 1996

Education Level	Poverty Headcount	Relative Poverty Risk
Elementary	14.3	+41
Apprenticeship	8.8	-13
Middle Vocational	10.1	-0
Complete Middle Vocational	8.2	-19
Complete Middle General	12.8	+26
Higher Vocational	11.1	+9
University	7.9	-22
Total average	*10.1*	*0*

Notes: The unit of observation is the individual. Poverty measured by total income and less than the minimum subsistence level. The *relative poverty risk* is calculated by dividing the group-specific poverty rate by the national average, then expressing the ratio in % terms (e.g. 14.3 divided by 10.1 equals 1.41 or +41%). *Source: 1996 Microcensus.*

The fact that we find a correlation between poverty and education does not necessarily imply that there is a causal relationship between the two. There could also be reverse causality (the poor are less able to invest in an education), or there could be some "third" variable that is related to both low education and poverty (such as less educated families living in more economically-depressed areas). In order to examine the ways by which education is associated with poverty, we calculate relative poverty risks by education after controlling for the partial effects of other factors.[8] For example, we can control for the region that people live in, or for the labor market status of the household head, and examine whether it is still true that those with low education are more likely to be poor.

To do this, we first run a regression of log equivalent consumption for each household on key sets of household characteristics (including demographic characteristics of the household; location; education; labor market status of the head; and some region-specific variables such as the share of Roma in the regional population). Then we use this regression to simulate income if one of these key characteristics would be identical across the population (thus "wiping" out the effect of that variable). We then calculate the relative poverty risk using these simulated incomes. These results are presented in Table 1.7.

The first column of Table 1.7 shows that the differences in poverty risk by level of education of the household head become slightly smaller when we control for the partial effects of demographic characteristics. In other words, the relationship between higher poverty and lower education is due in part to the fact that those with lower education have less favorable demographic characteristics. Take the first row as an example. We see that the relative poverty risk for households where the head has only an elementary education decreases once we "wipe" out the effects of demographics: it falls from +41 percent (Table 1.6) to +28 percent. This means that families with less educated heads tend to have demographic features (such as larger families) that would of themselves be associated with higher levels of poverty. Once we take the unfavorable demographic factors out, their risk of poverty falls. But they still have a higher-than-average risk of being poor. Compare this to the case of those with university education: their relative poverty rate stays relatively unchanged when we control for demographics.

---

[8] For a detailed description of the methodology used in these calculations, see Luttmer (2000).

This indicates that the demographic features of university graduates tend to be "poverty-neutral".

Table 1.7 Pathways for Poverty Risk by Education of Household Head
(poverty risk for group relative to average risk, in percent)

Education of household head	(1) Household size, age, gender etc.	(2) Regions	(3) Labor market	(4) Education	(5) % Roma in region	(6) All factors
Elementary	28.01	18.77	25.39	19.91	41.81	-27.43
Apprenticeship	-19.49	-27.74	11.49	-13.08	-15.45	-48.94
Middle vocational	-22.58	-22.08	22.99	-0.05	-0.13	-44.33
Complete middle vocational	-29.14	-25.80	6.91	-1.70	-19.69	-25.43
Complete middle general	-0.73	10.21	55.51	25.00	26.19	-19.86
Higher vocational	-1.78	-5.31	20.23	26.73	9.46	14.65
University	-22.7	-27.86	-8.36	17.95	-21.68	1.92
Memorandum item:						
Overall poverty rate (with controls)	8.73	8.67	11.73	10.99	10.11	7.37

Notes: Omitted education group are those under age 15. The unit of observation is the individual. Poverty measured by total income and less than the minimum subsistence level. Relative poverty risks are relative to the national uncorrected poverty rate (10.1 percent).
Source: 1996 Microcensus.

As seen in Columns (2) and (3), the differences in poverty risk across education groups also become smaller when we control for location (region) and for labor market status. The relative poverty risk for those with only elementary education, for example, falls from +41 percent to +18.7 percent when we control for region; and from +41 percent to +25.7 percent when we control for labor market status. This suggests, again, that part of the observed correlation between poverty and low education comes about because those with lower education tend to live in poorer regions and are more likely to be unemployed. Controlling for the relationship between education and mean income -illustrated in Column (4)—also diminishes differences in relative poverty, indicating that much of the relationship between education and poverty comes about because higher education tends to command higher incomes. The percentage of the regional population that is Roma does not have a significant impact on differences in poverty risk by education. Finally, when we control for all factors at once we find that the relative poverty risks get "inverted", with the relative risk for those with less education being less than the average, that of university graduates being close to the average, and that of higher vocational being actually higher than the average. What this means is that the residual or "unexplained" part of poverty is actually more negative for those with higher education than for those with lower education. Since we know that the variance of incomes tends to increase with education, this simply means that as education goes up, it is harder to predict (or explain) why a family with an educated head would be poor, as it is likely to reflect very household-specific reasons (e.g., health problems, etc). Another way to think about this is to turn it around: poverty among those with low education is explained by observable factors such as the combination of their demographic characteristics, their labor market status, the region they live in, and the fact that those with lower education command lower incomes on the job market.

Labor Market Status

A second important correlate of poverty is the labor market status of the household head. As we can see in Table 1.8, households where the head is unemployed have several times the poverty risk of those were the household head is employed or is a pensioner. Strikingly, pensioners have a poverty risk that is much below the average (and this finding remains even after we start controlling for the partial influences of other factors). This points to the extremely important role that pensions have played in preventing poverty. It also says something about the design of policy: clearly, policymakers have paid a lot of attention to protecting this particular vulnerable group.

Table 1.8 Poverty Risk by Labor Market Status of Household Head (%), 1996

Education Level	Poverty Headcount	Relative Poverty Risk
Employed	9.0	-11
Unemployed	44.7	+347
Pensioner	6.0	-41
Other	41.0	+305
Total average	*10.1*	*0*

Notes: The unit of observation is the individual. Poverty measured by total income and less than the minimum subsistence level. Relative poverty risks are relative to the national uncorrected poverty rate (10.1 percent).
Source: 1996 Microcensus

Instead of looking at the labor market status of the household head, we can also examine poverty by the labor market status of each individual. This yields very similar findings: poverty risks for the unemployed (41.6 percent poor) are almost six times those of the employed (7.8 percent poor), and more than nine times those of individuals that are out of the labor force (4.9 percent poor). These results are discussed further in the corresponding paper in Volume II of this study (Steele, 2001).

As we did in the case of education, we can examine the pathways through which labor market status is associated with poverty (Table 1.9). We can see that unlike with education, controlling for demographic variables does not seem to have much impact on the relative risks of poverty by labor market status: households headed by an employed person or by a pensioner continue to have a much lower risk of poverty than those headed by an unemployed person. The same is true when we add in controls for region of residence, for education or for the percent of regional population that is Roma. Thus, the relationship between labor market status and poverty appears to reflect mainly the direct link between labor market status and household income. It is only when we control for all these factors simultaneously, including the link between labor market status and income, that the relative poverty risks tend to equalize themselves across labor market categories.

Table 1.9 Pathways for Poverty Risk by Labor Market Status of Household Head
(poverty risk for group relative to average risk, in percent)

Labor market status of household head	(1) Household size, age, gender etc.	(2) Regions	(3) Labor market	(4) Education	(5) % Roma in region	(6) All factors
Employed	-22.70	-22.82	31.02	-0.30	-11.62	-24.58
Unemployed	232.02	282.80	90.54	346.48	342.66	-20.64
Pensioner	-39.89	-53.63	-47.97	-37.40	-41.39	-42.86
Memorandum item:						
Overall poverty rate (with controls)	8.73	8.67	11.73	10.99	10.1	7.37

Notes: Omitted group are "other" e.g. students; housewives etc. The unit of observation is the individual. Poverty measured by total income and less than the minimum subsistence level. Relative poverty risks are relative to the national uncorrected poverty rate (10.1 percent).
Source: 1996 Microcensus.

Location

A third important correlate of poverty is location. Table 1.10 presents poverty rate by region and for rural/urban areas for 1996. As the table clearly shows, there are important differences in poverty risks both across regions, and between urban and rural households within the same region. Overall, the highest relative poverty risks are found for Kosice (+40.7 percent higher than the average) and Trencin (+20.3 percent higher than the average).

Table 1.10 Poverty Risk by Region (%), 1996

	Urban	Rural	Total	Relative poverty risk
Bratislava	9.0	20.8	9.4	-7.7
Trnava	7.0	8.6	7.6	-25.7
Trencin	13.0	8.6	12.2	20.3
Nitra	11.6	7.1	9.9	-2.2
Zilina	7.9	10.5	8.6	-15.7
Banska Bystrica	8.5	10.4	8.9	-12.7
Presov	10.1	7.6	9.7	-4.2
Kosice	13.5	16.4	14.3	40.7
Total	*10.1*	*10.1*	*10.1*	*0*

Notes: The unit of observation is the individual. Poverty measured by total income and less than the minimum subsistence level. Relative poverty risks are relative to the national uncorrected poverty rate (10.1 percent).
Source: 1996 Microcensus.

As with education and labor market status, we can also examine the pathways through which region of residence is associated with differential poverty risks. When we do this, we find that most of the differences in poverty rates between regions (with the notable exception of Bratislava) tend to go away once you control for education, labor market status of households and demographics. We find that these factors all contribute to explaining a large part, if not all, of observed regional differences—e.g., the regions which have higher levels of poverty are those with lower education rates, higher unemployment and larger families. The only genuine "regional" effect is that of Bratislava: poverty there is lower than would be expected even after including all the controls. This probably reflects the impact of being the capital city, with all that implies in terms of receiving more foreign direct investment and having more new job opportunities. In fact, when we look at the interaction between labor market status of households and region, we find clear evidence that part of the reason Bratislava has lower relative poverty is that it has better employment outcomes than the rest of the country.

Although the figures above indicate that the risk of poverty is significantly higher in certain regions, it is also interesting to examine also the *distribution* of the poor across regions. As shown in Table 1.11, there are actually poor households in all regions of the country (even in Bratislava). Thus, policies to help the poor that are mainly geographically targeted would be unlikely to work well in Slovak Republic as it would miss some important pockets of poverty.

Table 1.11 Distribution of the Poor by Region, 1996

Region	% of All Households	% of Poor Households	% of All Individuals	% of Poor Individuals
Bratislava	13.4	12.4	11.7	10.8
Trnava	10.4	8.0	10.4	7.7
Trencin	11.1	12.8	11.3	13.6
Nitra	14.2	14.4	13.7	13.2
Zilina	11.9	10.4	12.6	10.7
Banska Bystrica	13.1	11.1	12.5	10.9
Presov	12.3	13.0	13.7	13.2
Kosice	13.7	17.8	14.1	19.9

Notes: Poverty measure based on total income and less than the minimum subsistence level.
Source: 1996 Microcensus

Demographics

The demographic composition of the household also has a significant impact on the risk of poverty. In particular, families with children appear to have a much higher risk of poverty than families without children, and the risk tends to increase significantly with the number of dependents. Families with three children or more, for example, represent only 6.3 percent of the population, but account for 18.1 percent of the poor. Single parents with children appear to be at a particular high risk (Table 1.12). It also seems that female-headed households have a higher risk of poverty than male-headed ones. However, the differences in poverty risks between male and female headed households largely go away once you control for all observable factors (education, demographics, labor market status, and region).

Table 1.12 Poverty Risk by Family Composition (%), 1996

Characteristic	Poverty rate	Relative poverty risk	Share of All Individuals	Share of Poor Individuals
Gender of Household Head				
Male	9.7	-4.0	81	78
Female	11.1	+9.9	19	21
Family Composition				
Single parent with children	27.8	+175.3	1.6	4.4
Other families with children	17.7	+75.3	42.9	62.2
Single elderly male	0.1	-99.0	0.6	0.0
Single elderly female	1.1	-89.1	2.6	0.3
Multiple elderly only	3.2	-68.3	3.8	1.2
Other families with no children	6.7	-33.7	48.6	32.0
Total	10.1	0	100	100

Notes: The unit of observation is the individual. Poverty measured by total income and less than the minimum subsistence level. Relative poverty risk for group is measured as the poverty rate for group *is* divided by national poverty rate, in percent.
Source: 1996 Microcensus

If we then look at the risk of poverty by age group, we find that children at are a higher risk of poverty than any other age group (Table 1.13). Children face a risk of poverty that is two times that of adults and four times that of the elderly. This is mainly because families with many children at are a high risk of being poor. But why? In part because they live in households with characteristics—such as low levels of education and low levels of female labor force participation- that lead to lower family earnings; but also because there are simply more mouths to feed in such households. Although we cannot identify ethnicity, Roma households tend to present all of these elements: low education, low labor force participation of women and many children, which combine to lead to higher poverty (see below).

Table 1.13 Poverty by Age Group, 1996

Age Group	Share of All Individuals (%)	Share of Poor Individuals (%)	Poverty Rate (%)
0-5	4.6	8.1	18.1
6-10	6.1	10.7	17.8
11-15	8.0	12.8	16.2
16-64	69.0	64.0	9.4
65+	12.3	4.4	3.6

Note: Individuals. Poverty measure based on total income less than the minimum subsistence level.
Source: 1996 Microcensus

Poverty Among the Roma

As discussed earlier, the situation of the Roma in Slovak Republic is difficult to quantify. For this reason, poverty and living conditions among the Roma are examined separately using mainly qualitative data (see Chapter 4).

It is interesting , however, to use what little quantitative information we have to see if, at first glance, there is any apparent correlation between Roma ethnicity and quantitative measures of poverty. The only data we have available on ethnicity are official population statistics from the last census. These statistics show that there are eight districts in which the Roma account for more than 5 percent of the total population.[9] These districts are found primarily in the eastern (poorer) part of the country. As illustrated in Table 1.14, those districts where officially more than 5 percent of the population are Roma, have poverty rates that are higher than the average for the corresponding region as a whole. While very weak, this evidence is suggestive of a likely correlation between ethnicity and poverty.

THE ROLE OF THE SAFETY NET

The Slovak Republic has an extensive social protection system that combines social insurance (unemployment compensation, pensions, sickness insurance etc.) with social assistance (minimum subsistence level, aid to families with children). These extensive transfers make it possible for many households whose earned incomes would put them in poverty to nevertheless reach a certain minimum subsistence standard. In order to examine the impact of the safety net on

Table 1.14 Poverty Risk in Districts with More than 5% Roman Population, 1996 (below minimum subsistence level)

REGION/district	% Roma	Poverty rate
BANSKA BYSTRICA	1.93	8.9
Revuca	5.29	14.9
PRESOV	3.84	9.7
Kezmarok	7.89	14.4
Levoca	6.26	13.5
Sabinov	5.78	5.4
KOSICE	4.24	14.3
Gelnica	7.30	23.3
Kosice-Satellite	5.13	18.9
Michalovce	4.98	23.3
Spisska Nova Vos	8.87	7.6
TOTAL	1.60	10.1

Notes: Individuals. Roma population percentages from Slovak Statistical Office. *Source: 1996 Microcensus.*

poverty, we take out all social transfers from household income, and then estimate what would be the poverty rate in the absence of these transfers. We perform this exercise in two ways: first we take out all social transfers except for pensions; then we also take out pensions.

As illustrated in Table 1.15, poverty rates would be much higher if households were not helped by social transfers. The overall incidence of poverty (measured using the MSL) would jump from 10.1 to 18.7 percent of all individuals in the absence of all transfers except for pensions—a huge increase. The increase in poverty would be even more marked for certain vulnerable groups. Among households where the head is unemployed, for example, poverty would increase from 44.7 to nearly 80 percent.[10] Poverty among households with little education (elementary or less) would increase by over 10 percentage points, as would poverty in certain regions. Poverty among children would also increase sharply.

The most striking finding pertains to the role of pensions. The overall incidence of poverty in the absence of pensions would jump to 38.3 percent. Not surprisingly, poverty among pensioners would be very high (nearly 80 percent). Interestingly, though, poverty would also increase among households headed by non-pensioners, indicating that

---

[9] These statistics show that 1.6 percent of the total population was Roma in 1996, which is clearly an underestimate.
[10] This abstracts from behavioral effects. In reality it would be lower, as many unemployed would not be unemployed in the absence of unemployment insurance and social assistance (see Chapter 3 of this study).

pensions contribute to improving the well-being of many non-elderly only households. This is because many elderly, all of whom receive pensions, live with non-elderly family members, and pensions contribute to the income (and hence the welfare) of the whole family. Pensions have been critical in preventing the elderly from falling into poverty, but have also helped many non-elderly.

Table 1.15 Poverty Profile, 1996 (less than the minimum subsistence level)

	With all social transfers	Without transfers, with pensions	Without transfers, without pensions
a. Economic Activity of Household Head:			
Employed	9.0	17.3	20.5
Unemployed	44.7	79.7	82.9
Pensioner	6.0	10.5	78.8
b. Education of Household Head			
Elementary	14.3	24.5	64.1
Apprenticeship	8.8	20.5	42.0
Middle vocational	10.1	21.8	36.2
Completed middle vocational	8.2	14.7	28.1
Completed middle general	12.8	22.5	38.3
Higher vocational	11.1	16.7	42.2
University	7.9	9.9	22.0
c. Location			
Urban	10.1	18.2	36.5
Rural	10.2	20.5	44.3
d. Region			
Bratislava	9.4	12.2	31.2
West	9.9	18.0	38.4
Central	8.7	17.3	37.9
East	12.0	23.5	41.4
e. Gender			
Male	9.7	18.1	35.5
Female	11.1	20.2	49.3
e. Total	*10.1*	*18.7*	*38.3*

Notes: Individuals. Regions defined using old classification for comparability with Table 1.16 below.
Source: 1996 Microcensus

The importance of social transfers to poverty alleviation is further illustrated in Table 1.16. The table shows that social transfers account for almost 60 percent of the total incomes of the poor. While poor and non-poor appear to receive roughly the same absolute amount of social payments, poor households receive higher actual payments of means-tested benefits such as child allowances. An analysis of the incidence of social transfers confirms that they accrue more to the poor than to the non-poor, and are thus fairly effectively targeted (see Steele, 2001). However, the analysis also shows that a non-negligible fraction of the poor (20 percent) do not report receiving any benefits.

Table 1.16 Share of Income from Social Transfers, 1996

	All Social Transfers		Child Allowances		Pensions	
	Korunas	% of Income	Korunas	% of Income	Korunas	% of Income
Income Decile[*]						
Lowest decile	23,001	79.1	3,170	6.4	15,021	60.3
Highest decile	29,609	9.9	4,224	1.3	18.987	6.8
Poverty[*]						
Poor	34,271	56.7	10,486	17.4	8,986	14.9
Non-Poor	36,155	23.4	6,082	3.9	23,943	15.5

Notes: [*]Based on total household incomes. *Source: 1996 Microcensus.*

CHANGES IN POVERTY BETWEEN 1992 AND 1996

Using data from the 1992 and 1996 Microcensus surveys, we can examine how poverty in the Slovak Republic has evolved over time. Table 1.17 shows that under three out of the four poverty lines, estimated poverty in the Slovak Republic more than doubled between 1992 and 1996. However, poverty decreased when using the MSL. A similar finding has been documented by Filipova and Valna (1999), who attribute the decrease to changes in the definition and calculations of the MSL. Indeed, if we "redo" our poverty estimates leaving the MSL unchanged in real terms from its 1992 values, we find that poverty increased sharply. The same is true if we use the 1996 values for the MSL and adjust backwards to the same real level in 1992. Although we cannot examine trends since 1996, most indicators would suggest that poverty would have continued to increase (Box 1.4).

Table 1.17 Poverty Headcounts in 1992 and 1996

	Households		Individuals	
	1992	*1996*	*1992*	*1996*
Below 50 percent median equivalent income	2.1	5.9	1.4	5.8
Below US$2.15 PPP per person per day	0.2	2.1	0.1	2.6
Below US$4.30 PPP per person per day	2.7	6.3	3.9	8.6
Below the minimum subsistence level	9.3	7.9	12.2	10.1
If kept at 1992 real values[*]	9.3	17.0	12.2	21.0
If kept at 1996 real values**	2.5	7.9	3.0	10.1

Notes: Poverty measure based on total income. [*] 1996 values computed using 1992 MSL inflate to 1996 using CPI; [**] 1992 values computed using 1996 MSL and deflating using CPI.
Sources: 1992 Luxembourg Income Study and 1996 Microcensus

Between 1992 and 1996, poverty increased not only in terms of the headcount but also in terms of depth and severity. Using the uncorrected MSL, the depth of poverty increased from 2 in 1992 to 3.4 in 1996, while the severity rose from 0.6 to 2. The increase in the depth and severity of poverty is even sharper when we use a line that has not fallen in real terms: at the US$4.30 per capita line, for example, the depth of poverty rose five-fold from 0.6 to 3, and the severity of poverty nine-fold, from 0.2 to 1.8. These quantitative trends are backed up by evidence from sociological surveys. Bednarik (2000), for example, reports a steady rise in the fraction of the population declaring that their incomes are insufficient to meet their basic needs. When asked to evaluate their situation relative to that three years earlier, a larger fraction of the population defines itself as being "poor".

Box 1.4 Poverty Trends Since 1996

The lack of nationally representative household-level data on incomes or consumption makes it very difficult to obtain an estimate of poverty after 1996. Faced with this problem, the recent National Human Development report for the Slovak Republic (2000) opted for using an alternative definition of poverty. They defined poverty as the number of people in material distress, which includes all applicants for social assistance payments independently of whether they qualified for payments or not. An upward trend in the number of people asking for social assistance is clearly discernible in Table B1.3.1. This suggests that poverty is likely to have increased since 1996.

Table B1.3.1 Population in Material Distress (end-year figures)

Year	Number of individuals in material distress	Share in total population
1993	386,323	7.2
1994	442,544	8.3
1995	408,507	7.6
1996	378,637	7.0
1997	392,927	7.3
1998	506,440	9.4
1999	584,941	10.8

Source: UNDP, National Human Development Report, 2000.

How have families coped with rising poverty? Sociological surveys suggest that mainly by either using savings or by borrowing (Bednarik, 2000). The evidence also suggests that support by families and friends plays a very important role. About 30-35 percent of Slovak households report receiving cash, goods or work from their families (compared to 7-9 percent for Poland; 8-10 percent for East Germany; and 6-13 percent for the Czech Republic). Among the lowest quintile of the income distribution, the fraction of households reporting help from their families increases to 43-44 percent.

As regards the characteristics of the poor, the comparison between 1992 and 1996 is not straightforward as the definition of some categories (e.g., region) changed between the two surveys. In addition, because we use the LIS version of the 1992 survey, some of the educational definitions are not entirely equivalent between the 1992 and the 1996 data. However, some rough comparisons are shown in Table 1.18. It is clear from these findings that the poverty profile has not changed very much, and that the same groups which were at a high risk of poverty in 1992, were also at a high risk of poverty four years later.

Table 1.18 Poverty Risk for Individuals, 1992 and 1996

	1992	1996
Economic Activity of Household Head*		
Employed	9.4	9.0
Unemployed	67.2	44.7
Pensioner	7.3	6.0
Education of Household Head*		
Elementary	18.1	14.3
Apprenticeship		8.8
Middle vocational	13.6	10.1
Completed middle vocational	11.5	8.2
Completed middle general	6.2	12.8
Higher vocational	7.5	11.1
University	2.2	7.9
Region*		
Bratislava	5.5	8.8
West	11.8	10.1
Central	10.8	8.7
East	15.6	12.0
Gender of Household Head		
Male	11.8	9.7
Female	14.5	11.1
Family Composition		
Single parent with children	32.0	27.8
Other families with children	16.9	17.7
Single elderly male	1.0	0.1
Single elderly female	2.7	1.1
Multiple elderly only	4.5	3.2
Other families with no children	5.5	6.7
Total	*12.2*	*10.1*

Notes: Individuals. Elderly defined as 65 or older and children defined as 0 to 15 years of age. Poverty based on total income and less than the minimum subsistence level. *These variables are not equivalent in the LIS version of the 1992 Microcensus and the Slovak Statistical Office version of the 1996 Microcensus.
Sources: 1992, Luxembourg Income Study; 1996, Microcensus

INEQUALITY

Inequality matters because it largely determines how the benefits of growth are to be distributed. Growth which accrues mainly to the top of the distribution may do little to improve the living standards of the poor and increases in inequality may easily swamp the positive impact of growth. Unless a society is highly mobile, the economic distance between the rich and the poor presents an important indicator of differences in values, aspirations, consumption patterns and lifestyles across groups. Inequality has many correlates: social exclusion, declining investment in human capital in low income areas, declining confidence in government, increased economic insecurity, and impaired functioning of democracy. Simply put, if the rich and the poor share no common economic and social realities, there will be little or no agreement on common social goals or vehicles to achieve these goals.

Historically, the Slovak Republic has been a very egalitarian society. According to the Luxembourg Income Study methodology, in 1998 the Gini coefficient (a common-use measure of inequality) was 0.19, significantly below that of Western Europe and neighboring countries, with the exception of the Czech Republic. However, inequality has increased sharply since then (Garner and Terrell, 2001). As shown in Table 1.19, between 1988 and 1996 the Gini coefficient increased by at least a third, and other measures of inequality essentially doubled in size. Most of this increase occurred after 1992, as an earlier study by Garner and Terrell (1998) showed almost no change in the Gini coefficient between 1988 and 1992. By world standards, the speed of the increase in inequality in such a short time-span (1992-96) is huge. However, compared to what has happened in other transition economies, it is relatively moderate (World Bank, 2000). And despite the increase in inequality, Slovak Republic remains one of the more egalitarian countries in the OECD (Figure 1.1).

The rise in inequality is not necessarily a bad thing. Some inequality is needed if the market is going to reward differences in productivity and effort. In addition, some inequality is associated with higher returns to entrepreneurship and risk-taking, and with a revaluing of education and of scarce skills. All of these are positive developments, and suggests that some degree of rising inequality in the Slovak Republic has to be viewed as positive. However, the process has to be managed carefully a huge increases in inequality, such as those witnessed for example in the countries of the FSU, can generate social tensions and undermine social cohesion. Increasingly, there is evidence that it can also undermine growth.

Table 1.19 Overall Income Inequality, 1988-1996

Indicator	1988		1996		% Change	
	LIS	Per capita	LIS	Per capita	LIS	Per capita
Gini	0.187	0.195	0.250	0.263	33.7	34.9
Log deviation	0.062	0.062	0.128	0.142	107.2	129.3
Theil	0.060	0.065	0.112	0.128	86.7	96.9
Coef. Var.	0.067	0.079	0.131	0.157	96.1	99.2

Notes: LIS is according to LIS equivalency scale. Total household income.
Source: 1988 and 1996 Microcensus, as reported in Garner and Terrell (2001).

What lies behind the rise in inequality? According to Garner and Terrell (see also Paper 2, Volume II) the main factor driving the rise in inequality is an increase in the inequality of earned non-agricultural incomes. Earnings from non-agricultural activities have become far more unequal over time. Most of this is coming from rising earnings disparities by education. As argued above, this is not necessarily bad: it simply means that the labor market is moving to reward skills and education as in more mature market economies (see also Chapter 2). Another factor contributing to rising inequality is 'other monetary income' (i.e., foreign income, etc.) because, although it represents only a small share of total household income, its distribution has become more unequal as its share at the top decile has increased considerably (from 1.4 percent of total household income in 1988 to 6 percent in 1996).

The increasing inequality of non-agricultural earnings has been partially compensated by the impact of social transfers. Since 1988, social payments have grown as a share of total income for the average household. In 1996, such payments represented roughly about 41 percent of total household incomes. The evidence also suggests that they have become more progressively distributed (Steele, 2001; Garner and Terrell, 2001).

Figure 1.1 Income Inequality in Slovak Republic and Other Countries

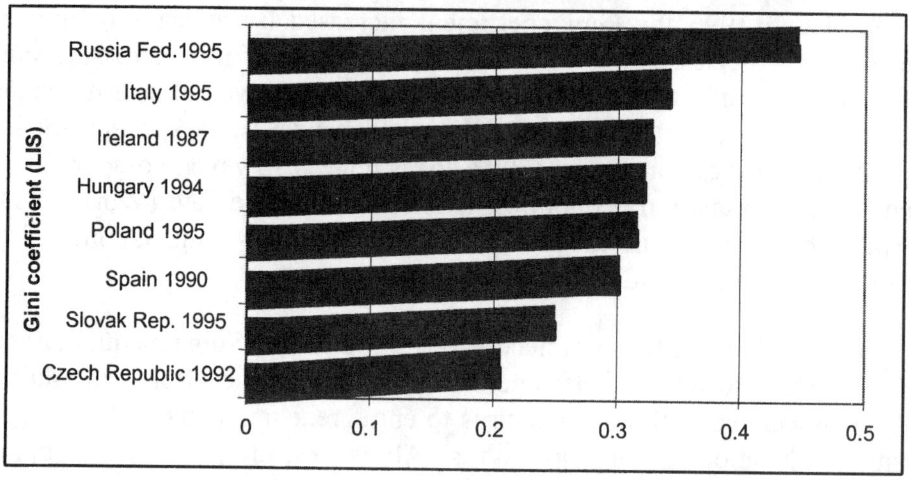

Overall, it seems that social transfers have been key not only to preventing more widespread poverty, but also to maintaining a relatively egalitarian distribution of income. These positive effects of the safety net, however, have come at a price. The broad scope and coverage of the generous safety net has undoubtedly created strong disincentives for the unemployed to actively look for jobs (see Chapter 3). This is particularly true among those with low education or skills, since the minimum living standard has been close to the minimum wage more often than not, and social assistance benefits use this subsistence level as a reference.

It is also important to notice that, in recent years, the growing number of recipients has generated some fiscal stress at a point in time when there is little room to maneuver, since there is substantial pressure to control the budget deficit and payroll taxes are already very high. Moreover, high payroll taxes –needed to finance the extensive safety net—have been identified as a factor contributing to unemployment, especially among the low-skilled.

CONCLUSIONS

In 1996, about 10.1 percent of the individuals living in the Slovak Republic were poor. Those at highest risk of being poor were those living in a household headed by an unemployed person or by someone with only elementary education. Families with children faced a higher risk of poverty than those without children, as did families living in either the Kosice or Trencin regions. By age groups, children faced the highest risk of poverty, while the elderly faced a much lower risk of poverty than other groups.

Poverty in Slovak Republic would be much higher if households did not receive very substantial social payments. These payments are particularly important for those at the bottom of the distribution, and appear to be fairly well targeted, even if they may cause some disincentive effects for those receiving them.

By most measures, poverty increased between 1992 and 1996. During this period, the profile of poverty remained fairly constant—with the same groups facing the greatest risk. However, some of the differentiation between groups has blurred, suggesting that poverty is spreading beyond easily defined groups. The lack of nationally representative data prevents us from examining what has happened to poverty since 1996. However, most indicators-such as the number of people requesting social assistance— would suggest that it has increased. Given the strong correlation between poverty and the employment status of the household head, the fact that unemployment among the latter is growing is a reason for special concern (see Chapter 3).

REFERENCES

Bednarik, Ratislav. 1999. "The Development of Slovak Income Distribution During the Transformation (1988-98)." Mimeo. Research Institute of Labor, Social Affairs, and Family, Bratislava, Slovak Republic.

Filipova, Jana and Silvia Valna. 1999. "Minimum Subsistence Income." Mimeo. Research Institute of Labor, Social Affairs, and Family, Bratislava, Slovak Republic.

Garner, Thesia I. and Katherine Terrell. 1998. "A Gini Decomposition Analysis of Inequality in the Czech and Slovak Republics During the Transition," The Economics of Transition, 6 (1): 23-46.

Garner, Thesia I. and Katherine Terrell. 2001. "Some Explanations for Changes in The Distribution of Household Income in Slovak Republic, 1988 and 1996." Paper 2, Volume II, "Slovak Republic: Poverty, Employment and Labor Market Study," Report N. XXXX, World Bank. Washington DC.

Luttmer, Erzo. 2000. "Poverty and Inequality in Croatia." Paper 1, Volume II, "Croatia: Economic Vulnerability and Welfare Study," Report N. XXXX, World Bank, Washington DC.

Ravallion, Martin. 1992. "Poverty Comparisons: A Guide to Concepts and Methods." Living Standards Measurement Study Working Paper, No.88. Human Resources Division, Population and Human Resources Department, World Bank, Washington, DC.

-----. 1998. "Poverty Lines in Theory and Practice". Living Standards Measurement Study Working Paper, No.133. Human Resources Division, Population and Human Resources Department, World Bank, Washington, DC.

Steele, Diane. 2001. "A Snapshot of Poverty and Living Conditions in the Slovak Republic." Paper 1, Volume II, "Slovak Republic: Poverty, Employment and Labor Market Study," Report N. XXXX, World Bank. Washington DC.

UNDP (United Nations Development Program) 2001. National Human Development Report: Slovak Republic 2000.Bratislava, Center for Economic Development.

World Bank. 2000a. Making Transition Work for Everyone: Poverty and Inequality in Europe and Central Asia. Washington, DC: World Bank

World Bank. 2000b. Attacking Poverty, World Development Report 2000/2001. Washington, DC: World Bank

THE CHALLENGE OF GENERATING EMPLOYMENT[11]

RISING UNEMPLOYMENT AND INACTIVITY

High unemployment is the Achilles heel of Slovak Republic's economic performance to date, and the country's most pressing social problem. Despite maintaining fairly robust growth rates, averaging 4.6 percent between 1994-2000, the number of unemployed in Slovak Republic has steadily mounted, reaching some 498,000 in the second quarter of 2000 (according to the LFS).[12] This represents about 18.7 percent of the labor force (Table 2.1)—the highest rate of unemployment in all of the OECD. Unemployment has risen in every region of the country—although much more in some regions than others—and among all groups of workers. Workers with only primary or secondary education have been more affected by unemployment than university graduates, but even among the latter unemployment has been rising. The largest increases in unemployment over time have occurred among young workers, with workers under 25 years of age facing an unemployment rate of 35 percent. Unemployment is significantly lower among prime-age workers, but has also been increasing: in the first half of 2000 the unemployment rate for workers aged 25-64, was 16 percent, up from 11 percent in 1996. Rising unemployment among prime-aged workers is a reason for concern, since these are workers in their prime productive years, and they usually bear a larger responsibility for supporting their families.

Table 2.1 GDP Growth, Employment and Unemployment, 1993-2000

	1993	1994	1995	1996	1997	1998	1999	2000	Avg. 94-00
GDP, constant 1995 prices,									
Annual % change	-3.7	4.9	6.7	6.2	6.2	4.1	1.9	1.8	4.6
Total employment,									
Annual % change	-2.6	-1.0	2.4	-1.4	-2.3	-1.0	-1.8	-1.4	-0.9
Unemployment rate									
Labor force survey	13.7	14.1	12.4	10.9	11.8	12.5	17.1	18.7	13.9
Registered	14.4	14.6	13.1	12.8	12.5	15.6	19.2	17.9	15.1
Labor force participation rate	--	70.8	70.9	70.7	67.6	66.8	66.3	66.6	68.5
Average wage, constant 1995 prices									
Annual % change	-3.9	3.0	4.3	10.6	6.6	1.7	-2.8	-3.1	2.9
Inflation, annual % change									
CPI	23.2	13.4	9.9	5.8	6.1	6.7	10.6	12.0	9.2

Source: Statistical Office of the Slovak Republic; National Labor Office, IMF.

As the rate of unemployment has increased so has the average duration of unemployment, so that at present more than 50 percent of all unemployed individuals have been so for more than a year (Table 2.2). The share of long-term unemployment in total unemployment has remained stable over time, and has not really responded to either business cycle fluctuations nor to reforms in the unemployment insurance system—

---

[11] This chapter draws on much existing literature on employment in the Slovak Republic, and on the background paper by Manuel de la Rocha (2001), Background Paper #3, Volume II of this study.

[12] Figures on *registered* unemployment, which are available on a more timely basis, are significantly higher. As of February 2001, some 558,726 were registered as unemployed, equivalent to 20.7 percent of the labor force.

pointing towards deep structural causes of unemployment. Moreover, flows in and out of unemployment are low, leading to very little turnover among the stock of unemployed.

Unemployment developments reflect only a part of the underlying negative employment trends, as many unemployed workers have become discouraged and left the labor force. According to Boeri (2000) up to one third of workers in Central Europe who leave the state of unemployment do not find a new job, but simply stop looking for one. Data from the LFS, which allows us to follow individuals over one year, suggest that over the course of a year some 5 percent of the unemployed will move out of the labor force. As unemployment spells lengthen, the proportion of unemployed exiting the labor force altogether goes up.

Partly as a result of this discouraged worker effect, labor force participation rates have fallen sharply.

Table 2.2 Distribution of Unemployment Spells by Duration.

	1994	1995	1996	1997	1998	1999	2000
< 6 months	32.4	30.3	32.3	32.8	32.1	30.83	24.45
< 12 months	49.9	44.9	46.9	47.4	48.8	50.88	44.95
12 + months	50.1	55.1	53.1	52.6	49.7	49.12	55.05

Source: Statistical Office. Labor Force Survevs (LFS).

Labor force participation for both sexes has fallen from nearly 71 percent in 1994 to 66.6 percent in 2000. As a result of the combined rise in unemployment and fall in labor force participation, employment as a share of working age population—a good measure of the extent to which Slovak Republic is employing its *potential* labor resources—has dropped to 50.3 percent. This is significantly below the EU average of 61.1 percent and much below the OECD average of 65.1 percent (Figure 2.1). It suggests that a large (and rising) share of the potential Slovak workforce is idle.

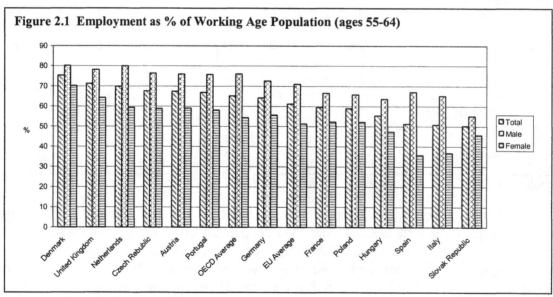

Figure 2.1 Employment as % of Working Age Population (ages 55-64)

Statistical Office of the Slovak Republic

26

When compared to other OECD countries, the low activity rates of Slovak men are especially striking: employment to working age population ratios for men average 71 percent for the EU and 76 for the OECD as a whole; as compared to only 55 percent for Slovak Republic (Figure 2.1 and Table 2.3). The only other countries with relatively low activity rates for men are Hungary and Poland, suggesting that there may be some common elements due to transition. Nevertheless, both Hungary and Poland have male employment to population rates above 60 percent. One likely explanation for low male activity rates in all three transition countries is to be found in the patterns of employment restructuring that have taken place, which have favored services and trade at the expense of the industrial sectors, which were traditionally more male-intensive. Such restructuring may have pushed many male workers, and especially older ones, out of the labor force altogether. Activity rates among Slovak women are also somewhat low when compared to the OECD, but the differences are much less pronounced: 45.6 percent of Slovak women of working age are employed, as compared to a EU average of 51 percent, and an OECD average of 54.3 percent. Among women, much of the adjustment to lower activity levels has taken the form of withdrawal from the labor force, bringing Slovak Republic's historically high female participation rates more in line with those of market economies. The possibility of early retirement may have also played a role in explaining why employment to population ratios among both men and women are low.

Table 2.3 Labor Market Status, by Gender (% of working age population, 15-65)

	1996			*1999*			*2000*		
	All	*Male*	*Fem*	*All*	*Male*	*Fem*	*All*	*Male*	*Fem*
Employed (at work)	54.13	62.58	46.15	50.64	57.23	44.28	50.27	55.11	45.60
Employed (on leave)	6.26	4.13	8.27	5.12	3.26	6.91	3.81	2.37	5.20
Unemployed	7.75	7.82	7.69	10.52	11.80	9.29	12.41	14.19	10.68
NLF (discouraged)	0.34	0.38	0.30	0.24	0.30	0.19	0.26	0.31	0.20
NLF	31.51	25.08	37.59	33.48	27.41	39.33	33.26	28.01	38.32

Source: Statistical Office, LFS.

Regardless of the cause, the fact that roughly only one-half of Slovak Republic's potential labor resources are employed means that the country is not fully exploiting its growth possibilities, and that economic and social policies are failing in one critical dimension: that of providing jobs to everybody willing to be gainfully employed.

Unemployment and Poverty

High unemployment has huge economic and social costs. First, it means people are idle, rather than gainfully and productively employed. Past investments in education and individuals' productive potential are not given the chance to bear fruit. Second, unemployment—and especially long-term unemployment—deprives people from a critical way to contribute to and integrate into society. It can also deprive them of access to key social networks, often necessary to getting a job and to otherwise participating in economic life. This can push people into an unemployment trap, and lead to growing social exclusion and marginalization. Third, unemployment greatly increases the risk of an individual and his or her family being poor. As we saw in Chapter 1, in 1996 households where the head was unemployed had five times the incidence of poverty (44.7 percent poverty rate) than those in which the head was employed (9 percent poverty rate).

The fact that unemployment has steadily increased since 1996 bodes ill for the evolution of poverty in the Slovak Republic. In 1996, almost one half of all households where the head was unemployed were found to be poor. At that time, only 7.4 percent of heads of household were unemployed (and the overall unemployment rate stood at 11 percent). Unemployment among heads of household has nearly doubled since then, to14 percent in the first half of 2000 (18.7 percent overall). If the risk of poverty for a household where the head is unemployed has not changed much over time—and there are many reasons to believe that it cannot have decreased much, since among other things unemployment benefits have become more stringent and of shorter duration—then in and of itself this development is likely to have had very severe consequences for overall levels of poverty.[13]

From a poverty point of view, it is of particular concern that unemployment has been rising the most precisely among heads of households (Table 2.4). While unemployment among heads is still lower than among secondary workers, the rate of increase since 1996 has been much faster.

Table 2.4 Employment and Unemployment Rates, by Position in Household

	1996			1999			2000		
	Head	*Spouse*	*Other*	*Head*	*Spouse*	*Other*	*Head*	*Spouse*	*Other*
Employed (at work)	86.10	75.50	74.60	83.36	77.19	68.21	82.19	77.88	66.87
Employed (on leave)	6.44	13.65	8.27	5.77	10.21	7.82	3.89	7.63	6.16
Unemployed	7.47	10.85	17.13	10.88	12.60	23.97	13.92	14.49	26.97

Notes: employed and unemployed both defined as percent of population in labor force. *Source: LFS 1996, 1999 and 2000.*

What Lies Behind the Sharp Rise in Unemployment and Inactivity?

Three main factors lie behind the spectacular rise in unemployment and inactivity in the Slovak Republic:

- The first factor is widespread *job reallocation* associated with transition, which has resulted so far in a net loss of jobs. A lag between the destruction of old, non-viable jobs and the creation of new ones is to be expected, but in the case of Slovak Republic this lag may have been accentuated by the reluctance of the previous administration to undertake widespread structural reforms, and by fundamental macroeconomic imbalances prevailing during 1996-1998;

- The second factor is the existence of severe mismatches between existing stock of labor resources and what is demanded in the new market economy. This mismatch has an important skills component—new jobs being created require skills that are very different from those offered by available workers—but also a location component as most of the emerging job opportunities are not located in the same geographical areas as the large pools of unemployed; and

---

[13] Unfortunately the lack of recent nationally representative data prevents us from estimating just how big the impact on poverty of rising unemployment may have been.

- The third factor results from the interaction of demographic changes, labor supply decisions and job search behavior patterns. Large cohorts entering the labor market have put upward pressure on unemployment, while job search behavior has been negatively affected by the existence of unemployment and social assistance benefits which are very generous relative to the minimum wage.

In this chapter we concentrate on the first two sets of factors, namely those affecting the demand for labor, and the matching of demand and supply. We begin by examining patterns of job creation and destruction, and how these may link to overall macroeconomic developments, and policy choices, including the role played by foreign investment and privatization policies. We then examine the extent of mismatches between the new jobs being created and the workers looking for jobs, and try to identify the reasons for this mismatch. We end by looking at policy measures that can help both enhance job creation and reduce the mismatch.

The next chapter (Chapter 3) then turns to analyzing those factors contributing to unemployment on the supply side, especially those affecting decisions to participate or not participate in the labor market; and those that influence job search behavior and incentives to work.

JOB REALLOCATION DURING TRANSITION

One of the main features of the transition process everywhere has been the massive reallocation of labor: first, from the state sector to the new private sector, comprising both new and privatized firms; and second, from the initially predominant industrial sectors to new activities in services and trade (EBRD, 2000). In most transition countries, the destruction of jobs in public enterprises has happened much more quickly than the creation of new private ones, hence leading to a rise in unemployment. Slovak Republic has been no exception to these trends, except that the lag between job destruction and new job creation seems to be even more pronounced than in its neighbors.

Employment, Output and Productivity

Total employment in the Slovak Republic has fallen sharply since the start of transition, with some of the largest drops coming very early on in the process. Between 1989 and 1993, GDP declined (in real terms) by a cumulative 21.7 percent, while total employment fell by about 15 percent. Most of this net loss in employment reflected widespread labor shedding in large state enterprises, which had until then hoarded significant amounts of surplus labor (Figure 2.2). Employment in the state sector fell by nearly 50 percent in this four-year span. Some of the hardest-hit sectors were machinery and equipment (-34.5 percent drop in employment, 1991-93 alone), electrical machinery (-34.4 percent), mining (-28.9 percent) and wood products (-28.5 percent).

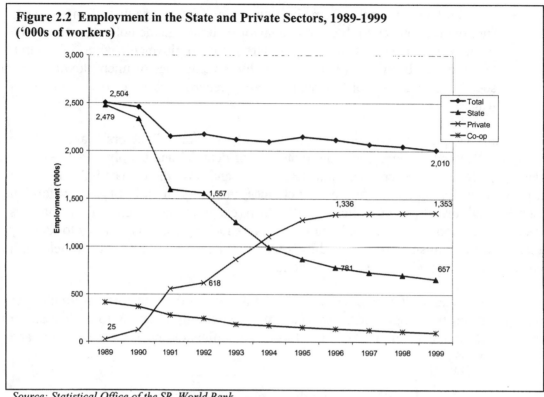

Figure 2.2 Employment in the State and Private Sectors, 1989-1999 ('000s of workers)

Source: Statistical Office of the SR, World Bank

Since 1993, GDP has grown by a cumulative 34 percent, but total employment has remained largely unchanged. During 1993-1999, total employment fell by a cumulative—2.4 percent. Employment in the state sector has continued to decline, while employment creation in the private sector has been largely stagnant. The composition of employment has, however, shifted dramatically as a result of the drop in public employment. At present, the private sector accounts for 70 percent of all employment.

If we look at the evolution of employment by sectors, we see that the declining trends in total employment has been accompanied by a significant shift toward services and away from agriculture and industry (including construction). Relative employment in agriculture has fallen by a cumulative 47.4 percent since 1991; in industry it has fallen by 26 percent; in construction by 42.5 percent. One consequence of this has been a marked increase in the weight of services in total employment (Table 2.5).

Table 2.5 Employment by Sector (% of Total Employment)

	1991	1992	1993	1994	1995	1996	1997	1998	1999
Agriculture	12.60	11.80	9.40	10.20	9.40	9.00	7.90	7.70	7.10
Industry	32.80	30.30	29.60	29.30	29.30	29.50	30.00	28.60	26.00
Construction	11.20	9.10	8.20	7.60	7.20	7.50	7.60	7.50	6.90
Services	48.00	52.60	54.20	55.10	55.50	55.00	54.40	55.90	59.10

Source: Administrative data. Statistical Yearbook of the Slovak Republic. Excluding persons on maternity and additional maternity leave and including employees with second job.

Because employment adjustment initially lagged the decline in output, labor productivity fell initially in both industry and agriculture. But since 1994 labor productivity has been increasing steadily in both agriculture and industry, and was increasing in construction until 1997 (Figure 2.3). The behavior of real wages has not followed that of productivity. Real wages in agriculture have stayed basically flat, despite substantial productivity gains in the sector, whereas real wages have shown an inverted u-shape in both industry and construction. The real wage increases in construction have been particularly noteworthy, given that productivity has increased less in that sector than elsewhere (Figure 2.4).

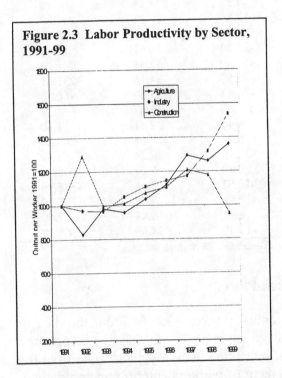

Figure 2.3 Labor Productivity by Sector, 1991-99

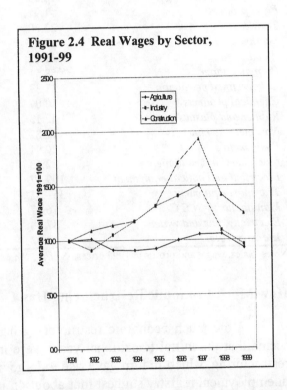

Figure 2.4 Real Wages by Sector, 1991-99

The evolution of labor productivity and real wages over the period is summarized in Table 2.6. The table clearly shows that cumulative labor productivity growth has clearly outstripped real wage increases in both agriculture and industry, but that real wage growth has exceeded productivity growth in construction.

Table 2.6 Real Wage Growth and Productivity, 1999 Relative to 1991

1991=100	Average Wage Index	Labor Productivity Index	Difference Index (AW-LP)
Agriculture	92.63	135.8	-43.1
Industry	95.76	153.8	-58.0
Construction	124.5	94.9	29.6

Source: Statistical Office of the SR, from Statistical Yearbook.

Table 2.7 takes a more disaggregated look at employment, labor productivity, profits, sales and wages by branch. What is remarkable is that there is essentially a zero correlation between changes in employment and changes in wages, and only a weak correlation between changes in employment and changes in either profits or sales.

However, there is a much stronger positive correlation between changes in wages and changes in sales, and between changes in wages and changes in profits. This suggests that workers are able to bargain over a share of profits or revenues, with employment would be being determined separately. It may indicate the existence of soft-budget constraints at the firm level, which could take the form of "soft", directed credits.

Table 2.7 Percent Changes in Sales, Employment, Wages and Profits 1991-99, by Sector

	Real Sales	Employment	Real Wages	Real Gross Profits
Mining and quarrying	-10.99	-30.79	13.01	-61.47
Food products	-1.91	-4.32	23.19	106.20
Textile	-22.60	-13.83	10.21	-224.80
Leather	9.92	-33.46	13.65	68.43
Wood	21.93	-20.20	16.61	-2.64
Pulp and paper	58.51	-17.89	42.46	1041.18
Coke, refined petroleum	27.37	-35.58	34.16	-231.21
Chemical products	10.07	-26.42	23.57	-60.84
Rubber and plastics	42.13	-1.80	25.67	-48.32
Non-metallic minerals	17.82	-16.44	28.41	31.10
Basic metals	20.91	-6.79	19.68	269.59
Machinery and equipment	22.63	-28.15	28.24	-52.49
Electrical and optical equipment	109.57	0.47	30.01	235.71
Transport equipment	351.32	-11.61	52.96	396.86
Manufacturing N.E.C.	16.57	-27.91	27.06	-18.37
Electricity, gas and water	87.28	8.21	14.49	-57.60
Industry Total	**43.02**	**-14.70**	**24.99**	**-60.29**

Notes: Sales, wages and profits in 1995 prices. *Source: Statistical Yearbook, SR Statistical Office.*

How Much Economic Restructuring Has Taken Place?

How much economic restructuring has actually taken place? From the data, it seems that the initial transitional years were indeed associated with massive layoffs and restructuring, which in turn gave rise to large inflows into unemployment. Data from the unemployment registry suggest that about 45 percent of workers entering unemployment in 1993-94 did so because they were "restructured" or laid-off (Table 2.8). During this period, inflows into unemployment more than doubled in size the outflows from unemployment into new jobs. However, as growth recovered and as the Government backed away from reforms, employment restructuring appears to have slowed down. By 1999, the fraction of workers entering unemployment who reported losing their job due to restructuring had declined to 27 percent. The bulk of those losing their jobs in 1999 and 2000, did so because their contract (usually a temporary one) ended. Although inflows into unemployment have picked up since 1997, there is no hard evidence that suggests that the increase is associated with deep restructuring per se. But hard budget constraints are likely to have been imposed through the restructuring and privatization of the remaining state banking system. The data, however, do not yet show a significant increase in the number of the unemployed who report losing their job due to layoff, nor do we see an increase in the incidence of involuntary part-time or temporary employment.

32

Table 2.8 Reasons for Ending Employment

Reason for end of employment:	Percent of workers reporting in year:			
	1993	1999	2000	Avg 1993-2000
Agreement	32.46	21.40	18.58	24.05
Involuntary (layoff)	45.41	27.44	30.13	32.77
Voluntary (quits)	4.17	2.99	2.96	3.76
Disciplinary	0.02	2.25	2.24	0.62
Termination of contract	17.94	45.93	46.09	38.80

Source: Unemployment Registry, NLO.

When we look at individual transitions from employment into unemployment; and from unemployment back into employment, we do not find evidence for a marked increase in restructuring or layoffs. As we can see from Table 2.9, flows from employment into unemployment were fairly similar between 1996 and 1999. The bulk of those who are employed stayed employed between the start and the end of the year, except for a small fraction (around 2 percent) than moves into unemployment, and a small fraction (1.5 percent) that moves out of the labor force. However, the pool of unemployed seems very stagnant. Less than a third of those who start the year unemployed have moved out of unemployment by the end of the year. Comparing 1996 and 199, suggests that if anything, exit from unemployment into employment is slowing down: the fraction of the unemployed going back into employment by the end of the year has decreased from almost 29 percent in 1996 to 19 percent in 1999. The deep structural reforms introduced by the current administration (starting in 1999) are likely to show a different picture vis-à-vis labor market dynamics.

Table 2.9 Transitions Across Labor Market States

Year 1996 Q=4 Q=1	Employment	Unemployment	Not in LaborForce
Employment	96.80	1.68	1.52
Unemployment	28.75	67.28	3.98
Not in Labor Force	3.61	3.76	92.63
Year 1999 Q=4 Q=1			
Employment	95.96	2.32	1.72
Unemployment	19.08	76.33	4.59
Not in Labor Force	2.54	4.93	92.54

All in all, the data suggest that there is very little net employment creation in the Slovak labor market. At the same time, economic restructuring appears to have slowed down significantly between 1994-1998. This points to a relatively sluggish labor market in which there are relatively few movements across labor market states (from employment into unemployment, and vice-versa). But is this truly the case? Evidence from other countries suggests that aggregate trends can hide a lot of labor churning. Recent work on Poland, for example, indicates that despite the conventional wisdom that held the Polish labor market to be sluggish and stagnant, evidence from the firm level indicates that on the contrary there is significant amount of job creation and job destruction going on hidden behind the aggregate numbers (World Bank, 2001). Could this be true for Slovak Republic as well?

Job Creation and Job Destruction

To answer this question, we look at firm-level data on jobs created and jobs lost. For this purpose we use data from the "Trend" firm-level database, supplemented as needed by those from the "Albertina" firm-level database (see Annex for details). The data cover the period 1993-98, and include information on total number of employees, revenues from sales and other activities, revenues from exports, personnel and other costs etc. These data pertain to both continuing and closing/entering firms, although it is likely that the sample under-represents closures.[14]

Table 2.10 presents gross job creation, gross job destruction, and gross job turnover rates by year.[15] As we can see from the table, a much larger share of job turnover is accounted for by job destruction than by job creation. It also seems that job creation rates have remained low but stable, whereas job destruction rates have fluctuated more widely. Figure 2.5 compares average turnover rates (1994-98) for the Slovak Republic to those for Poland and some OECD countries. Clearly, gross job turnover in Slovak Republic is much lower than in Poland or other OECD economies: 5.59 percent on average for 1994-98, as compared to 17.5 percent for Poland, or 15.3 percent for the United Kingdom.

Table 2.10 Job Creation and Job Destruction in the Slovak Republic, 1994-91

Year	Gross Job Creation	Gross Job Destruction	Gross Job Turnover
1994	0.10	1.68	1.78
1995	2.29	5.29	7.58
1996	2.31	1.33	3.64
1997	2.61	3.70	6.31
1998	2.01	6.93	8.94
Avg 94-98	1.86	3.73	5.59

Notes: [1] Average annual rates as percent of total employment.
Source: TREND, ALBERTINA.

There are a number of reasons, however, why the Slovak data may understate true job turnover. First, the data tend to exclude many small and medium enterprises, which often have higher turnover. Nevertheless, the bias towards larger firms exists also in the data for other countries, so this alone would not explain why turnover rates are so much lower in Slovak Republic. Second, as suggested above, the data may under-represent firm closures. For this reason, it may make more sense to compare the Slovak figures to turnover rates in other countries which pertain to continuing firms only. However, even

---

[14] In principle, the annual databases comprise firms operating that year. However, when firms exit from the sample between years it is unclear if it is due to closure, merger or simply dropping out of the sample. For this reason, we treat our estimates as pertaining to all firms. It is likely, though, that they more accurately reflect the situation of continuing firms. See Annex 1 for details.

[15] The gross job creation measures the sum of all employment gains in expanding firms in a given year, divided by total employment at the beginning of the year. The gross job destruction rate measures the sum of all employment losses in shrinking firms in a given year divided by total employment. Gross job turnover is the sum of gross job creation and gross job destruction.

in this case (see Figure 2.5), the gross turnover rates for Slovak Republic are significantly below those found for other countries. This is mainly due to differences in gross job creation. Job creation in Slovak Republic—even among continuing firms only—is significantly below that recorded for the other OECD countries.

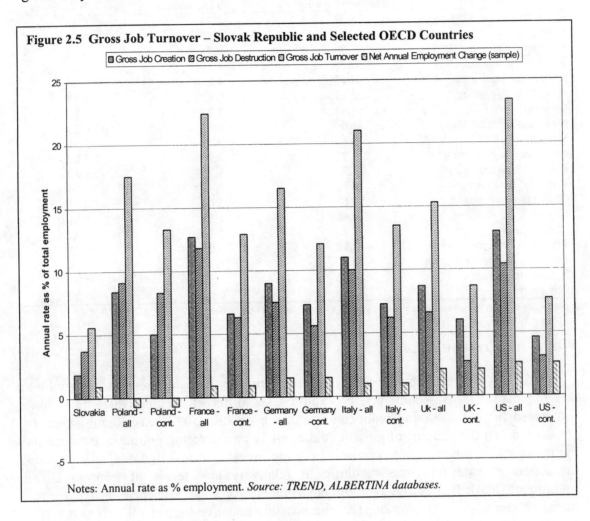

Figure 2.5 Gross Job Turnover – Slovak Republic and Selected OECD Countries

Notes: Annual rate as % employment. *Source: TREND, ALBERTINA databases.*

Most of the new jobs are being created in services and in a few manufacturing industries such as metal products; transport equipment; leather, wood and paper (Table 2.11). What is interesting is that several of these industries also have the highest rates of job destruction. The fact that most job destruction takes place in the same industries that are creating most new jobs indicates that a large share of job reallocation occurs within industries, as the result of labor moving from declining firms to expanding ones. This feature is not unique to Slovak Republic, but has been found for Poland (World Bank, 2001) and other countries as well (Haltiwanger, 2000). It indicates that economic restructuring and job creation often go hand-in-hand—i.e., that you need to allow job destruction in order to create new jobs. This suggests that excessive employment protection could ultimately stifle job creation. It also suggests that factors leading to job creation act primarily at the firm level, and not at the level of an industry. Thus policies aiming at creating (or saving) jobs at the industry level may be completely misdirected. What matters is ensuring that there is a favorable operating and investment environment at the firm-level.

Table 2.11 Job Creation and Job Destruction in Selected Industries, 1994-98

Industry	Gross Job Creation	Gross Job Destruction	Gross Job Turnover
Agric. forestry and fishing	1.57	4.74	6.33
Mining	0.07	6.59	6.66
Food products	3.56	0.74	4.30
Textiles and apparel	0.16	4.35	4.51
Leather, wood & paper	4.67	4.87	9.54
Publishing & printing	0.35	0.82	1.17
Chemicals	1.43	3.72	5.15
Non-metallic minerals	1.06	3.15	4.21
Metal products	3.13	9.31	12.44
Machinery & equipment	2.36	2.71	5.07
Electrical machinery	1.70	3.71	5.40
Transport equipment	3.72	1.47	5.19
Other manufacturing	0.61	3.62	4.23
Utilities	0.86	1.15	2.01
Construction	2.78	2.51	5.29
Wholesale and retail trade	2.98	6.05	9.03
Transport & communication	0.67	0.17	0.84
Real estate, finance	4.02	1.92	4.94
Other services	36.1	0.01	36.2

Notes: annual rates in percent of total employment; average for 1994-98. *Source: TREND, ALBERTINA.*

Why is Job Creation so Low?

Clearly Slovak Republic faces a problem of very low job creation. But why is this the case? This section briefly explores six different factors which may have influenced the extent of job reallocation and job creation in Slovak Republic during 1994-1998: (i) the patterns of growth, and a policy mix favoring public investment and the non-tradable sector at the expense of private investment and tradable; (ii) the weak investment climate for firms resulting in relatively low levels of Foreign Direct Investment (FDI); (iii) the unfavorable environment for small and medium enterprises, often the engines of job creation; (iv) the possible negative impact of high taxation of labor; and (v) the role of labor market rigidities. An extensive set of reforms have been taken during 1999-2000. While it is expected that those reforms will eliminate some of the old impediments to job creation data is still unavailable to observe expected changes in trends.

Patterns of Growth

During 1994 and partially in 1995, economic growth and recovery was mainly fueled by export growth. However, export performance started to deteriorate in 1996 as a result of an appreciating exchange rate, and continued to deteriorate further in 1997. Growth in real exports of goods and non-factor services slowed down to only 3 percent in 1995 (down from 14.2 percent in 1994), and to—0.3 percent in 1996. As export growth slowed, domestic demand—and investment demand in particular—took over as the main engine of growth. After declining in 1993-94, fixed investment increased in real terms by 5.3 percent in 1995, by 39.8 percent in 1996, and by 14.5 percent in 1997. Much of this, however, represented investment by the public sector and by a few large parastatals, and was financed through borrowing from abroad. During this period, the other components of domestic demand—private and public consumption—also increased substantially, at a rate of 6 to 8 percent per annum. Largely as a result, the current account shifted from a large surplus in 1994 and 1995, to very large deficits in 1996-98. Did this shift in the composition of the sources of growth have implications for job creation?

There are several ways to try to examine this. One way is to try to decompose changes in employment at the sector level into changes in domestic demand, exports, imports and labor productivity. This approach was followed recently, for example, in a World Bank report on the Polish labor market (World Bank, 2001). Following the methodology developed there, the decomposition is based on the following accounting identity:[16]

$$r_E = r_D(D/Q) + r_X(X/Q) - r_M(M/Q) - r_P$$

where r represents, respectively, the rate of change of employment (E), domestic demand (D), exports (X), imports (M), productivity (P) defined as Q/E, and Q represents total output.

We apply this decomposition to 16 industries over the 1994-99 period. The results are summarized in Table 2.12. The table clearly shows a strong job-creating effect of exports early on (1994/95), which declines quickly as export performance deteriorates. Domestic demand takes over as the main positive impact on employment change starting in 1996, but its positive impact is partially offset by imports. The table also shows that, on average, the job-creating impact of exports was smaller than the job-displacing impact of imports. The relationship between employment and productivity growth is clearly negative, offsetting much of the positive impact of exports and domestic consumption.

Table 2.12 Decomposition of Employment Change, 1994-99 (Median Industry Values) Percent Change (%)

All industries – median	1995/94	1996/95	1997/96	1998/97	1999/98	AVG94-99
Employment	-0.55	-1.72	-1.41	-5.81	-4.86	-3.14
Domestic consumption	25.80	18.10	2.78	22.27	-1.37	15.34
Exports	27.55	-0.55	3.87	4.43	4.20	8.93
Imports	-32.21	-6.68	-2.24	-27.87	-11.78	-13.77
Productivity	-17.30	-7.34	-11.71	-12.61	-11.95	-11.56

Source: Own calculations using merged NACE-SITC data at 2-digit sector level.

An alternative way to look at the employment impact of the shift from export-led growth to domestic-demand led growth is to go to our firm-level data and look at the differential behavior of firms serving the export market versus those serving the domestic market. Table 2.13 presents average annual growth in net aggregate employment, gross job creation rates, and gross job destruction rates for exporting and non-exporting firms.

---

[16] See World Bank (2001) for details on how to derive this decomposition. A similar approach was used earlier by Freeman and Katz (1989), and by Revenga (1990) for the United States.

Exporting firms are defined as those that export two-thirds or more of their production.[17] The table shows that exporting firms have had more net employment growth, and much more gross job creation. They have also experienced lower gross job destruction, and higher real wage growth.

Table 2.13 Net Employment Growth and Job Creation, Exporting vs. Non-Exporting Firms (%)

	1994	1995	1996	1997	1998	Avg. 94-98
Exporting Firms						
Net employment growth	-5.19	3.89	6.84	4.92	3.57	4.31
Gross job creation	0.13	2.59	3.75	2.74	2.95	2.29
Gross job destruction	-1.67	-2.51	-1.53	-2.85	-4.98	-2.56
Non-Exporting Firms						
Net employment growth	-5.73	-4.03	1.88	-0.92	-2.95	-1.71
Gross job creation	0.06	2.03	1.48	2.52	1.42	1.67
Gross job destruction	-1.68	-7.71	-1.21	-4.26	-8.14	-4.83

Source: Own calculations from ALBERTINA and TREND firm databases.

This evidence is just illustrative and much more in-depth work would be needed to ascertain what the employment impact of the shift in the composition of growth has been. Nevertheless, the findings suggest that the export-oriented sector was the most dynamic in terms of job creation during the early transition years, and that the slowdown of exports starting in 1996 may have been a factor contributing to weak employment performance.

Throughout much of the 1990s, the Slovak Government maintained a notionally "pro-investment" stance built on special incentives introduced under the privatization process and on large government-sponsored road and power infrastructure projects. Partly as a result, Slovak investment rates through most of the 1990s have been among the highest in all of Central Europe (Figure 2.6). Has this contributed positively to employment creation?

---

[17] Changing the "cutoff" level for classifying a firm as exporting by plus or minus ten percentage points did not have a significant impact on the results.

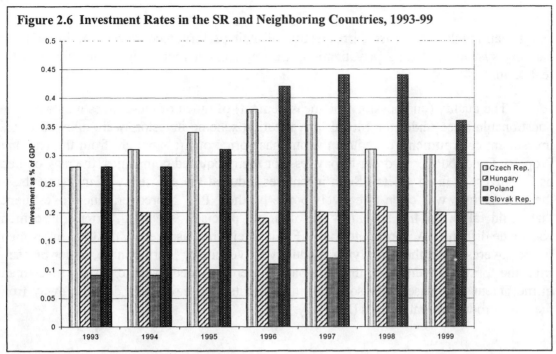

Figure 2.6 Investment Rates in the SR and Neighboring Countries, 1993-99

Source: Statistical Office of the SR, World Bank

Since the start of transition, investment has been recognized—both in theory and in practice—as a key vehicle for economic restructuring.[18] But it has also been recognized that what matters is *productive* investment. Investment rates in the former soviet block were very high, but a large amount was unproductive and growth was elusive in the 1980s. If firms face soft budget constraints, investment could reflect a waste of resources as the firms may use these funds for survival rather than for restructuring. Indeed, in the case of Slovak Republic, indirect government subsidies through the banking system to former SOEs have continued in a large scale through most of the 1990s. This may have undermined the use of investment as a means for restructuring. To the extent that it may have allowed the "survival" of inefficient firms, such policies may have slowed down job destruction in dying industries, but at a large cost. Without restructuring, and with inefficient investments and indirect subsidies going to non-viable firms, investment opportunities and hence job creation in truly viable alternatives may have been seriously dampened.

If we look at the composition of investment in the SR, we can see that much of it has been carried out by the public sector or by parastatals, which were formerly publicly owned. As a share of total investment, public investment declined from: 60 percent in 1993 down to 36 percent in 1999. But much of this apparent decline was due to the shift of parastatals from the public category at the beginning of the decade to the private category by the end. In reality the bulk of investment during 1994-1998 was carried out by very large firms, and by the four main public utilities (post, telecommunications, railways and electricity). In 1998, for example, nearly 70 percent of all investment was carried out by large firms (firms with more than 250 employees), even though these accounted for only 40 percent of total employment, and for less than 3 percent of the total number of firms. Many of these firms have easier access to credit from state owned

---

[18] See, for example, Aghion, Blanchard and Burgess (1994), and Blanchard, 1997.

39

banks than regular enterprises, irrespective of their performance. Recent reforms in the banking system, including privatization, are imposing harder budget constraints to the real sector.

The quality (and possibly the measurement) of much of these investments may be questionable since under the Slovak privatization scheme investors were allowed to use investment commitments to reduce the purchase price of firms bought from the National Property Fund (NPF). In order to pay less for their acquired companies, the new owners had to invest in fixed assets. Such incentives reduced the efficiency of investments, as the cost of them was often effectively borne by the NPF. Moreover, since investments that could fall under this scheme were often not precisely specified, strict enforcement was made difficult. According to the IMF it is likely that, as a result, the total investment figures overestimate the underlying productive investment. Furthermore, under pressure from the former Government, the state banks often provided loans to sustain investment in inefficient enterprises. By so doing investments may have been diverted away from the most productive enterprises (Box 2.1).

        VSZ, the giant steel mill located in eastern Slovakia is a good example of poor corporate governance, over investment, corruption, lack of strategic direction and close ties with the political elite. VSZ used to produce 9 percent of the Slovakia's GDP and generate 12 percent of Slovakia's exports. Privatized in several steps, first through vouchers (65 percent), then through some non transparent operations, the company was controlled by its managers and trade union which formed independent companies (Manager and Hutnik) that acquired part of VSZ at prices well below market.

        VSZ became a giant conglomerate/holding company with no clear strategic direction but with close ties to the government of PM Meciar. By 1996, VSZ had majority stake in 86 companies and the minority stakeholder in another 35 companies. The holding group included the Czech football club AC Sparta Prague (91 percent), daily newspapers Narodna obroda (86 percent) and Luc (77 percent), several investment companies and Slovenska poistovna (Slovak insurance company, 20 percent). Other companies were linked to VSZ through third parties. Stakes in the Slovak investment bank IRB, which was at that time the third largest bank in Slovakia, added up to 55 percent, of which VSZ direct ownership was 15 percent and through third parties at least 40 percent. This link made access to credit by VSZ easily available. By 1998, VSŽ held stakes in 102 companies in Slovakia and 16 abroad.

        During 1994–97 VSZ recorded profits, but by 1998 the company was in the red and eventually failed to service US$35 million of its foreign debt in 1999. The total debt of the company amounted to SK13bn. Since VSZ employed approximately 25,000 employees and impacted the jobs of 100,000, the government initiated negotiations with the creditors in an effort to prevent bankruptcy and massive layoffs. The Minister of Finance announced that the State was the largest creditor of VSZ with claims in amount of SK5bn for unpaid taxes. Eventually the government took back control (and partially renationalized the firm buying shares in the market), a foreign manager was put in place and VSZ began to restructure, selling some subsidiaries, including the football club AC Sparta Prague, some luxurious cars, garages, apartments, its jet aircraft and 100 pieces of art. The Company started paying interests (12 month delay) and wanted to solve its liabilities with the government (SK4bn), banks (SK18bn) and small suppliers (SK1.6bn). Consolidations of core activities followed, and negotiations to sell VSZ to a strategic foreign investor initiated. US Steel became the owner of all metallurgy related assets and also some significant liabilities of VSZ. US Steel offered in total US$425-475million, of which US$325million were for liabilities and US$15 million for past-due taxes. New investments for the next 10 years were promised in the amount of US$700million. No dismissal of labor was planned upfront, as the firm has a natural retrenchment rate of 6-7 percent annually. Around 25-30 managers were to come to VSZ from the US.

        Privatization and corruption. During the voucher privatization period of 1992-93, 65 percent of the company shares were privatized to the general public. On March 11, 1994, VSZ managers founded the company, Manager. The same day, parliament issued a vote of no confidence on the government of PM Merciar. However, three days later, the government approved the sale of 10 percent of VSZ's shares to Manager at a price of SK200 per share. That price was three times lower than the market price. The link between the government and VSZ was then constituted by the Minister of Finance and former manager of VSZ, Julius Toth. In 1995, Hutnik, a company founded by the VSZ's trade union, bought another 10 percent of the VSZ shares at the same price SK200 per share, even though the market price at that time was twice as high. The National Property Fund sold the remaining 15 percent of VSŽ shares to Ferrimex, s.r.o in July 1995, at SK200 per share. Ferrimex was owned by Hutnik (25 percent) and ARDS (75 percent), controlled by some of VSZ's managers. At that time, Alexander Rezes, the most important VSZ owner and Minister of Transport, Posts and Telecommunications, became the link with the government. Rezes obtained favorable transport prices for VSŽ at the cost of the state railways. Prior to the parliamentary elections in 1998, he worked as the leader of the election team of the then ruling HZDS.

Source: Marcincin (2000): Enterprise Restructuring, in Marcincin, A. and Beblavy, M. (eds.) Economic policy in Slovakia 1990-99, Bratislava.

        In terms of sectors, most investment has gone into non-tradable. Investment in industry and agriculture have declined steadily throughout the 1990s. The manufacturing sector, which accounted for 90 percent of exports and about 25 percent of GDP during 1994-98, received only about 20 percent of total investment during this period. Investment in market services increased sharply, and accounted for about 43 percent of total investment in 1999. At a more disaggregated level, it is possible to see that sectors such as chemicals, food, metal products have seen very little new investment; while transport equipment, communications, wholesale and retail trade, and other market services have seen the largest increases. What this means in terms of job creation is hard to infer, as some of these sectors—transport equipment, for example—have been among the more dynamic ones in creating jobs. At the same time, other dynamic sectors, more dominated by small firms such as leather or food products, are clearly not seeing new investment, which could be holding back the creation of jobs.

An interesting perspective on the allocation of investment resources across firms is given by data on banking system credit to enterprises. As can be seen in Table 2.14, since independence the state sector has absorbed, and continues to absorb, a very large fraction of all banking system credit. This fraction would be even higher if privatized parastatals had not been moved into the "private enterprise" category starting in the mid-90s.

Table 2.14 Banking Sector Credit (in billion of Slovak Koruna, end-year)

Credit:	1993	1994	1995	1996	1997	1998	1999*	2000**
Total	264.5	266.7	306.5	362.2	370.0	391.3	409.1	415.6
In SKK	256.4	252.3	283.8	331.4	334.6	346.9	356.9	362.1
Priv.	237.8	235.8	268.5	313.6	314.2	320.4	321.0	320.0
State	123.4	115.5	93.1	94.8	75.5	63.9	118.9	156.0
State/SKK	48.1%	45.8%	32.8%	28.6%	22.6%	18.4%	33.3%	43.1%
State/Priv.	51.9%	49.0%	34.7%	30.2%	24.0%	19.9%	37.1%	48.7%

* Bad loans moved to special financial agency; ** through 9/30/2000. *Source: NBS.*

We can use the firm-level data to get a first impression of whether banking system credit is being allocated to the most dynamic firms, or whether it is being used to "prop up" large firms that are in trouble. Table 2.15 presents some very simple statistics: employment size, net employment creation, growth in labor productivity and export orientation for firms that report not having or accessing bank loans versus those that do.[19] Although again, this is not hard evidence, the table clearly seems to suggest that firms who are not accessing credit tend to be smaller and have seen much more net employment growth. They also show higher average labor productivity (value added per worker), faster real wage growth, and a slightly higher export orientation. For some reason, the more dynamic firms in the sample—when it comes to generating employment—do not seem to be accessing bank credit, which during 1993-98 was going to larger, more sluggish firms.

Table 2.15 Banking Credit and Employment Performance

Use/access to banking credit:	Avg. number of employees	Avg annual employment growth	Avg. value added per worker ('000s SKK)	Share of exports in total sales
No	279	14.2%	1076.5	54.2%
Yes	1216	-0.64%	766.3	43.0%

Source: Own calculations from ALBERTINA and TREND datasets, 1993-98.

[19] We use a simple zero-one variable rather than any continuous measure of access to bank credit because: at the firm level we cannot really differentiate between the stock of loans and the current flow (in some cases we can, but in many the information on current flows is missing).

All in all, it seems that the public sector and large well-connected enterprises were absorbing a large share of available credit resources. Much of this was due to the past practices of "soft" lending by banks to poorly-performing but well-connected firms. Largely as a result of these bad lending practices, the Slovak state owned banking sector was faced with a massive crisis in the late 1990s. Banking practices are now being tightened, but one of the immediate impacts is that there is very little credit available for private firms other than very short term. And what is available is very expensive due to the high restructuring cost and the quality of the holding portfolio of the banks. This may prove to be a major constraint to the expansion of profitable firms in the near term, especially among small and medium enterprises (see below). There has clearly been a crowding out of private investment in the past, the effects of which are still being felt today and will probably continue to be felt in the near future.

Poor Investment Climate and Weak FDI Flows until 1998

It is widely acknowledged that the Slovak Republic's privatization process was far from transparent, and that it was plagued by cronyism and by numerous delays and changes in the methodology.[20] This was particularly true between 1994-1998. Most observers think that this contributed to making the country much less attractive to foreign investors. FDI flows were in fact been very modest during this period, amounting to only about 2 percent of total capital formation during the 1993-98 period. FDI flows to Slovak Republic were much lower than those pouring into its neighbors in Central Europe (Table 2.16). For example, at the end of 1998, cumulative FDI on a per capita basis equaled only US$340, or about

Table 2.16 Net Foreign Direct Investment in the Slovak Republic and Selected Countries (% of GDP)

	1992	1993	1994	1995	1996	1997	1998	1999	2000ϵ
Czech Republic	3.3	1.6	1.8	4.9	2.2	2.4	4.7	9.2	7.1
Estonia	1.9	4.0	5.4	4.2	2.5	2.7	11.0	4.2	6.1
Hungary	3.9	6.0	2.8	10.0	4.4	3.8	3.3	3.5	3.0
Poland	0.3	0.7	0.5	1.0	2.1	2.0	3.2	4.0	2.8
Slovak Republic	0.9	1.1	1.6	1.1	1.0	0.4	1.8	3.6	8.0
Slovenia	0.9	0.9	0.9	0.9	0.9	1.6	0.8	0.2	0.2

Source: IMF.

seven times less than in Hungary. Moreover, since 1994 the annual flow of net foreign direct investment fluctuated widely, in response to a few key investments per year. Low levels of FDI have prevented Slovak Republic from strengthening its export potential through capital injections from abroad, along with better management and technological know-how.

Several factor help explain why FDI flows have remained smaller in Slovak Republic compared to other neighboring countries:

- Lack of transparency, consistency and predictability in the implementation of investment-related laws that have resulted in the absence of legal protection for the rights of investors and in weak market regulations;[21]

---

[20] See, for example, IMF (1998 and 1999); OECD (1999)

[21] OECD 1999, pp. 73.

43

- Slow pace and reports of "cronyism" in the privatization process, in particular in the sectors attractive to major international investors; banking, telecommunications and infrastructure;

- Concerns over the macroeconomic environment and political stability, and a hostile environment for foreign investors (including numerous legal restrictions;[22]

- Slow, cumbersome, and sometimes corrupt company registration process for foreign investors;

- Relatively high and burdensome taxes. The corporate income tax rate was 40 percent until 1999, the highest in Central Europe, while the property transfer tax is unreasonably high and discriminates against foreign investors. In addition, Slovak Republic's tax holiday regime is complex and restrictive, and among the least attractive in the region;[23] and

- Increasing high level of external debt and the troubles plaguing the banking and enterprise sector.

Significant efforts have been made by the current administration to change the international perception about Slovak Republic. This effort has been successful. In combination with the recent OECD membership and a renewed and transparent privatization effort, particularly in the financial sector, increasing FDI flows to Slovak Republic have been the norm since 1999. By 2000 FDI flows to Slovak Republic are estimated to have reached 8 percent of GDP, over four times the level attained in 1998 and almost seven times the average reached during 1994-1998.

A recent survey of German investors,[24] suggested that most were generally satisfied with business in Slovak Republic. The situation was described as good by 38 percent of investors surveyed, satisfactory by 44 percent, and unsatisfactory by the remaining minority. This suggests that if some of the problems mentioned above relating to corruption, legal uncertainty or political stability were sorted out, FDI could flow into the country at similar levels than in neighbor Eastern European countries.

FDI is fairly concentrated both in terms of country of origin—with Germany and Austria jointly accounting for nearly 40 percent of the total stock of FDI—and in terms of sector of destination. Most foreign investment has concentrated in manufacturing (49.4 percent), trade (19.2 percent) and financial intermediation (19.6 percent). By number of firms, in 1997 just under 10 percent of private enterprises had foreign participation and a further 10 percent had mixed ownership—fairly low figures by the standards of the region. FDI flows have also been extremely concentrated in the Bratislava area, which attracted roughly two-thirds of all FDI that has come into the country. This may be one factor explaining why Bratislava's employment performance has far surpassed that of other areas.

---

[22] Remaining restrictions on non-resident purchases of shares in domestic-controlled banks were removed in February 1998.

[23] FIAS 1999.

[24] Quoted by Lukas, Zdenek. 1999, pp.31

What has been the impact of foreign participation on employment and labor productivity? Unfortunately, there is very little hard data that can be used to examine this. However, there are many reasons to believe that greater FDI flows would be very beneficial to employment creation. When it has come in, foreign ownership has usually been associated with greater restructuring, improved technological know-how and increased efficiency (Toth, 2001). Positive spillover employment effects can also be expected from the impact of a large foreign investor on local sub-contractors and SMEs.[25] In the short term, many foreign investments (at least those into existing firm) may not lead directly into expanded employment, but they help set the foundation for employment growth later on. Greenfield investments are more immediately beneficial from a job creation standpoint.

Evidence from Hungary shows that foreign-owned firms there were responsible for the creation of 75 percent of all new jobs between 1992-97.[26] In Hungary these enterprises absorbed a large fraction of workers released form state sector. Foreign-owned enterprises also saw labor productivity (and wages) rise much more than in either state-owned or domestic privately-owned firms. One can imagine that greater foreign ownership and/or foreign participation in Slovak firms could have equally positive effects on job creation.

What was needed to attract more FDI? According to many outside observers, a key factor was improving Slovak Republic's deteriorated international image.[27] This required establishing a credible track record on policy, a more transparent and investor friendly environment, and macroeconomic and political stability. The current administration has moved forcefully in these directions, implementing a series of needed reforms and bringing economic fundamentals to manageable levels (see Box 2.2). It may also be important to invest in key infrastructure bottlenecks (especially transport) in some of the less favored regions, where the lack of adequate infrastructure constitutes a major deterrent to foreign investors.

---

[25] See UNDP, 2001; de la Rocha, 2001.

[26] Kaminski and Riboud, 2000.

[27] See, for example, OECD (1999) and EBRD (2000).

Box 2.2 Reform Efforts since 1999

       In the Fall of 1998 a new coalition Government took office and immediately announced its intentions to reverse the policies that threatened Slovak Republic's economic and political stability. Since coming to power, the new government has successfully stabilized the economy and has launched an ambitious program of structural reforms. The Government's efforts have been recognized by the international community as indicated by the resumption of accession negotiations with the EU in November 1999, Slovak Republic's entry into the OECD in May 2000, the continuous improvement in the country's credit ratings, and the sharp decline in borrowing spreads.

Stabilization Efforts since 1999:

- The primary budget deficit was cut by nearly 2 percent of GDP;

- Primary expenditures were cut by 11 percentage points of GDP;

- The import surcharge has been eliminated (after 5 years) and corporate income tax rates have been reduced from 41 percent to 29 percent;

- The granting of Government guarantees has been significantly curtailed;

- Large privatization revenues have been used mostly to retire explicit and implicit Government liabilities;

- Administered prices (gas, electricity, heating, post, and railways) have been increased in 3 large steps;

- The current account deficit was reduced from 10 percent of GDP to 3.5 percent of GDP;

- The tightened fiscal stance has allowed the NBS to ease monetary policy;

- The improved policy mix has contributed to a sharp reduction in real interest rates, a nominal appreciation of the currency, an increase in foreign reserves, a rapid decline in the secondary market spreads on Slovak eurobonds, a rapid increase in export growth, and a rapid increase in the inflow of FDI (both greenfield and privatization-related). In fact, in 2000 FDI inflows amounted to nearly 10 percent of GDP (the highest among transition countries in 2000) and similar flows are expected in 2001 and 2002.

Structural Reforms since 1999:

- Banking sector reform has included the restructuring and privatization of the three large State banks, the consolidation of the medium and small banks, reform of the deposit insurance system, significant improvements in the legal and regulatory framework, and improvements in bank supervision;

- Enterprise sector reform has included the privatization of utilities and other state-owned enterprises, the workout of non-performing claims on enterprises, a comprehensive set of legal reforms designed to improve collateral and bankruptcy regimes, and improvements in corporate governance;

- Public sector reforms have improved the budget process and increased fiscal transparency; most extra-budgetary funds have been merged with the State budget, new rules prevent Parliament from submitting proposals that would result in an increase in the agreed budget deficit, medium-term financial planning has been strengthened, a functional classification of State expenditures will be introduced shortly, and a treasury system will be created in 2002 to improve overall public finance management. In addition, a comprehensive reform of tax administration is being implemented.

- The Government is preparing a comprehensive pension reform which will include the introduction of a multi-pillar system which is expected to become effective in 2004;

- The Government will also begin to prepare a comprehensive reform of health care to improve the efficiency and quality of health care services.

Source: The World Bank.

Obstacles to Small and Medium Enterprises

In much of Central-Eastern Europe, micro, small and medium enterprises have played a key role in employment creation. In Slovak Republic, the number of entrepreneurs and of workers employed by firms with up to 19 employees increased by 46 percent between 1994 and 1998 The bulk of these new jobs (74 percent) arose in the internal trade and market services sectors. A good example of how small enterprises are changing the composition of employment is found in less capital-intensive industries such as leather, textiles and food products. In this sectors, there is a visible process of de-concentration going on, with employment falls in large firms being compensated by employment gains in small firms. The mix of small versus large firms is moving more in line with what characterizes these sectors in more advanced economies. By 1998, small and medium firms were employing around 58 percent of total employment in Slovak Republic with important differences among sectors. In industry, large enterprises (more than 250 employees) still retain more than 60 percent of the employment, whereas in trade or construction, SMEs employ between 75 and 90 percent of all workers. Despite these developments, however, small firms in Slovak Republic appear to face some serious obstacles in their expansion and development.

In 1999 the European Bank for Reconstruction and Development (EBRD) conducted a major survey, in collaboration with the World Bank, on business environment and enterprise performance in transition economies in Central and Eastern Europe (BEEP survey), receiving feedback from over 3,000 enterprises in 20 countries of the region. Some 138 firms from Slovak Republic were interviewed, 25 of them public and 113 private. Among the firms interviewed, 11 had some kind of foreign participation, 58 percent were in the service sector and 42 percent in manufacturing. By size, 56 percent of the companies surveyed had less than 50 full-time employees and 21 percent had more than 200. Given the quality and thoroughness of the survey, as well as the number of countries encompassed and companies interviewed, the EBRD survey is a very complete tool of analysis for cross-country comparison of the private sector environment in Central and Eastern Europe. In this section, we use the data form this survey to identify some of the main concerns affecting SMEs in the Slovak Republic.[28]

Small firms identified the *high cost of borrowing*, the *high level of taxes*, the complexity of *tax regulations*, and *restrictive entry procedures* as the four main obstacles for their business. Corruption was not mentioned among the top obstacles for firms, although some 16 percent of them deemed it to be a problem. Low quality and inefficiency of public services was also mentioned, with Slovak Republic receiving the second lowest valuation after Bulgaria (among small firms in CEEC countries) when assessing the public sector's efficiency in delivering services.

---

[28] See de la Rocha (2001) for a more detailed discussion of this analysis.

Figure 2.7 Main Financial Obstacles for Small Enterprises in Central and Eastern Europe

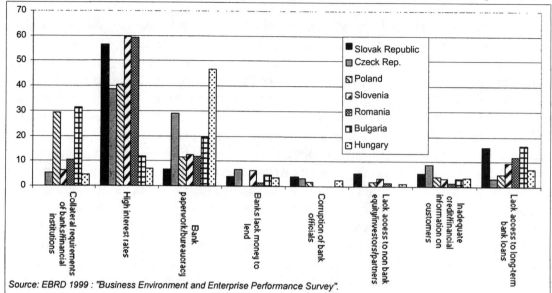

Source: EBRD 1999 : "Business Environment and Enterprise Performance Survey".

High borrowing costs were deemed to be a critical problem by 56.6 percent of small firms surveyed, followed by lack of access to long-term banking loans (see Figure 2.7). In the majority of Slovak enterprises the share of reported bank loans in assets is minimal, which points to the important role of self-financing through internal funds or retained earnings. This is especially true for SMEs. For example, 75 percent of small firms reported a zero credit burden to banks, while medium-size ones had bank loans below 22 percent of assets. Figure 2.8 below shows the average answers from Slovak firms in the EBRD survey about their sources of funding. Self-finance represented 73 percent of the total funding for small firms—ten points more than for the average of all firms and much higher than in Poland, Hungary or Czech Republic. Leasing arrangements and supplier credits were reported as the most important outside source of funding for all firms but representing each less than 10 percent of the total funds. Moreover, local banks were providing substantially less funding to small firms than to larger firms.[29] High levels of intra-firm indebtedness combined with difficult access to working capital from banks and suppliers suggests that many firms, especially small companies, are obtaining finance by way of defaulting their payments.

High taxes were mentioned by 62.3 percent of small firms as a major impediment to their business (compared to 55.6 percent among all firms). Compared to other CEEC countries, Small enterprises in Slovak Republic were the second most concerned after Hungary, and followed closely by Bulgaria. A 1997 FIAS study comparing the tax burden in Slovak Republic and neighboring countries showed that Slovak Republic's tax system appeared to be the most unfavorable for investors, especially foreigners, due mainly to the combined result of its rather high corporate income tax and the property transfer tax rate (20 percent at the margin). However, the reduction of the corporate income tax in late-1999, from 40 percent to 29 percent has gone a long way to bring Slovak Republic's corporate taxes more in line with those applied in the rest of Central

---

[29] See de la Rocha (2001)

and Eastern Europe. As in most of its neighbors, SMEs in the Slovak Republic enjoy certain benefits and tax exemptions. For example, VAT exemptions apply to small business with annual turnover below US$23,000, and new firms enjoy substantial tax reductions during the fist three years of operations. However, no special simplified tax regime applies currently to SMEs.

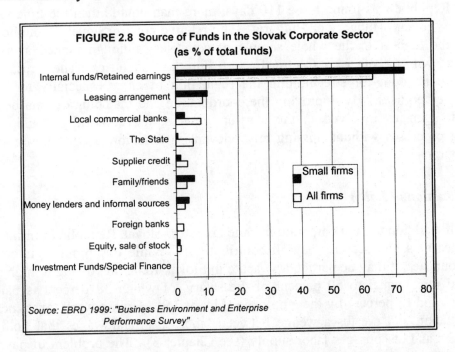

FIGURE 2.8 Source of Funds in the Slovak Corporate Sector (as % of total funds)

Source: EBRD 1999: "Business Environment and Enterprise Performance Survey"

Tax procedures and tax-related regulations were mentioned as a major problem for business by 55 percent of the small firms surveyed, versus only 25 percent of large companies. The FIAS' survey reports that while investors feel that the legal procedures for tax registration, collection and appeals are well developed in Slovak Republic, there are many problems and complaints about the lack of transparency and clarity in the interpretation of the law, which is very often left to the discretion of the tax official. Small companies are then discriminated versus larger companies since they are often worse prepared in lawyers or tax experts and hence, lack of transparency or clarity in the tax system implies higher costs in money and time than it does to larger firms.

The third main obstacle to business identified by Slovak Republic in firms were *entry regulations*. Some 6.4 percent of small firms considered it to be a major obstacle, more than twice the number than in any other CEEC country; some 19.5 percent considered it to be a moderate obstacle. Indeed, establishing a business enterprise in Slovak Republic tends to be cumbersome, slow and bureaucratic. Regulations are described by investors and lawyers as often confusing, and some times, non-existent. The company registries are decentralized, fragmented, and housed in the courts, which are severely over-burdened. Overall, according to FIAS, the process of starting up an enterprise in Slovak Republic is lengthier than in most other Central European countries, usually in the range of two to six months.[30]

---

[30] FIAS 1999.

A recent study published by the National Bureau of Economic Research,[31] which examined the required procedures governing entry regulations in seventy-five countries, confirms these findings. Slovak Republic was ranked 54 out of 75 regarding the burden, time and cost of setting up a company, falling behind every other Eastern European country analyzed. In particular, the standard time required to start up a business in Slovak Republic was found to be 110 days, more than double than the time required in Slovenia, Poland, Hungary or Bulgaria. The relative cost in Slovak Republic was also among the highest in the whole sample of countries, although ranked average when compared with the other six Central Eastern European countries. These results suggest that there is room for streamlining the regulation of entry especially for small and medium enterprises. By improving the coordination and matching of data between the different agencies involved in the start-up process, the authorities could streamline existing processes without missing any relevant information needed for prudential or safety purposes.

High Taxation of Labor

In addition to high corporate income tax rates, Slovak Republic in firms face very high rates of social security payroll contributions. While this problem is common to many countries, it may be particularly acute in Slovak Republic, owing to high (and flat) marginal rates, equal to 50 percent of the salary, of which 38 percent is paid by the employer and 12 percent by the employee (Figure 2.9). High payroll taxes increase the cost of labor, and creates a wedge between labor costs and wages that both burdens employers and discourages labor supply (see Chapter 3). The problem of payroll taxes may be particularly acute for SMEs, for whom the costs of complying with payroll taxes and with the necessary administrative procedures are likely to be higher than for big firms.

---

[31] S. Djankov and R. La Porta; 2000.

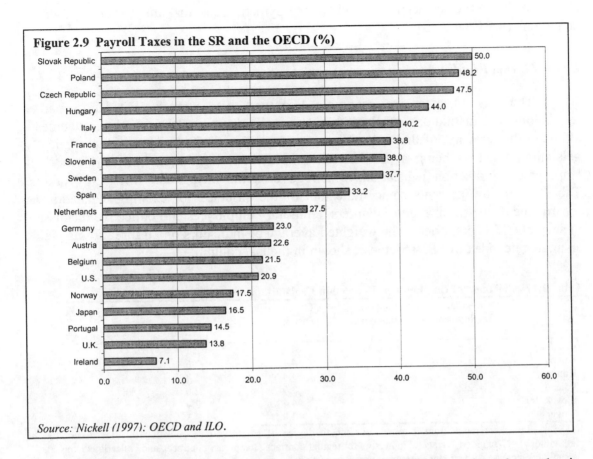

Figure 2.9 Payroll Taxes in the SR and the OECD (%)

Slovak Republic	50.0
Poland	48.2
Czech Republic	47.5
Hungary	44.0
Italy	40.2
France	38.8
Slovenia	38.0
Sweden	37.7
Spain	33.2
Netherlands	27.5
Germany	23.0
Austria	22.6
Belgium	21.5
U.S.	20.9
Norway	17.5
Japan	16.5
Portugal	14.5
U.K.	13.8
Ireland	7.1

Source: Nickell (1997): OECD and ILO.

High payroll taxes may introduce a bias against unskilled labor since the wedge is more burdensome at lower incomes. For higher-skill workers, business can more easily separate compensation into a wage and non-wage component; in addition it is also easier to understate true incomes for workers at the top of the scale. But for workers with lower skills, whose wages are already close to the minimum wage, there is much less margin to maneuver. The choice for enterprises is either to shy away from hiring low-skill workers, or to hire them "off the books", expanding the informal economy and inducing a loss of revenue for the state and other social costs. High payroll taxes may also discourage part-time employment: the employer needs to follow exactly the same procedures and encourage similar fixed costs as with a full-time employee, for fewer hours of weekly work.

In this context, reducing social security contributions could help boost job creation and reducing employment in the gray economy. Such reductions would reduce the wedge between gross and net salaries, increasing both labor demand and incentives to work. However, these cuts need to be very carefully designed to avoid further straining the government budget. Preferably, they should be carried out only within the context of a general reform of social security benefits and unemployment insurance, in order to eliminate the perverse incentives and unemployment traps that the current system is generating (see Chapter 3).[32]

Labor Market Rigidities

There is an extensive economic literature that suggests that labor market regulations and institutions can have a significant impact on labor market outcomes-- although the direction of that impact is not always clear.[33] One aspect which typically gets highlighted as being a problem for employment creation is the "strictness" of employment protection legislation, which governs the hiring and firing of workers. Table 2.17 below presents some indicators of the strictness of existing legislation as regards the dismissal of regular workers, temporary employees and collective dismissals in several CEEC countries. The weighted average of indicators on all three fronts yields an aggregate index of EPL strictness, shown in the last column.

Table 2.17 Strictness of Employment Protection Legislation, Late 1990s[1]

	Regular Employment	Temporary Employment	Collective Dismissals	Overall EPL strictness	
				Index[/2]	Rank[3/]
Czech Rep.	2.8	0.5	4.3	2.1	3
Estonia	3.1	1.4	4.1	2.6	5
Hungary	2.1	0.6	3.4	1.7	1
Poland	2.2	1.0	3.9	2.0	2
Slovak Rep.	2.6	1.4	4.4	2.4	4
Slovenia	3.4	3.1	4.8	3.5	6

Notes: [1/] Indicators range from 0 to 4 according to degree of strictness (see Nickell, 1997 for description of methodology). [2/] Weighted average of indicators for regular contracts, temporary contracts, and collective dismissals. [3/] Rankings increase with strictness of employment legislation.
Source: OECD 1999 and World bank staff estimates. Summarized in forthcoming paper by Riboud, Sanchez-Paramo and Silva-Jauregui (2001).

As one can see from the table, the Slovak Republic falls somewhere in the mid-range of the CEEC economies. Hungary has the most flexible labor legislation, closely followed by Poland, and the Czech Republic, while Slovenia stipulates more restrictions on employment issues. When extended to include also the OECD economies, Slovak Republic continues to fall in the middle range; ahead of many EU countries but behind notoriously flexible labor markets such as those of Australia, Denmark, Ireland, New Zealand, Switzerland, the United Kingdom, or the United States. Nevertheless, the degree of employment protection legislation in the Slovak Republic is far below that seen in more traditionally "rigid" labor markets, such as those of Italy, Spain or Portugal. It thus seems unlikely that low employment growth and job creation in Slovak Republic can be attributed to these firing rigidities per se. These restrictions, however, could tend to exacerbate the negative impact of other types of shocks and constraints. Take an example: economic and political uncertainty is more likely to have a negative impact on new employment creation if firms are concerned with not being able to adjust their workforce later on in response to a sudden downturn.

---

[32] A deeper analysis of Social Security and Unemployment Insurance is included in other background papers of this study.

[33] See, for example, Nickell (1997).

Three other features of the labor market which are important to its functioning are: (i) the characteristics of collective bargaining and strength of union representation; (ii) the design of policies aimed at supporting the unemployed; and (iii) the extent and design of active labor market policies. On all of these fronts, the Slovak Republic tends to score in the middle of the pack and on a par with most other CEEC economies (Table 2.18). As regards to other European and OECD economies, Slovak Republic ranks quite high in the degree of union coverage. Greater union coverage tends to be associated (across countries) with higher unemployment (Nickell, 1997). But this can be offset by greater employer and union coordination on wage setting, on which the Slovak republic also ranks highly. As regards the other features, Slovak Republic is not especially generous in its treatment of the unemployed relative to continental European countries, but it is much more generous than the Anglo-Saxon countries. It is not clear, however, what the overall effect of this is on labor supply and unemployment. As discussed in Chapter 3, there are reasons to believe that the UI system may generate some disincentive effects, but there is also some evidence that it may help with job search and with finding a better ultimate match between the job seeker and available jobs.

Table 2.18 Other Features of the Slovak and other CEEC Labor Markets

	Union Density (%)	Union Coverage Index	Coordination		Benefit Replacement (%)	Benefit Duration (months)	Active LMP[5] (%)
			Union	Employer			
Czech	42.8	2	1	1	50	6	2.0
Estonia	36.1	2	2	1	10[6]	6 - 3	0.8
Hungary	60.0	3	1	2	64	12 [1]	5.1
Poland	33.8	3	2	1	40[7]	12 - 24 [2]	2.6
Slovak	61.7	3	2	2	60	6 - 12[3]	4.4
Slovenia	60.0	3	3	3	63	3 - 24[4]	10.6

Notes: [1] Requires 4 years of employment. [2] Raising with previous employment tenure (up to 2 years). [3] Linked to period of contribution. [4] Average duration in 1996 was 13.1 months. Potential eligibility depends on the years of service. [5] Estonia, Czech Republic and Slovenia data are for 1998, Hungary data for 1997, and Poland and Slovak Republic for 1996. [6] Benefits are set at 60 percent of minimum wage, which amounts to around 10 percent of average wage. [7] The replacement ratio is set at 40 percent of average wage in the preceding 12 months. The ratio than increases by 3 percent for each year of tenure, and decreases monthly by 4 percent in the second half of the year. Minimum and maximum amounts are set at 75 percent of the minimum wage and 60 percent of the previous wage.

Source: OECD Employment Outlook (1999), Table 2.5., column 10 and 11. World Bank estimates for Estonia and Slovenia, utilizing the labor code for Estonia, and the new draft for labor code for Slovenia. World Bank (1999) Czech Republic: Toward EU Accession, World Bank Country Study, Labor Market Chapter. World Bank (1998) Slovak Republic: A Strategy for Growth and European Integration, World Bank Country Study, Labor Market Chapter. IMF, Article IV consultation with the Slovak Republic.

On the whole, it seems unlikely that any of these factors would be a major contributor to the level of unemployment, but they are likely to be a significant contributor to the composition of the unemployed. Other structural measures, especially those introducing at the beginning of the transition from command to market economy are likely to have contributed more to the creation of unemployment. Any contribution from institutional factors may have been masked by the size of the adjustment produced by other structural reforms.

THE IMPORTANCE OF REGIONAL AND SKILLS MISMATCH

Section B above focused on factors that may have negatively affected the demand for labor—on aggregate and at the level of firms and industries—and hence led to stagnant employment growth and rising unemployment. However, demand factors yield only one part of the overall picture. An equally important determinant of employment and unemployment outcomes is the process by which labor demand and labor supply get matched: or in other words, how the labor market and its institutions mediate the process of transiting from old jobs (or no jobs) to new jobs.

This matching process has several critical dimensions. A first important dimension is the extent to which the skills demanded in the new jobs are offered by (or available among) those looking for jobs (whether these individuals be new entrants in to the labor force, unemployed, or out-of-the labor force waiting to be pulled back in). A second important dimension is the extent to which jobs are being offered in the same places where there are available workers; or the extent to which workers can migrate without difficulty to the location of the new jobs. On both of these dimensions, the Slovak labor market gives evidence of serious matching problems.

Indicators of Mismatch in the Labor Market

A first indicator of mismatch can be gleaned from the existence of wide disparities in unemployment outcomes across regions and localities. Although the Slovak Republic is not a large country, the differences in unemployment rates between prospering areas and disadvantaged areas are huge. The district with highest unemployment is Rimavská Sobota, with a rate of 37.6 percent; the district with the lowest rate of unemployment is Bratislava IV, with only 4.8 percent unemployment—nearly eight times less. As shown in Table 2.19, the variability of unemployment rates across and within regions has been increasing over time, both in absolute and relative terms. Both the coefficient of variation of district unemployment rates (a measure of relative variability) and the standard deviation of district unemployment rates (a measure of absolute variability) have increased sharply since 1991.

Table 2.19 Variability of Unemployment, by Regions and Districts, 1997-2001[1]

	Unemployment rate			Standard deviation[2]			Coefficient of variation[3]		
	1997	2001	Rank[4]	1997	2001	Rank[4]	1997	2001	Rank[4]
Bratislavský	4.60	6.6	1	2.2	3.1	2	0.457	0.472	8
Trnavský	11.48	16.6	3	2.9	3.6	4	0.264	0.216	4
Trenčiansky	9.10	14.1	2	3.3	4.1	6	0.338	0.289	6
Nitriansky	15.04	23.7	5	2.5	3.7	5	0.162	0.157	2
Žilinský	11.69	18.2	4	3.1	3.5	3	0.247	0.194	3
Banskobystrický	15.87	24.2	6	6.3	7.6	8	0.382	0.314	7
Prešovský	18.86	25.4	7	3.3	3.0	1	0.168	0.119	1
Košický	18.33	27.0	8	5.6	6.8	7	0.311	0.251	5
Total SR	13.37	19.8	--	6.0	7.8	--	0.426	0.394	--

Notes: [1] Refers to 12/31/1997 and 1/31/2001. [2] The SD is a measure of absolute variability. [3] The CV is a measure of relative variability (equal to the SD divided by the mean). [4] Rank is for 1/31/2001.
Source: World Bank

As can be seen from the table, the region with the highest unemployment is Kosice (27 percent); that with the lowest is Bratislava (6.6 percent); but even in low unemployment regions there is very high variability. This indicates that there are districts with high unemployment in close proximity to districts with low unemployment. The fact that these differences exist and are persistent (and growing) over time, suggests that there are important barriers to labor mobility: unemployed workers do not seem to be able to move to the districts where the new jobs are located (see also section 3 below).

A second, commonly-used, indicator of mismatch is the ratio of job seekers to job postings—that is the number of unemployed per vacancy. Figure 2.10 plots these ratios for the Slovak Republic as a whole, and by region. The table shows that for country as a whole the number of unemployed per vacancy has increased more than fourfold, from 18 at end-1997 to 84 at end-2000. For certain depressed regions, the increase has been even shaper: for example, by end-2000 in the Kosice region there were 266 unemployed (or potential job seekers) per posted vacancy. Clearly, the expectations of getting a job for an unemployed individual in Kosice are very low.

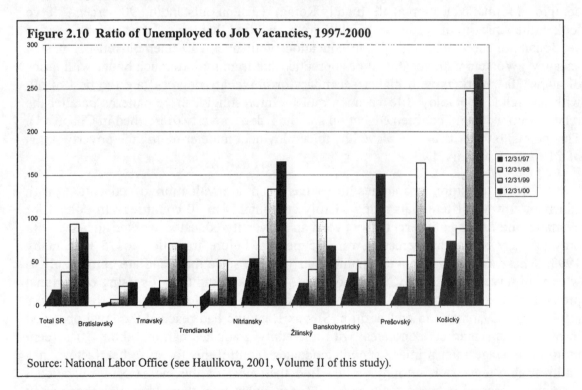

Figure 2.10 Ratio of Unemployed to Job Vacancies, 1997-2000

Source: National Labor Office (see Haulikova, 2001, Volume II of this study).

These vacancy figures could be overstating the seriousness of the problem, since they correspond to "official" vacancies, drawn from the lists complied by the National Labor Office, and they could be missing some of the activity going on in the labor market. Indeed, in many other countries, official labor offices capture only a fraction of existing vacancies. However, in Slovak Republic, posting a vacancy is mandated by law, and both anecdotal evidence and the opinion of Slovak experts seems to indicate that the figures are fairly accurate. If anything, official figures are likely to underestimate vacancies at the top end of the job spectrum, where professional networks and connections play a more important role in job search (Buerkle and Guseva, 2000). But this would not alter much the dismal job opportunity picture for workers with lower skills. And while some lower-skill jobs exist which are never officially posted—those filled informally or through temporary arrangements—they do seem numerous enough to alter substantially the trends portrayed in Figure 2.10.

A Widening Skills Gap

In addition to a geographical dimension, mismatch in the labor market also seems to have a skill component. A big fraction of the stock of the unemployed are workers with basic or less than basic education (including those who have not completed any formal schooling). Yet all evidence suggests that new jobs are demanding a higher level of skills.

Workers with basic or less than basic education represent almost a third of the total unemployed, and nearly 40 percent of the long-term unemployed (those unemployed for over a year). Unemployment rates for workers with completed basic education are hovering around 30 percent; while those for the small group of workers with no completed formal education at all (mainly Roma) reach an outstanding 90 percent. If we look at the structure of vacancies by skill group, we find that the most unfavorable ratios are found for those with only basic education, with over 130 unemployed per posted vacancy. Workers with vocational or apprenticeship training fare much better with ratios of about 30. Workers with higher secondary or university degrees fare the best of all, with negligible unemployed to vacancy ratios. Interestingly, these patterns parallel the relationship we found between education and the risk of poverty (described in Chapter 1). This points to the critical role played by unemployment in determining the poverty status of a family or an individual.

In all transition economies there has been a revaluation of education, with educational wage differentials rising sharply and quickly in all countries. In Poland for example, the earnings differential between an university-educated worker and one with only primary education increased from 35 percent before transition to 75 percent by 1993. These differentials have remained fairly stable since then, and are comparable to what is observed in other OECD economies. A similar trend towards rising educational premiums is evident in Slovak Republic. According to Filer, Jurajda and Planovsky (1999), by 1997 returns to education in Slovak Republic had reached the level observed in more mature market economies, with university graduates earning about 70 percent more on average than primary school graduates (controlling for all other factors in a multivariable regression setting). They find that most of the increase in educational premiums occurred between 1995 and 1997--somewhat later than what was observed in Poland.

Wage differentials are increasing not only across education groups, but also across industries and across occupations. The average gross wage of an unskilled worker, for example, has fallen in relative terms to about 30 percent of that of a scientist or technical specialist; and to less than a fourth than that of a "legislator or leading professional", the top occupational category. Prior to transition, wages of unskilled workers were almost two-thirds those of the top occupational category. In this regard, Slovak Republic's wage structure is simply starting to resemble that of more mature market economies. But the underlying increasing demand for skills bodes ill for the stock of unemployed, who do not have these skills and who may even lack the education foundation needed to acquire them.

Despite the signs that point towards a widening skills gap between the unemployed and the skills demanded in new jobs, firms surveyed do not highlight "lack of skilled labor" as a significant problem in the Slovak Republic. Most firms surveyed do not report having a surplus of unskilled labor nor a shortage of skilled workers, with the slight exception of small firms who do report an excess of unskilled workers (from the BEEP survey).[34] A parallel survey of foreign investors, as reported in the EBRD's *Transition Report 2000*, suggests that foreign firms in Slovak Republic and neighboring countries view both their skilled and unskilled workers as only moderately less productive than workers in their own countries (varying between 60 and 78 percent of productivity of foreign workers, depending on skill category). The same firms report that workers on average would need between four and six months of training to achieve Western standards of productivity (interestingly, the training period required is shortest for workers with vocational training, and is as high for university graduates as for primary education grads). Lack of general flexibility or adaptability is by far the greatest perceived deficiency across all educational categories. Firms also find that workers with vocational education tend to lack the necessary IT skills; not so for university graduates, who on the other hand were found to lack technical and managerial capacity. All in all, this suggests that firms do not face critical barriers in getting the quality of workers they need, and that deficiencies can be made up through training.

Barriers to Labor Mobility

As mentioned above, the existence of large and persistence differences in unemployment rates across regions and districts suggests that there are significant barriers to labor mobility. Table 2.20 shows that, in fact, the extent of internal mobility has declined by almost 25 percent since the 1980s. So clearly people are not moving more in response to differentials in employment opportunities and incomes. Somewhat surprisingly, the structure of migration: within districts, between districts or across regions has not changed very much. There is no notable increase in migration flows across districts or across regions, even as geographical differences in unemployment outcomes have widened.

Table 2.20 Internal Migration among Districts and Regions

	1980	1990	1991	1993	1994	1995	1997	1998
Number of migrants ('000s)	115.6	100.8	93.1	85.0	82.6	68.3	82.5	84.8
O/w % shares:								
within district	56.5	59.4	60.2	59.6	58.7	55.8	43.5	44.0
within regions	24.0	22.5	21.5	22.2	21.9	23.5	33.4	33.8
across regions	19.5	18.1	18.3	18.2	19.4	20.7	23.1	23.2

Note: Migration defined as change of permanent address. Data for 1996 among regions not available due to administrative reform.
Source: Statistical Office of the SR, reported in Lubyova (2000).

---

[34] See de la Rocha (2001), in Volume II; and EBRD (2000).

Some labor mobility could take the form of commuting, and not involve a change of residential address. In this case, it would not be adequately captured by the migration statistics. Indeed, anecdotal evidence points towards some increase in commuting, especially around Bratislava region. But unfortunately, hard statistics on this are lacking.

Why are Slovak families not moving more? The biggest problem seems to be the housing market. A first deterrent is the high cost of home purchase in better off regions, such as Bratislava (which combined with a weak mortgage market puts home buying outside the possibilities of most families, and especially those from depressed regions). A second barrier is a narrow and expensive rental market, especially in the Bratislava region. And a third barrier is the continued existence of complex administrative regulations and requirements governing a change of permanent address. Data on housing expenditures is scarce, but some insights can be gleamed from the 1999 Household Budget Survey (which, unfortunately, does not include some of the worse-off groups of the population such as the unemployed). Housing and rental expenditures per quarter (averaged for the full year) are summarized in Table 2.21. Reported quarterly expenditures on housing do not seem to be significantly different across regions, and are only slightly higher in Bratislava than in the rest of the country. However, these figures could be deceptive, since most people own their house. What is not captured here is the differential in the value of a house in Bratislava versus other regions--and thus the extra one-time expenditure that would be needed to move from a poorer region to the Bratislava area. Probably a better picture of the problems in the housing market can be drawn from the information on rents. Here, it is clear that rent payments in Bratislava are noticeably higher than in other regions (with the exception of Banska Bystrica, which also has high rents).

Table 2.21 Expenditures on Housing and Rent, 1999 (average for all four quarters)

Region:	Housing expenditures (SKK per quarter)	As % of total household expenditure	Rent payments (per month)
All Regions	*6,523.9*	*12.0*	*571.3*
Bratislava	6,895.2	12.8	741.6
Trnava	6,238.7	12.4	541.7
Trencin	6,544.7	10.7	412.6
Nitra	6,345.8	12.1	516.9
Zilina	6,540.9	12.0	447.1
Banska Bystrica	6,294.1	12.2	809.7
Presov	6,809.5	11.8	492.9
Kosice	6,506.6	11.8	543.7

Source: Own calculations from 1999 Household Budget Survey family records.

Another reason why families may be reluctant to move away from depressed regions is because of social networks and the importance of family and friends as a means of support—especially when someone is unemployed. In Chapter 1 we mentioned that the amount of aid Slovak households receive from family and friends is very significant, and higher than in other CEEC countries. These networks are also very important to finding jobs. To the extent that moving residences may imply moving away from these support networks, it could have a large dampening effect mobility. In fact, the worse the situation gets for an unemployed family, the more difficult it may be to move, since the support network becomes more and more important as a means for survival and the resources at people's disposal to finance a move become smaller. A similar phenomenon, for example, has been documented in Spain, where family support networks and changes have proved critical to the unemployed. The role of family support has been one factor explaining the persistence of regional unemployment differentials there.

Until recently, information flows on job opportunities between districts and regions were also limited, hence making it more difficult for families to move. This was corrected in 1998, when labor offices across regions and districts started to coordinate and share their information on job seekers and vacancies.

Finally, with regards to commuting, the biggest barrier seems to be relatively high costs of transport in the Slovak Republic.

ENHANCING EMPLOYMENT CREATION: CONCLUSIONS AND POLICY RECOMMENDATIONS

The Slovak labor market has been characterized during the 1990s by its rising unemployment, low net employment growth, and sluggish job creation. All in all, job creation in Slovak Republic is low, and below that seen in neighboring countries. Some of the evidence from 1994-1998 found suggests the reluctance to allow more restructuring, while it may have postponed the inevitable job destruction, may have also affected the ability of the Slovak economy to create new, better jobs. A pattern of growth biased against exports has not helped either, as it has stifled the most dynamic part of the Slovak economy—at least in terms of job creation. Moreover, new private firms may have been crowded out of the credit market by huge public borrowing and public investments, and by the directing of credit to well-connected large enterprises at the expense of smaller, more dynamic ones. Again, at the cost of job creation.

All in all, it is clear that generating employment is one of the country's most pressing economic and social problems. Tackling this problem, however, will require addressing some of the underlying causes of slow job creation outlined above. The changes in economic policy introduced since 1999 are steps in the right direction and are likely that in time will help reinvigorate the labor market and improve the economy and business conditions so that the private sector can create more jobs to reduce the large unemployment rates.

Creating a More Favorable Economic Environment for Private Firms and Investors

The first priority for job creation is building a more appropriate environment for successful firms to function, grow and create employment. This requires continued macroeconomic and political stability, and establishing the credibility of policy vis-à-vis both domestic and foreign investors. Significant progress has been made in this direction by the new Slovak Government, but the threat of reversals still exists, with potentially discouraging effects on both domestic and foreign investors.

Creating a more favorable environment for firms to grow also requires, very urgently, profound reforms of the financial sector to ensure that the banking system is solvent, and that credit is available and flows to the most viable and dynamic firms. This too is a key element of the current reform agenda. Reducing the public sector's absorption of scare investment and credit resources will be key, as well, to allowing resources to flow to firms that have the potential to expand and create jobs. It will also contribute to reducing the high cost of credit, once the problems in the banking system are resolved and the portfolio of the banks improved.

Another top priority is addressing policy biases that favor domestic demand led growth at the expense of exports. Without improved export performance, Slovak Republic's chances of sustaining labor productivity and employment growth over the long term are poor. Recent trends in FDI flows are encouraging and should be a boost to both productivity and export performance.

A clear pro-export orientation, sounder financial system and greater transparency and credibility in administrative regulations and procedures will also help attract even more of the much-needed foreign investment. Such foreign direct investment, especially of the greenfield type, holds substantial potential for creating new jobs, and for generating positive spillover effects onto domestic firms. Experiences from other transition economies in the region, particularly Hungary and the Czech Republic, demonstrates the potential gains from FDI.

Supporting the Development of SMEs

Small and medium enterprises have the potential to be one of the engines of job creation. SMEs have been the key for job creation in other transition economies of CEE. However, the environment for SMEs in Slovak Republic needs to be improved if they are to play such an important role. A first priority is tackling the scarcity of credit which affects SMEs most of all. As argued above this requires, first of all, a sound financial sector reform, to ensure the solvency of the banking sector and its efficient operation. This is well underway. However, even relatively well-functioning financial systems can fail to serve small borrowers. From the point of view of the lender, monitoring small loans is much more expensive (as a function of loan size) than monitoring larger loans; moreover, the cost of enforcing repayment, if forced to go through the legal system, may be higher. What additional measures can be taken to promote wider access to credit among small entrepreneurs? Micro-credit schemes or schemes specifically targeted at small borrowers have some potential, but such programs have to be run on a strictly commercial basis. What can help small enterprises are not subsidized loans, but rather simplified procedures, tailored documentation and capital requirements and tailored treatment of collateral. Other measures which can improve the availability of credit to small borrowers are establishing or strengthening credit bureaus, improving the legal framework for leasing and factoring, and fostering the development of credit unions.

Another ingredient which may be important to facilitating the emergence and expansion of SMEs is the simplification of regulations and administrative procedures, and especially of licensing requirements. "Single-window" arrangements that allow entrepreneurs to comply with most administrative requirements at one time can be very helpful at encouraging and facilitating entry.

Measures to simplify the tax regime for SMEs may also help their development and help boost job creation. The National Agency for the Development of Small and Medium Enterprises (NADSME) has identified two serious tax-related problems affecting small and medium enterprises: first, the obligation to transfer tax funds according with the tax base of the previous year, without taking into account changing market situations; second, the impossibility of deducting investments from the taxable income base. In 1999, NADMSE proposed a number of changes in the way SMEs calculate their tax base in order to make them simpler and more favorable. These proposals included a gradual lowering of the tax rate, including increasing the amount exempt from income tax; allowing for deductions in the tax base for investments; improving the depreciation policy of tangible investments making it more favorable for SMEs; and simplifying the accounting requirements for tax purposes for small traders. Such proposals could significantly support the growth and development of SMEs. An alternative approach to simplifying the tax regime for SMEs, which has been implemented in many countries, is to opt for lump-sum presumptive taxation for certain categories of enterprises, or other simplified mechanisms (see Box 2.3).

Increasing Wage Flexibility and Reducing Labor Costs

Unlike some neighboring countries (e.g., Poland), Slovak Republic does not seem to face a problem of wage flexibility. Minimum wages are low, and do not appear to be binding even in the poorer regions. The minimum wage represents only between 20 to 25 percent of the average wage (depending on the region). Very few workers, according to the 1999 HBS, report earning the minimum wage even in lower-income Presov or Kosice. The only group for whom the minimum wage could have an effect is for unskilled young workers (new entrants) in poorer regions, but even among these individuals the minimum wage still represents less than 40 percent of the average wage. This is the usual "cutoff" point above which the minimum wage is deemed to have negative employment effects. It thus seems unlikely that the minimum wage is having serious negative employment effects.

Box 2.3 Simplified Taxation Schemes for SMEs

One way to simplify the tax regime for SMEs is to introduce presumptive taxation or lump-sum taxes for small business, which simplifies compliance procedures and therefore reduces the scope for arbitrary interference. The experience of other European economies may provide useful lessons for Slovakia in this regard. An example from an EU country with a corporate sector structure similar to that of Slovakia is Spain. In Spain, like in Slovakia, the share of self-employed (75 percent) and micro enterprises (22 percent) in the total number of business is much higher than elsewhere in the European Union (50 percent). To tackle the problem of tax evasion and tax regulations for small business, during the last decade the Spanish authorities have introduced a number of measures aimed at these kind of companies:

First; since 1995 a special tax rate applies to small business with turnover of less than ESP 250 million (US$1.3 million). They benefit from a reduced corporate tax rate of 30 percent, up to the first ESP 15 million (US$0.07 million) of taxable profits; additional taxable profits being taxed at the normal 35 percent rate.

Second; small business, self-employed and other professionals are subject to the personal income tax, and may qualify for special simplified regimes. SMEs, with turnover below ESP 100 million (US$0.52 millions) may choose between two simple taxation systems:

- a "forfaitaire" system, introduced in 1992, relying on objective assessment of taxable income. Under this system the income assessment to calculate the tax amount relies on ex-ante business activity indicators—for instance the number of employees, power consumption, workshop surface, etc. By 1996, about 75 percent of small and micro business were taxed according to the "forfaitaire" system; and

- A "simplified direct estimation" system, based on simple accounting rules which came into effect in 1998 replacing the "simplified flat rate system" which was a mixture of a "forfaitaire" system and estimation based on accounting rules. In 1996 10 percent of small and micro business were subject to the "simplified direct estimation".

Moreover, both systems allow for more liberal depreciation deductions for tangible assets according to simplified rules and giving more freedom to SMEs in spreading the capital depreciation expenses over time.

These fiscal measures for SMEs have proved useful for containing tax avoidance and simplifying tax-compliance. Hence, the introduction of a "forfaitaire" system, or reduced rates for SMEs, in a country like Slovakia where small and micro enterprises make up more than 85 percent of all business, could boost job creation and lead to a reduction of tax fraud and an increase in the transparency of the tax regulations. At the same time, however, reduced rates for small business can lead to under-invoicing in order to be eligible for the lower rate. Furthermore, a drawback of the "forfaitaire" system is that it can increase taxpayer inequity, since firms whose taxes are underestimated by the relevant activity indicators may free ride in the system. If a similar system were to be implemented it is therefore suggested that as the use of accounting becomes more widespread among small business the "forfaitaire" system be replaced by a "simplified direct estimation" scheme.

Source: de la Rocha (2001), Volume II of this study.

What could be having more negative effects are wage settlement and negotiation procedures, especially as pertains to collective bargaining. Wage bargaining in Slovak Republic occurs at three levels: (i) nationwide tripartite bargaining which sets broad guidelines to be followed throughout the economy; (ii) industry-wide agreements which are binding for all firms in the sector; and (iii) enterprise-specific bargaining agreements on top of what was agreed at the industry level. This structure is fairly similar to that which exists in much of continental Europe. However, this type of structure can pose some wage flexibility problems. Some critics argue, for example, that while nationwide agreements offer a useful overall coordination framework for bargaining, industry-level agreements can have damaging effects on employment by putting upward pressure on wages. Indeed some evidence suggests that to the extent industry-wide agreements that apply to all firms irrespective of particular situations, they can put additional pressure on wages, as they in fact create a floor for successive wage bargaining at the firm level.

However, the evidence on this is far from uniform, and other experts argue that decentralized bargaining in union-dominated systems can be just as damaging by creating "leapfrogging" behavior by unions, who take an earlier pay settlement in a related sector as a baseline to be exceeded in its own negotiations. Regardless of the model chosen, what is important as long as union representation is strong, is to ensure that there is: (i) coordination across unions and between unions and employers; and that (ii) the bargaining framework allows individual firms and workers to adjust their pay settlements to the specific situation of the firm and workers involved so that wages an productivity changes are better linked.

Another possible reason for concern as regards the flexibility of wages is the extent to which wage bargaining is de-linked from the consequences of wage decisions. Slovak Republic has seen significant growth in the use of temporary contracts. If bargaining is done mainly by unions who represent permanent workers, and short-term employment adjustments are borne mainly by temporary workers, there can be a dangerous disconnect between wage demands and the situation in the labor market. This is exactly what happened in Spain during the second half of the 1980s, following the introduction of widespread temporary contracts (Bentolila and Dolado, 1997) Hard empirical evidence on whether this is actually happening in Slovak Republic does not exist, although anecdotal evidence and conversations with union leaders suggest it is not the case at present. It may, however, become a problem in the near future, if the use of temporary contracts continues to spread and if unions do not sufficiently take into account the welfare of temporary workers in the bargaining decisions.

Although there is little indication that wage flexibility poses a problem in Slovak Republic, it is clear that firms face very substantial non-wage labor costs. As seen above, at 50 percent the payroll tax is by far the highest in the region. If you add personal income taxes and a corporate tax which applies to self-employed individuals, it is clear that the overall tax burden on labor incomes in Slovak Republic is very high. Such a high tax wedge is bound to have effects on both labor demand and labor supply. On the supply side, the high wedge could at the margin be discouraging potential workers from entering the labor market, and contributing to low employment to population ratios. It may also be feeding a welfare dependency trap (see Chapter 3). On the demand side, high non-wage costs are contributing to reducing overall labor demand, and may introduce a bias against low skill workers. While lowering the tax wedge will not provide the solution to Slovak Republic's employment problem, it would be a positive step towards facilitating job creation.

Lowering the payroll tax has to be a critical part of lowering the overall tax wedge. However, this has to be done as part of an overall reform of the social security, pension and unemployment insurance system and in coordination with a sound fiscal stance. Tightening the rules on sickness and disability insurance will also be important. Options to reduce the personal tax on labor income could include, among others, increasing tax deductions for families with at least one working adults, introducing lower-income tax credits. Lowering the tax burden is critical but needs to be accompanied by a similar effort in the expenditure side of the budget to avoid the large fiscal deficits that weakened the Slovak economy in the past.

There is little evidence that labor regulations and institutions are introducing important rigidities in the Slovak labor market. Firing restrictions are on a par with those of neighboring countries and below levels seen in much of Western Europe. There is also little evidence that severance requirements are preventing firms from adjusting their labor force, or that they are a significant factor in low job creation. Avoiding measures that increase rigidities in the labor market and its institutions should remain in the governments agenda.

Investing in Worker Skills and Training

Measures to increase labor demand and labor supply will have little effect on final employment outcomes if workers entering or re-entering the labor market do not have adequate skills. As discussed above, there seems to be a wide and growing gap between the skills being offered by those in search of jobs—especially among unemployed workers and new entrants—and those demanded in the new jobs.

Long-term solutions to the skill mismatch problem involve a comprehensive reform of the education and training system, so as to improve overall qualification levels and align them better with the demands of the labor market. The discussion of such reforms go significantly beyond the scope of this paper, and will not be addressed here. However, in a more narrow sense, measures are needed in the immediate and short term to address the skill deficiencies of those who are already in the labor market and of those who are now unemployed. There seems to be broad consensus among policymakers, union representatives, academics and other experts that Slovak Republic needs to encourage continued participation in adult education and training programs among all its workers, and not only the unemployed. The problem is how to do this. Publicly financed investments in external training have largely proven to be ineffective worldwide, unless targeted to very specific categories of workers. Job search assistance and other complementary measures have proven to be more cost-effective in helping the unemployed, and may prove more useful in the Slovak context as well. But in terms of equipping workers, unemployed or not, with new skills the most promising avenue is to encourage firms to do training themselves.

There are several possible directions to go in, many of them complementary: (i) allow costs of training unemployed hires to be tax deductible, or even partially subsidized; (ii) allow workers to use fraction of their unemployment insurance to pay for such on-the-firm training or to privately purchase and invest in training; (iii) introduce apprenticeship contracts that allow firms who hire new entrants to pay below stipulated industry minimums in exchange for engaging in on-the-job training; (iv) consider loans for individuals to finance education and training on their own; and (v) encourage the development of privately-supplied training and job-matching services. Regardless of type of program chose, constant monitoring and evaluation to continually assess the impact of the programs is key. Moreover, the choice and extent of such programs should be carefully balanced against their financial cost—especially at a time where mounting demands for social spending are at odds with a need for fiscal restraint.

Enhancing Labor Mobility

The Slovak labor market seems to suffer from important barriers to labor mobility. Mainly these seem to have their route in the housing market. Large housing price differentials between poorer and richer regions; absence of an effective mortgage market that allows households to borrow against a future stream of earnings; and a narrow rental market were identified as the main problems. Tackling these problems is complex and has to be done in the context of overall housing policy and reform strategy. But it is clearly a priority in terms of encouraging labor mobility and reducing regional disparities in unemployment.

High transport costs may also be a problem in discouraging commuting and in keeping people from taking up jobs that are far from their home. One option for reducing the burden of transport costs and encourage commuting would be to make them in part tax deductible, as is done in may countries.

Other measures to facilitate mobility include: (i) ensuring that information on job vacancies and opportunities flows quickly and accurately across regions and districts, through the NLO offices but possible through alternative mechanisms as well; (ii) liberalizing and encouraging the emergence of private job placement and temporary agencies, which can help mediate the supply of and demand for jobs; and (iii) ensuring that the design and implementation on the ground of existing unemployment insurance, social assistance, and job search assistance programs do not, unintentionally, discourage labor mobility.

REFERENCES

Aghion, P., O. Blanchard and R. Burgess. 1994. "The Behavior of State Firms in Eastern Europe Pre-Privatization", *European Economic Review*, 38 (6), 132-273.

Bentolila, S. and J. Dolado. 1994. "Labor Flexibility and Wages: Lessons from Spain". Banco de España Documento de Trabajo 9406.

Blanchard, O. 1997. *The Economics of Post-Communist Transition.* Oxford: Clarendon Press.

Boeri, T. 1998. *Mediating the Transition: Labour Markets in Central and Eastern Europe.* London: CEPR.

De la Rocha, M. 2001. "Corporate Sector and SME Environment in the Slovak Republic". Background Paper for the World Bank, "Slovak Republic: Living Standards, Employment and Labor Market Study."

Djankov, S. and R. La Porta. 2000. "The Regulation of Entry". NBER Working Papers. September.

EBRD 1999 "Business Environment and Enterprise Performance Survey".

EBRD, 2000. Transition Report 2000.London: EBRD.

Filer, R., S. Jurajda and J. Planovsky 1999. "Returns to Market: Valuing Human Capital in the Post-Transition Czech and Slovak Republics". CERGE-EI, Prague. Processed.

Haltiwanger, John (2000). "Aggregate Growth: What Have We Learned from Microeconomic Evidence?". University of Maryland, processed.

Kaminski, B. and M. Riboud 2000. *"Foreign Investment and Restructuring: The Evidence from Hungary",* World Bank Technical Paper No. 453. Washington DC: World Bank

Lubyova, M. 2000. "Labor Market", Chapter 7 in A. Marcincin and M. Beblavy, eds., Economic Policy in Slovak Republic 1990-1999. Bratislava: Center for Social and Media Analysis; Research Center of the Slovak Foreign Policy Association, and Institute for Economic and Social Reforms.

Marcincin (2000): Enterprise Restructuring, in Marcincin, A. and Beblavy, M. (eds.) Economic policy in Slovakia 1990-99, Bratislava.Nickell, S. (1997). "Unemployment and Labor Market Rigidities: Europe versus North America", Journal of Economic Perspectives, II(3), 55-74.

OECD (1999). Employment Outlook. Paris: OECD.

Riboud, Sanchez-Paramo and Silva-Jauregui (2001).

United Nations Development Program 2001. *National Human Development Report: Slovak Republic 2000.*Bratislava, Center for Economic Development.

World Bank 1999 Czech Republic: Toward EU Accession, World Bank Country Study, Labor Market Chapter. World Bank 1998 Slovak Republic: A Strategy for Growth and European Integration, World Bank Country Study, Labor Market Chapter. IMF, Article IV consultation with the Slovak Republic.

World Bank 2000. *Making Transition Work for Everyone: Poverty and Inequality in Europe and Central Asia.* Washington DC: The World Bank.

World Bank (2001). *Poland: Labor Market Study.* World Bank Country Study, Washington, DC.

UNEMPLOYMENT, SKILLS AND INCENTIVES: THE ROLE OF THE SAFETY NET SYSTEM[35]

INTRODUCTION

Following independence in 1993, the Slovak government inherited the social security system in place in the former Czechoslovakia. This system was then adjusted and modified several times throughout the 1990s in response to the country's changing economic, political, and social conditions. Like other safety nets, the role of the Slovak system is twofold. It provides income for those who are not employed and whose income falls below the poverty level,[36] and it aims to stimulate these individuals to find a job and obtain their own means of subsistence. As argued in Chapter 1 of this study, the safety net has been tremendously effective in achieving the first goal. Poverty in Slovak Republic would be some 10 to 19 percent higher if its social assistance/support and unemployment insurance programs were to disappear[37] (see also Steele, 2001).

However, while effective in fighting poverty, such a generous social safety net can also have negative effects-specifically it can alter the incentives of workers and individuals to look for a job and pull themselves out of poverty. And it can, if poorly designed, create a "poverty trap" for certain groups—for example, by excessively penalizing those who do manage to find a job and pull themselves just above the "cut-off" level for benefit recipiency. These types of phenomena have been extensively documented in many OECD economies.

In this chapter we examine the potential incentives/disincentives effects of the Slovak safety net, using new, very detailed data on benefit recipiency from the Unemployment Registry (1990-2000) and the Labor Force Survey (1996, 1999, and 2000). In order to do so, we use a flexible approach that allows us to identify behavioral changes that may occur as the quantity and duration of the benefits change over time, as well as behavioral differences between benefit recipients and non-recipients. The data and methodology are described in more detail in the background paper by Sanchez-Paramo (2001), in Volume II of this study. Here we concentrate mainly on the results.

---

[35] This paper is a synthesis of the longer and more detailed background paper by C. Sanchez-Paramo, in Volume II of this study (Sanchez-Paramo, 2001).

[36] Although there is no official poverty line in the Slovak Republic, the Minimum Living Standard (MLS) is used as such for the purpose of benefit eligibility, etc.

[37] It is important to notice that the total income figures used for this calculation *include* pensions.

We find that there are important behavioral differences between those who receive benefits and those who do not. The former tend to spend more time unemployed, but they also look for employment more actively than their counterparts, have more demanding preferences regarding their future jobs, and find jobs in the private sector more often. In addition, these jobs turn out to be better matches than the ones obtained by non-recipients (where match quality is measured as duration of the match).

Moreover, the behavior of recipients varies tremendously depending on whether they are actually receiving benefits or not. In particular, **once benefits are exhausted**, they exit the registry at a higher rate, search more actively, and move into private-sector jobs more often. So when we use these workers as their own control group, we *do* find strong evidence that both unemployment insurance and social assistance/support have important disincentive effects, not only on unemployment duration, but also on search behavior and on exit-to-employment.

OVERVIEW OF THE UNEMPLOYMENT INSURANCE, SOCIAL ASSISTANCE AND SOCIAL SUPPORT

The Slovak Republic provides cash benefits and support services to many jobless individuals and families through a web of programs. The scope of these programs as well as their coverage are broad, even for European standards, with total cash payments (including pensions) exceeding SK 95 billion, or 14 percent of GDP, in 1999. The system as it stands today is the product or numerous reforms, implemented throughout the last decade. Such changes have not only had budgetary repercussions, but have also altered the rules of the game for the unemployed.

Unemployment Insurance System.

After its creation in 1993, the country inherited the unemployment insurance system in place in the former Czechoslovakia. A system which had already undergone a major reform in 1992, due to soaring payments associated with growing unemployment. At that time the original 12-month entitlement period was halved and eligibility conditions were tightened. Replacement ratios also decreased slightly. These changes were applied retroactively onto old entitlements as well as onto new ones, and they implied for many unemployed an earlier-than-expected switch from non means-tested unemployment insurance to means-tested social assistance/support benefits.

Contrary to what other transition economies were doing at the time, in 1994-97 the Slovak government relaxed the unemployment insurance system, partially reversing the steps taken in 1992. In particular, entitlement conditions went back to pre-1992 levels, and the duration of the benefits was lengthened according to the age of the unemployed. Replacement ratios were kept constant except for those with no previous work experience, who saw their benefits decrease from 60 to 45 percent of the minimum wage, and those involved in -public- retraining programs, who lost their privileged status. These measures caused a partial shift from social assistance to unemployment insurance, reversing the previous trend, and coincided in time with changes in the safety net financing mechanism. While initially all benefits were financed through the government budget, in 1994 unemployment insurance became the responsibility of the so-called Employment Fund, supported by the insurance contributions of employers and employees. This meant that the relaxation of the unemployment insurance system had no immediately-visible adverse budgetary effects (in fact, public expenditure actually decreased after the changes), and this no doubt contributed to the oversight of potential disincentive effects associated with the proposed reforms.

In 1998, with the economy slowing down and unemployment growing again, a second round of restrictive reforms came around. Benefit duration was made a function of the contributive history of the individual, rather than her age; a measure most likely to affect those with interrupted labor market careers (i.e., women). In addition, the entitlement period was cut by 3 months for those who had quitted their job voluntarily and without *serious reason*. Similar changes were implemented in 1999, shaping the system as it stands today. Entitlement duration was reduced to 6 months for those having contributed for a maximum of 15 years, and 9 months for those with more than 15 years of contributions. Replacement ratios were cut, while the maximum benefit payment became a function of the Minimum Living Standard (i.e., poverty line), rather than the minimum wage. Finally, conditions for entitlement were relaxed slightly by requiring 6 months of contribution history during the 3 years prior to the benefit claim, instead of 12.

The share of unemployed receiving benefits has fallen sharply as a consequence of the reforms, from 82 percent in 1991, to 33 percent in 1992, and 27 percent in 1999 (Table 3.1).[38] However, such a decrease has been vastly compensated by an increase in the number of social assistance/support recipients among the unemployed, so that overall almost the same percentage of the unemployed received help from the state in 1999 than in 1993.

Table 3.1 Registered Unemployed Receiving Unemployment Insurance (UI) and/or Social Assistance (SA)

	Registered unemployed	Receiving UI (Total)	Receiving UI (%)	Receiving SA (Total)	Receiving SA (%)
1991	301,951	247,728	82.00	NA	-
1992	260,274	87,322	33.55	NA	-
1993	368,095	122,853	33.37	101,607	27.60
1994	371,481	85,032	22.89	168,416	45.33
1995	333,291	89,995	27.00	147,101	44.13
1996	329,749	93,517	28.36	135,440	41.07
1997	347,753	92,914	26.72	155,345	44.67
1998	428,209	119,931	28.01	193,706	45.24
1999	535,211	144,690	27.03	272,813	50.97

Source: Social Policy. Ministry of Labor, Social Affairs and Family.

Furthermore, total annual expenditure in unemployment benefits has increased substantially, from SK 1.7 billion in 1992 to SK 7.2 billion in 1999 (Table 3.2). This is a reflection of both the growth in the absolute number of unemployed workers receiving

---

[38] It is important to notice that these numbers represent the fraction of unemployed workers who *are receiving* UI in any given year, and not the fraction of unemployed workers who *are entitled* to UI at the beginning of the spell. This figure is actually much higher.

unemployment insurance, from 87,322 in 1992 to 144,690 in 1999, as well as an 84 percent increase in the average monthly benefit during the same period (from SK 1,583/month to SK 2,916/month).

Table 3.2 Expenditure on Social Assistance and Labor Market Policies (in millions SK)

	Social Assistance		Labor Market Policies		Benefits to registered unemployed (Total)
	Total	To registered unemployed	Passive (UI[A] benefits)	Active	
1991	NA	NA	NA	NA	NA
1992	2,218	1,526	1,711	3,812	3,237
1993	3,120	2,200	1,859	1,107	4,059
1994	5,134	3,824	1,710	1,896	5,534
1995	5,517	4,058	2,181	3,899	6,239
1996	5,510	3,850	3,063	4,290	6,913
1997	5,891	4,154	3,989	3,098	8,143
1998	7,978	5,813	5,484	2,289	11,297
1999	11,599	8,790	7,292	474	16,082

[A] Unemployment Insurance.
Source: Social Policy. Ministry of Labor, Social Affairs and Family.

It seems that, more often than not, changes in the unemployment insurance system have responded to budgetary concerns, rather than to the need for a rationally designed and efficient system. Unfortunately, this policy has done little to minimize the potential disincentive effects associated with unemployment insurance benefits.

Social Assistance and Social Support.

Unemployed workers who are not eligible for Unemployment Insurance are covered by the Social Assistance and Social Support systems, designed to guarantee basic living conditions for everyone.[39, 40] Social assistance/support benefits are calculated with reference to the subsistence level (i.e., Minimum Living Standard, described in Chapter 1). The concept of a MLS was introduced by legislation in 1991. Its level is a function of the individual's age and position within the household, and it is adjusted according to the cost-of-living index for low income households. In particular, an adjustment is made when this index increases 10 percent or more. Because this process is not automatic, during certain periods the MLS has been very close to the minimum wage, which may have had a negative effect on the incentives of the unemployed to actively look for a job.

---

[39] Basic conditions are described as "one hot meal per day, necessary clothing and shelter" (*Social Policy, 2000*).

[40] Under the SA system, the needy are classified with respect to the reason for their deprivation, and the amount of the benefits depends on the type of need. Individuals can be in *objective* need if they are "trying to help themselves" (e.g., registered at the unemployment office and actively searching for a job), or in *subjective* need if they are not doing so. The former represent 64 percent of all recipients and receive the full MLS, while the latter (29 percent) are paid only 50 percent of the MLS. Finally, in the case of employment, income is topped up by social benefits to a 1.2-multiple of the MLS (This premium for employed individuals is about to disappear, since the reform currently under discussion in Congress does not contemplate such a measure anymore. The authorities believe that incentives to work should arise from the wage structure rather than from payments received from the State).

The total number of individuals receiving social assistance/support benefits increased from 199,127 to 297,688 between 1994 and 1999 (Table 3.2).[41] Most of this growth has occurred in the last 2-3 years and among couples with dependent children. Simultaneously, during 1994-99, expenditure went from SK 5.1 to SK 11.6 billion and the average monthly payment grew from SK 2,130 to SK 3,426—a 60 percent increase.

Table 3.3 Persons in Material Destitution Receiving Social Assistance (SA)

	Persons in material destitution	Recipients of SA (Total)	Recipients of SA (%)	Couples with dependent children	Individuals or couples w/o dependent children
1991	NA	NA	-	-	-
1992	NA	NA	-	-	-
1993	NA	NA	-	-	-
1994	442,544	199,127	44.99	89,214	90,718
1995	408,507	176,705	43.25	79,525	83,364
1996	378,637	160,788	42.46	72,679	78,443
1997	392,927	174,971	44.53	71,153	97,255
1998	506,400	222,655	43.96	NA	NA
1999	584,941	297,688	50.89	93,799	202,805

Source: Social Policy. Ministry of Labor, Social Affairs and Family.

As a complement to the social assistance/support benefits, the SS system grants child and parental allowances, both of which are among the programs most often blamed for providing disincentives to job search and to further employment. These benefits are usually means-tested (but without tapering), which implies that there exists a threshold for household income,[42] above which marginal increases in labor income will cause an absolute decrease in total income due to the loss of the allowance. Moreover, both child and parental allowances require the qualifying person to provide care for the dependent child. That is, a parent who finds a job and starts working loses the allowance.

Child allowances are granted independently for each child in the family, and the quantity of the benefit varies according to the household income and the age of the child. As a result, disincentives increase with the number and age of children. The number of recipients has over time, from 682,045 in 1995 to 568,951 in 1999, as so has expenditure (from SK 10 to SK 9 billion over the same period). These trends have translated into a moderate 8 percent increase in the average monthly allowance, which, given inflation, corresponds to a fall in real terms (Table 3.4).

---

[41] SA payments are formally administered for two broad reasons: assistance to families with dependent children and assistance to socially deprived persons. Couples with dependent children constitute the largest group of recipients, growing from 90,718 individuals in 1994 to 202,805 in 1999. Couples/individuals without dependent children are the second largest group of beneficiaries, with their number increasing at a lower rate over this period from 89,214 to 93,799 (Table 3.3).

[42] In fact there are two such thresholds for each household: 1.36 and 1.99 of the corresponding MLS.

Table 3.4 Social Support Programs

	Child allowance		Parental allowance	
	Number of recipients	Expenditure (in million SK)	Number of recipients	Expenditure (in million SK)
1995	682,045	10,002	154,012	2,519
1996	653,938	9,982	144,101	2,758
1997	594,219	9,119	142,134	4,116
1998	603,445	9,925	139,876	4,479
1999	568,951	9,190	137,931	4,417

Source: Social Policy. Ministry of Labor, Social Affairs and Family.

Parental allowances are only applicable to children under the age of three, a restrictive condition for a population with a very low fertility rate. As a consequence, the number of recipients has also been falling over time, from 154,012 in 1995 to 137,931 in 1999. Expenditure, however, has exhibited a positive trend during the same period, growing from SK 2.5 to SK 4.4 billion. Altogether this translates into a 100 percent increase in the average monthly benefit.

BRIEF SIMULATION ANALYSIS OF THE DISINCENTIVES PROVIDED BY UNEMPLOYMENT INSURANCE, SOCIAL ASSISTANCE, AND SOCIAL SUPPORT

The ample coverage provided by the unemployment insurance and social assistance and support systems, sometimes for unlimited periods of time, is likely to have disincentive effects on job search and re-employment. In addition, the co-existence of all these different programs makes the Slovak safety net a complex system, both for its administrators and its beneficiaries, and such complexity could create undesirable opportunities for unintended misuse or even fraud.

How sizeable are these potential disincentive effects? In this section we use a series of quantitative examples to identify their likely importance. For the purpose of the analysis, we concentrate on unemployment insurance, social assistance and social support, and ignore social insurance. We construct a series of hypothetical examples that examine the situation of different types of households receiving unemployment insurance or social assistance/social support, and use such examples to identify what features of these programs are most likely to generate disincentive effects, and what groups are most susceptible to them.

We also try to distinguish between individual-level effects and household-level effects, where the latter take into account the labor supply decisions of other members of the family. We perform these simulations for several different types of households, including a single individual, couples with two children (of varying age), and couples with a large number of children. The details of these simulations are described in detail in the background paper by Sanchez-Paramo (2001). Here we summarize the findings for two types of households for whom the disincentive effects are particularly noteworthy: (i) a couple where there is one working adult and where the spouse either does not work or, if working, earns only the minimum wage; and (ii) a couple with five children, which could proxies the situation of some of the more disadvantaged households identified in Chapter 1 poverty.

74

A Couple With Two Small Children

We assume that both children are under the age of six. In this case, the household is entitled to SK 1,260/month[43] in the form of child allowances if their total income is below a 1.36-multiple of the MLS, or SK 840/month if it is between a 1.36- and a 1.99-multiple of the MLS, as long as one of the parents stays at home taking care of the children.. The MLS for a family of four with these characteristics is SK 8,410 per month.

Adult 2 Unemployed or Out of the Labor Force

We first assume that adult 2 makes no monetary contribution to family income (i.e., he does not work nor receive unemployment insurance). Adult 1 used to be employed but becomes unemployed and hence eligible for unemployment insurance. If adult 1 used to earn the average wage when employed, she would receive SK 5,400 during her first three months of unemployment, and SK 4,297 for the rest of the entitlement period (Table 3.5, row 1).[44] This amounts to 49 percent, and 45 percent, respectively, of her potential wage in case of re-employment (and assuming she return to work at her old wage). If adult 1 had been earning the minimum wage only, then the corresponding replacement ratios would be 90 percent (Table 3.5, row 3). Once her unemployment insurance ends, adult 1 is entitled for social assistance. If she were living alone, this would amount to some 29 percent of her potential labor income (when earning the average wage). However, because this individual is part of a household with larger needs, the actual payments they receive are higher than those an individual would receive. In particular, since the second adult does not work and they have two children, the family's income is below the minimum subsistence level for a family of four with their characteristics. This implies they qualify for social assistance benefits, as well as for the highest possible child allowance. Including all these payments, the family income becomes SK 9,670 (Table 3.5, row 2), which represents 79 percent of its potential level were adult 1 to work for the average wage, and 100 percent of its potential income were she to work at the minimum wage (rows 2 and 4).[45] At these replacement ratios, there may not be a strong incentive for adult 1 to find a job.

Table 3.5 Replacement Ratios for a Couple with 2 Children; Adult 2 Not Working

Benefit regime Income	UI First 3 months (RR 50%)	UI After first 3 months (RR 45%)	SA/SS (Objective)
Adult 1's income	5,400	4,927	3,230
(average wage)	(0.49)	(0.45)	(0.29)
Household income	9,670	9,670	9,670
(average wage)	(0.79)	(0.79)	(0.79)
Adult 1's income	3,230	3,230	3,230
(minimum wage)	(0.90)	(0.90)	(0.90)
Household income	9,670	9,670	9,670
(minimum wage)	(1.00)	(1.00)	(1.00)

Source: own simulations based on UI and SA/SS entitlements (see Sanchez-Paramo, 2001).

---

[43] For both children.

[44] UI benefits are capped at 1.5-multiple of the minimum wage (or, most recently, of the MSL).

[45] When interpreting these results, it is important to notice that, since one adult 2 remains unemployed, the household is still entitled to child allowances and the proposed 'replacement ratios' are really the lower bound of all possible values.

Adult 2 Employed at Minimum Wage

Now assume that adult 2 is employed, but earns only the minimum wage. In this case, the perverse disincentive effects are still strong. At the individual level the situation is identical to the one where adult 2 is unemployed or out of the labor force. If adult 1 can earn the average wage, the replacement ratio varies from 49-45 percent while on unemployment insurance, to 29 percent with social assistance/support, and these numbers become 90 percent if she can only get a minimum-wage job (Table 3.6).

Similarly, if adult 1 can earn the average wage, the household replacement ratio is around 70 percent when receiving unemployment insurance and 67 percent otherwise. If adult 1 can only earn the minimum wage, these numbers go up to 112 percent. This implies that total household income would actually decrease as a result of the adult 1's re-employment due to the loss of child allowances (which require that at least one parent be at home with the children). Notice that this is also the reason why the replacement ratio here is actually higher than that calculated for case A. Clearly, the system is designed in a way so as to penalize the return to work of adult 1, if she can only aspire to earn the minimum wage. The disincentive effects are significantly smaller, if both adult 2 and adult 1 can aspire to earn at least the average wage.

Table 3.6 Replacement Ratios for a Couple with 2 Children; Adult 2 Working at Minimum Wage

Benefit regime Income	UI First 3 months (RR 50%)	UI After first 3 months (RR 45%)	SA/SS (Objective)
Adult 1's income	5,400	4,927	3,230
(average wage)	(0.49)	(0.45)	(0.29)
Household income	10,260	9,787	9,670
(average wage)	(0.71)	(0.67)	(0.67)
Adult 1's income	3,230	3,230	3,230
(minimum wage)	(0.90)	(0.90)	(0.90)
Household income	9,670	9,670	9,670
(minimum wage)	(1.12)	(1.12)	(1.12)

Source: own simulations based on UI and SA/SS entitlements (see Sanchez-Paramo, 2001).

A Couple with Five Children

The second example considers the case of a large family with five young children. As argued in Chapter 1, these families tend to exhibit much higher risks of poverty than other groups. We assume that all five children lack any independent means of subsistence, and that their age distribution is as follows: one of them is under 3, one more is between 3 and 6, two are between 6 and 15, and the eldest if above 15. These differences allow for variation in the amount of the child allowance corresponding to each child, and help us bring into the analysis the disincentives associated not only with the number of children, but also with their age. Moreover, because education levels tend to be low among such large families, and because usually women in large families do not work outside the house, we only consider the case where adult 1 was previously employed at the minimum wage and adult 2 is unemployed or out of the labor force.

76

Under the above assumptions and rules, the minimum subsistence level for this family is SK 12,790, and child allowances can amount to SK 3,700/month. This implies that if both adults are unemployed the full household monthly income is SK 16,490 (Table 3.7). Most important, should one of them find employment at the minimum wage level, that amount would continue to be the same because social assistance/support would complement their income to bring it up to the minimum subsistence level, and the family would still receive child allowances. In these circumstances, there is very little reason for either adult to look for a job, and even less so for both of them to do so, since that would deprive the family of child allowances, making them worse off overall.

Table 3.7 Replacement Ratios for a Couple with 5 Children; Adult 2 Not Working

Benefit regime Income	UI First 3 months (RR 50%)	UI After first 3 months (RR 45%)	SA/SS (Objective)
Adult 1's income (minimum wage)	3,230 (0.90)	3,230 (0.90)	3,230 (0.90)
Household income (minimum wage)	16,490 (1.00)	16,490 (1.00)	16,490 (1.00)

Source: own simulations based on UI and SA/SS entitlements (see Sanchez-Paramo, 2001).

Even though each example has its own specificities, a few general conclusions can be drawn from the analysis:

- Individuals who expect to be re-employed at the minimum wage level have few incentives to look for a job (except maybe those whose spouse works for the average wage). Moreover, if we are willing to accept that workers on minimum-wage jobs are most likely workers with low levels of education, this means that the disincentive effects of unemployment insurance and social assistance/support should be strongest for this group;

- Disincentives are stronger when receiving unemployment insurance than when receiving social assistance/support because the payments are larger under the former (i.e., replacement ratios are higher). However, the unlimited duration of social assistance/support, together with its conditionality, can also have pervasive effects, especially at the household level;

- The smaller the worker's potential contribution to total household income, the more important the opportunity cost of working and the weaker the incentives for job search and further employment. This mechanism is specially relevant in the case of secondary earners;

- Disincentive effects are aggravated by the presence of children and the payment of child (or parental) allowances, since these bring the replacement ratio of actual income to potential income closer to one, or even above one in the case of families with low levels of education/low income; and

- Finally, all this implies that it is possible for certain households to be worse off when both adults are employed than when only one of them is because the potential net contribution to total household income of the secondary earner is very small, or even negative.

EMPIRICAL ANALYSIS OF DISINCENTIVE EFFECTS

The above simulations suggest that, on theoretical grounds at least, there are likely to be some serious disincentive effects for families with low earning potential. However, there is still a large gap between what theory may predict and what may actually happen. For this reason, we try to go beyond simple simulations and carry out an actual empirical analysis of the behavior of unemployed individuals, both for those who are receiving support and those who are not; and for those who received support at some point in time and have since exhausted it.

The methodologies used to carry out these analysis have been extensively used in many country settings, but can be somewhat complex. For this reason, the full description and discussion of the methodology is left to the corresponding background paper in Volume II (Sanchez-Paramo, 2001), along with the full set of results. Here we concentrate on explaining: (i) the type of data used for this analysis; (ii) the basic approach and objective of the empirical methodology; and (iii) the main results and conclusions.

Data

The empirical analysis combines two different data sources, the Unemployment Registry (collected by National Labor Office) and the Labor Force Survey (carried out by the Slovak Statistical Office).

The Unemployment Registry Data

The first data source (the Unemployment Registry) contains very detailed information on unemployment duration and unemployment insurance payments for a sample of (anonymous) individuals during the 1990-2000 period. The data come from the administrative records of the NLO, and contain information on the beginning and the ending dates of each unemployment spell, as well as on the quantity and duration of unemployment insurance benefits when received. Since information is organized by individual rather than by spell, the records only contain complete demographic information on the last unemployment spell of each unemployed individual. However, we are able to construct individual histories using archival data on past unemployment spells, and adjusting the necessary demographic variables accordingly.

The Unemployment Registry sample contains 30,714 spells corresponding to 18,141 individuals. The number of spells per individual ranges from one to five, although more than 50 percent of all individuals in the sample experience only one unemployment spell. The duration of such spells also varies substantially, with 36 percent lasting less than 3 months and 25 percent lasting for more than a year. The average spell duration is 10.4 months, and almost 60 percent of all spells end with a transition into private-sector employment. Also, 44 percent of all observations correspond to spells during which the individual received unemployment insurance benefits. It is important to distinguish this number from the percentage of unemployed individuals that, at a certain point in time, are receiving unemployment insurance. As was mentioned in Section C, this number is much smaller, about 25-30 percent since 1995.

However, there are certain drawbacks associated with the use of the data from the Unemployment Registry. First, a registered worker is not necessarily an unemployed worker according to ILO standards (i.e., did not perform paid work for more than an hour during the week prior to the interview, is looking for a job, and is able to start working within the next two weeks), and it is impossible to determine who is actually 'unemployed' using such criteria because no information is collected either on search behavior or on availability. Second, the Unemployment Registry contains no information on social assistance/support payments or on household-level variables, although both are potentially very relevant for out analysis. Fortunately, the Labor Force Survey (LFS), which has been administered by the Slovak Statistical Office on a quarterly basis since 1994, provides fairly rich information on both of these issues, so we will use the LFS data both to expand the scope of the analysis, and to check on the robustness of the results obtained when using the Unemployment Registry.

The Labor Force Survey Data

We use data from the LFS for the years 1996 and 1999, together with the first two quarters of 2000. In each quarter, the Labor Force Survey sample contains approximately 10,000 households (about 0.1 percent of all Slovak households), or 30,000 individuals. The survey follows a 20 percent rotation scheme across every two consecutive quarters, which implies that we can trace individuals for a maximum of five quarters.

The fact that individuals are only observed for a limited period of time, together with the absence of retrospective questions in the survey, implies that, in order to obtain accurate information on benefit entitlement and recipiency, we need to impose additional conditions when constructing the sub-sample we will work with. In particular, we select only those individuals who become unemployed during the survey period or who have been unemployed for less than three months at the time of the first interview. This way we follow individuals from the beginning of their unemployment spells and can correctly identify their recipiency status. This selection rule has the added advantage of allowing us to avoid stock sampling bias (i.e., over-representation of long spells). The sample then contains 2,465 unemployed individuals, where the definition of unemployment accords with ILO standards. We observe a single spell per individual, which can be completed or censored, given that individuals remain in the sample for *at most* five quarters. Almost 50 percent of all (observed) spells last for less than three months, while about 4 percent last for more than a year.

Approximately 53 percent of all individuals are paid unemployment insurance during the unemployment spell, while 31 percent receive social assistance/support. There is some overlapping between both programs, with 18 percent of those receiving unemployment insurance, also getting social assistance/support. Moreover, 10 percent of the unemployed live in households where some other member receives unemployment insurance, and 18 percent in households where some other member receives social assistance/support. Finally, about 90 percent of the sample is registered at the Employment Office, almost half of it declares to be searching actively for a job (i.e., using search channels other than registration at the Employment Office), and 15 percent finds employment during the survey period. Notice, however, that this figure is an underestimate of the percentage of workers who *eventually* find a job, since we do not observe workers for the totality of their spell.[46]

A Guide to the Empirical Strategy

For the sake of clarity and internal logic of the presentation, we have structured the analytical work around three building blocks, namely, the effects of benefits on (i) unemployment duration, (ii) on exit-to-(private sector) employment, and (iii) on job search and match quality. The evidence presented in first block relies on survival analysis,[47] while the second and third blocks uses probability models[48] (see background paper by Sanchez-Paramo, in Volume II for details).

Since the contents of our two datasets—the Unemployment Registry and the Labor Force Survey—are somewhat different, we use either source depending on its comparative advantage in addressing the question at hand. Table 3.8 below summarizes the empirical strategy, together with the information on each dataset:

---

[46] In fact, this will be very important when we interpret the results on the effect of benefits on exit-to-employment.

[47] **Survival models** are commonly used to determine which variables have an effect on the duration of a certain event. In our case, this event is unemployment. Thus, observed unemployment duration, expressed in some measure of time (e.g., months), is the left-hand variable in the model, the variable we are trying to explain. Then, on the right hand side, we would like to include all those factors that we believe may have an effect on unemployment duration, such as the demographic characteristics of the individual or information on his/her recipiency status.

[48] **Probability models** are used to study the determinants of the likelihood of a certain event or behavior. For instance, here we will use this type of models to determine what factors affect the probability that an individual finds a job in the private sector, or the probability that a worker looks actively for a job while unemployed. A peculiar feature of these models is that, while we directly observe from the data whether something actually happens or not (e.g., the worker find a job), the model will only produce a predicted probability that such event occurs. That is, the model will tell us how likely it is that a certain individual will find a job, given his characteristics, rather than whether the individual actually finds a job or not. In terms of the data, this implies that the left-hand side variable is an indicator that takes a value of one if we observe the event or behavior we are trying to explain, and a value of zero otherwise, while the outcome produced by the model will be a number between zero and one (and, most likely, different from zero and one), a predicted probability. The right-hand side of the model will again include all those factors that we believe to have an effect on the event we are trying to explain.

Table 3.8 Summary of Data and Empirical Strategies

Data Set	Unemployment Registry	Labor Force Survey
Comments:	**ADVANTAGES** - Completed unemployment spells - Very detailed information on unemployment insurance benefits. **DISADVANTAGES** - No information on social assistance/support - Information available only at the individual level **MAIN USE** - Analysis of unemployment insurance	**ADVANTAGES** - Information on social assistance/support - Information available at the individual and household levels **DISADVANTAGES** - Limited information on unemployment insurance/social assistance/support - Individuals observed for a limited period of time (censored unemployment spells) **MAIN USE** - Analysis of social assistance/support - Analysis of household factors
Outcome Variable:	**STRATEGY (variable):**	**STRATEGY (variable):**
Unemployment duration	Survival model (unemployment spell)	Survival model (unemployment spell)
Exit-to-employment	Probability model (exit to job)	Probability model (exit to job)
Job search and match quality		Probability model (search)

Source: World Bank

An Illustrative Example

Given the relative complexity of the safety net system, we expect tremendous variation to exist both between and within individual experiences. For this reason, it is necessary to take into account not only benefit recipiency, but also differences in the type/quantity of the benefits received. For instance, once an individual becomes unemployed, she may or may not qualify for unemployment insurance benefits. If indeed she is entitled, the duration of such benefits would be a function, among other factors, of the her contributive history. Although, in a regression context, the use of an indicator variable for recipiency would get at the issue of entitlement, it would not be very useful at identifying behavioral differences between recipients with dissimilar contributive histories.

Similarly, the experience of any given recipient also varies over time due to the two-tier nature of the unemployment insurance system, and to the limited duration of the benefits. For example, a worker who is entitled to 5 months of unemployment insurance benefits and who remains unemployed for 10 months, will receive high-level benefits (high replacement ratio) for 3 months, low-level benefits (low replacement ratio) for an additional two-month period, and finally no payments at all for the rest of the spell. There is no reason to believe that the behavior of this worker will remain unchanged during the ten months that she is unemployed, so we distinguish between these three different scenarios in the empirical analysis. The three different scenarios can be illustrated as follows:

➢ *Case 1: Individual entitled to benefits (recipient) during her full spell*

Receiving UI *(1)*

T=0   T=N=exit from unemployment

➢ *Case 2: Individual entitled to benefits (recipient); exhausts benefits during her spell*

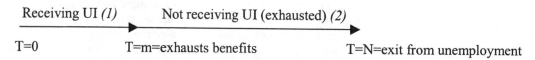

Receiving UI *(1)*   Not receiving UI (exhausted) *(2)*

T=0   T=m=exhausts benefits   T=N=exit from unemployment

➢ *Case 3: Individual not entitled to benefits (non-recipient)*

Never received UI *(3)*

T=0   T=N

MAIN RESULTS

As discussed earlier, we focus on four main sets of outcomes: (i) unemployment duration (e.g., the length of time spent unemployed by an individual); (ii) exit-to-employment: understood as exit to employment in the private sector (e.g., we exclude those who leave unemployment to go into public works); (iii) job search behavior and preferences on future employment (measures how actively and selectively individuals look for a job); and (iv) match quality, measured as the duration of the new job.

Unemployment Insurance, Social Assistance and Unemployment Duration

The first part of the analysis examines the relationship between different features of the unemployment insurance system and the *duration of* unemployment. In particular, we pay special attention to the duration of the benefits and to changes in the benefit quantity associated with the two-tier nature of the unemployment insurance system—i.e., high and low replacement ratios.

As a first cut, Table 3.9 presents separate unemployment spell distributions for those individuals who receive unemployment insurance and those who do not, using the Unemployment Registry. It can be seen

Table 3.9 Unemployment Duration by Unemployment Insurance (UI) Recipiency

Duration of spell (in months)	% of all spells with UI	% of all spells without UI
Less than 3	21.40	48.35
4 to 6	21.02	16.19
6 to 12	25.90	14.38
12 to 24	19.92	11.17
More than 24	11.77	9.92

Source: Unemployment Registry, 1990-2000.

that those with no unemployment insurance exit the Registry sooner than those with it: almost 50 percent of all spells with no unemployment insurance last less than three months, while this number is 21 percent for spells with unemployment insurance. Interestingly, this difference tends to disappear as we move towards longer spells. Given that benefit duration is limited, such pattern would be consistent with the existence of disincentive effects associated with recipiency. To explore this issue further, we explicitly account for the duration of benefits (Table 3.10), and find that those who receive unemployment insurance actually leave the Registry when or soon after their benefits come to an end.

In addition, part of the differences between recipients and non-recipients, in terms of unemployment duration, could be a product of the different demographic composition of both groups of workers. For instance, women may be less attached to the labor market than men, and

Table 3.10 Distribution of Spells by -Actual- Duration of Benefits (months)

Benefits	0-3	4-6	7-9	10-12
Spell				
0 to 3	61.05			
4 to 6	15.06	31.10		
6 to 12	13.98	29.24	49.47	23.80
12 to 24	6.25	23.83	33.50	55.40
More than 24	3.66	15.83	17.03	20.80
Number of spells	4,790	6,903	1,417	204

Source: Unemployment Registry, 1990-2000.

therefore have a higher probability of exiting the Registry at any point in time, independent of their recipiency status. Since the fraction of female workers is higher among non-recipients, this could lead to a larger share of shorter spells among non-recipients that is unrelated to benefit entitlement.

These issues motivate the use of regression analysis, so as to separate the effect that unemployment insurance recipiency may have on unemployment duration from the effects associated with other variables such as gender. As we discussed earlier, we use a proportional hazard model for this purpose.[49] The estimation results are summarized in Table 3.11. In addition to the variables presented in the table, the models also include detailed demographic variables (age, education, gender) and controls for previous experience, occupation, sector, region, and year/quarter of observation. Full estimation results, along with a detailed discussion, are presented in the background paper by Sanchez-Paramo (2001), in Volume II. With respect to the effects of the demographic variables, we find that women tend to experience longer spells than men, and so do single workers. Those between 26 and 45 years of age spend less time unemployed than younger workers (under 25), while those above 46 spend more. Duration also decreases with education, and those with no previous employment experience are actually faster to exit the Registry. These effects are fairly robust to different specifications.

The first two columns of Table 3.11 contain the results for models that include either an indicator for whether the individual ever received unemployment insurance during that particular spell, or a measure of the duration of such benefits. From the first model, it seems that benefit recipiency increases unemployment duration. In particular, those who receive unemployment insurance experience spells that are, on average, 30 percent longer than the ones of individuals without unemployment insurance. If we

---

[49] We estimate a Weibull model. For a more detailed discussion on hazard models, the reader can consult Lee (1992).

instead control for the duration of unemployment insurance, each extra month of benefits increases duration by 15 percent.

However, the quantity of the benefits varies over time, as the worker moves from the high-replacement-ratio regime to the low-replacement-ratio one. There is no reason to expect that the effect on unemployment duration of an extra month of high benefits is the same as that of an extra month of low benefits. Thus, in order to capture any potential differences across regimes, we also include two different variables the duration of high and low replacement periods (column III). Surprisingly, the coefficients of both variables are very similar in size; that is, one extra month of high replacement unemployment insurance has the same effect on unemployment duration as one more month of low replacement unemployment insurance (namely, a 15 percent increase in duration).

Yet these results are subject to an important criticism: they do not capture behavioral differences associated with *actually* receiving or not receiving unemployment insurance, but rather differences associated with *ever* receiving or *never* receiving unemployment insurance. This second comparison is not fully satisfactory since, once unemployment insurance is over, those who were entitled to benefits find themselves in the same situation as those who never received them. To address this issue, for each individual we create a series of pseudo spells so that the indicators for unemployment insurance recipiency, and for high/low replacement ratios are allowed to vary over time—i.e., to be turned on and off, so to speak, as individuals move across the different regimes.

These new results not only strengthen our previous conclusions, but also provide new evidence on how the behavior of those who receive unemployment insurance varies over time (columns IV and V). The effect of unemployment insurance recipiency on unemployment duration is even more evident than before, with those who are actually receiving the benefits spending almost 50 percent more time unemployed than those who never received any payments. More interestingly, because this methodology allows us to capture changes in the behavior of unemployment insurance recipients, we can now see that, once unemployment insurance is over, those entitled to unemployment insurance leave the Registry at much faster rate than those who never received any benefits. This result confirms the basic intuition arising from Table 3.10.

In addition, there is now a clear difference between those who receive high replacement unemployment insurance and those who receive low replacement unemployment insurance, with the former exhibiting lower exit probabilities (and, hence, longer unemployment duration). In particular, while unemployment duration is almost 50 percent longer for those receiving high level benefits than for those with no benefits, this percentage falls to 25 percent when the quantity of the benefits decreases. Furthermore, once unemployment insurance payments end, those entitled tend to exit the Registry at a higher rate than those who have not.

Columns VI-VIII of Table 3.11 present similar estimations but using the data from the Labor Force Survey (LFS), rather than from the Unemployment Registry (UR). The results are very similar to hose found with the Registry lending additional credence to the findings. In addition, the LFS results allow us to examine the impact of social assistance/social support and of household-level variables, which was lacking from the UR data. Interestingly, social assistance/support seems to have the same effects as unemployment insurance, only more pronounced: social assistance/support recipients spend, on average, almost 50 percent more time unemployed than non-recipients. This appears to be entirely due entirely to the fact that social assistance/support duration is unlimited, since the marginal effect associated with an extra month of benefits is almost equal for both programs. With respect to household-level variables, only the individual's position in the family seems to have explanatory power, with household heads and their spouses spending more time unemployed than other members of the household (although this result is only significant for the latter).

In sum up: we find that both unemployment insurance and social assistance/support recipiency increase unemployment duration; and that the behavior of those individuals who are entitled to benefits varies over time, depending on whether they are actually receiving the payments or they did so in the past. In particular, exit rates for this group increase substantially after their benefits are over.

Table 3.11 Hazard Estimates for Duration of Unemployment Spell

Variables	I UR	II UR	III UR	IV UR	V UR	VI LFS	VII LFS	VIII LFS
Receives unemployment insurance (UI)	0.684** (0.011)			0.529** (0.009)		0.783** (0.098)		0.643** (0.088)
Receives social assistance (SA)						0.481** (0.064)		0.470** (0.069)
Duration of UI spell (months)		0.852** (0.002)					0.815** (0.029)	
Duration of SA spell (months)							0.852** (0.043)	
UI w/ high replacement ratio			0.838** (0.007)					
UI w/ low replacement ratio			0.862** (0.004)					
Duration of UI w/ high RR					0.532** (0.010)			
Duration of UI w/low RR					0.770** (0.018)			
Ever received UI				1.735** (0.027)	2.033** (0.034)			0.950 (0.248)
Other variables	YES	YES	YES	YES	YES	YES	YES	YES
Number of individuals	18,141	18,141	18,141	18,141	18,141	2,465	2,465	2,465
Number of observations	30,741	30,741	30,741	39,711	46,577	2,465	2,465	2,680

Coefficients represent hazard ratios (Note: A hazard ration greater (smaller) than 1 indicates that such variable decreases (increases) unemployment duration).
Robust standard errors in parentheses (errors clustered at the individual level).
** Significant at the 5 percent level. * Significant at the 10 percent level.
Baseline comparison: Illiterate single male, 16-25 years old, with previous employment experience, but with no recorded employment prior to current unemployment spell.

Source: Unemployment Registry, 1990-2000 (columns I-V) and Labor Force Survey, 1996.1-1996.4, 1999.1-1999.4 and 2000.1-2000.2 (columns VI-VIII)

What it all means, at a glance

Graphical analysis can help illustrate the magnitude of the effects we have been discussing. We start by comparing the actual distribution of spells, with what would exist had everybody[50] (nobody) received unemployment insurance. Not surprisingly, increases in the coverage rate (i.e., share of

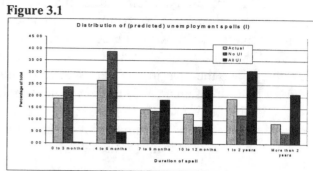

Figure 3.1

Source: Unemployment Registry.

workers entitled to unemployment insurance benefits) cause average unemployment duration to increase. Graphically, this translates into a rightward shift of the spell distribution (Figure 3.1). For instance, while 18 percent of all spells last less than three months given the actual allocation of benefits, this number increases to about 24 percent when no benefits are distributed (i.e., more workers leave the Registry early on), and decreases to almost 0 when everybody is entitled to 12 months of unemployment insurance (i.e., almost no workers leave the Registry during the first 3 months of unemployment). The same patterns arise for longer spells.

Similarly, we explore the role of (maximum) benefit duration by comparing the distribution of predicted spells corresponding to systems with a maximum unemployment insurance duration of 3, 6, 9 or 12 months (Figure 3.2). Again more generous unemployment insurance benefits, this time in terms of duration, shift the distribution of spells to the right.

Figure 3.2

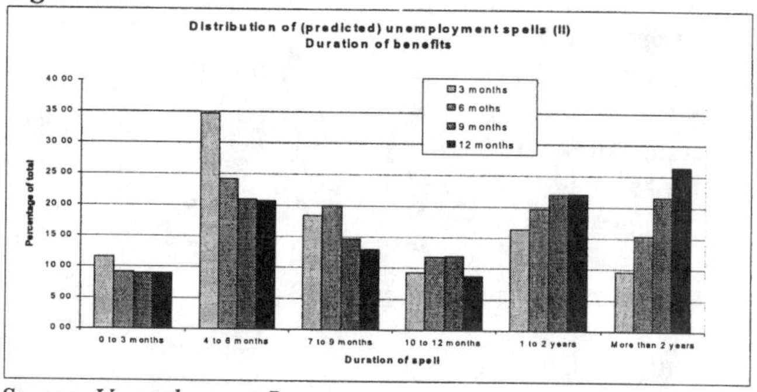

Source: Unemployment Registry.

Finally, we compare the actual distribution of spells with that generated by substituting high replacement unemployment insurance with low replacement unemployment insurance. That is, actual recipients are still entitled to the same number of unemployment insurance payments (in months), but they only receive low-replacement benefits, and non-recipients remain so. The effects are qualitatively similar to the ones obtained in the previous

Figure 3.3

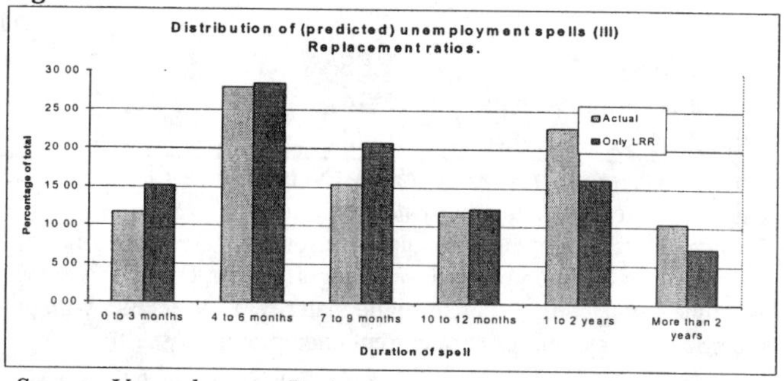

Source: Unemployment Registry

---

[50] We apply 1999 rules and provide the maximum UI.

examples: exit rates increase when we reduce the amount of the benefits (i.e., its generosity) and the distribution of spells shifts leftwards (Figure 3.3).

Exit-to-Employment

As we mentioned above, there is substantial variation in the behavior of unemployment insurance recipients over time. In particular, although their unemployment spells are longer on average than those of non-recipients, they tend to abandon the Unemployment Registry faster than their counterparts once the benefits are exhausted. The question then arises as to what it means to leave the Registry, since exit does not necessarily imply employment. For instance, it could be the case that, once unemployment insurance is exhausted, workers have no further reason to remain registered. The policy implications associated with each scenario are fairly different, so we explore this issue further.

Using the Unemployment Registry data, we estimate a probit model for the probability of exit-to-employment,[51] where employment means private sector work. As before, in addition to the benefit-related variables, the regressions include controls for demographics and other factors. With respect to the latter, we find that women and married workers have a slightly higher probability of finding a job, and so do prime-aged and/or more educated individuals (Box 3.1). These effects are fairly robust to different model specifications.

Results are summarized in Table 3.12. When we consider benefit entitlement, workers who receive unemployment insurance are more likely to find a job in the private sector than those who do not (about a 9 percentage-point increase in probability). There also seems to be some stigma associated with longer spells (e.g., the longer the spell, the less likely the individual will exit into a job). This could potentially hurt recipients since they spend more time unemployed on average, but this effect is very small compared to the impact of unemployment insurance one (a 1 percentage-point decrease in probability for every tow extra months).

As we did when analyzing unemployment duration, we want to differentiate between "currently receiving unemployment insurance' and 'having ever received unemployment insurance" to allow for potential behavioral differences related to changes in the recipiency regime. Once we do so, we find that the probability of exit-to-employment for recipients is actually very low while receiving unemployment insurance, and that it increases substantially once the benefits are over. In particular, workers who are currently receiving unemployment insurance are 40 percent less likely than non-recipients to move to a private sector job, while those who have exhausted their benefits are 35 percent more likely to do so. Similarly, when we distinguish between high and low replacement unemployment insurance, it appears that the probability of finding a job in the private-sector is smallest while the worker is receiving the former. In sum,

---

[51] Only exit to employment in the private sector was considered as a successful exit. Qualitatively and quantitatively equivalent results are obtained when exit to both employment in the private sector and employment in a public employment program are considered instead.

workers who are receiving benefits are the least likely to exit-to-employment, and workers whose benefits have ended are the most likely to do so. When we repeat this exercise using the Labor Force Survey, we obtain results that are very qualitatively similar (see Sanchez-Paramo, 20001,in Volume II).

Table 3.12 Probability of Exit to Employment in the Private Sector

Variables	I	II	III
Receives unemployment insurance (UI)	0.087**	-0.413**	
	(0.006)	(0.004)	
Duration of spell	-0.006**	-0.009**	-0.009**
	(0.000)	(0.0003)	(0.0003)
UI w/ high replacement ratio			-0.417**
			(0.004)
UI w/ low replacement ratio			-0.387**
			(0.003)
Ever received UI		0.351**	0.477**
		(0.005)	(0.005)
Other variables	YES	YES	YES
Number of individuals	18,141	18,141	18,141
Number of observations	30,741	39,711	46,577

Notes: Coefficients represent marginal effects evaluated at sample means. Robust Standard errors in parenthesis. All specifications include controls for demographic variables, previous experience, occupation, sector, region, and year/quarter dummies.
See Sanchez-Paramo (2001) in Volume II for full set of results.
** significant at 5 percent level; * significant at 10 percent level.
Source: Own calculations from the Unemployment Registry, 1990-2000.

Job Search and Job/match Quality

In principle, there is no single explanation for the link between unemployment insurance recipiency and a higher likelihood of exit-to-employment. One can think of the probability of exit-to-employment as a function of the number of job offers that a worker receives, which in time depends on the individual's search effort and his willingness to accept any given offer. It may be the case, then, that unemployment insurance payments, by lowering the opportunity cost of unemployment, allow these workers to search more (and more selectively), and to therefore find a match more often. And since the search process is time-consuming, these workers also experience longer unemployment spells. On the other hand, it is possible that receiving benefits increases workers' reservation wages, making them less willing to accept job offers, and hence decreasing their probability of exit (i.e., increasing unemployment duration). We believe it is important to distinguish between these two hypotheses, and we attempt to do so here using the Labor Force Survey.

Both the unemployment insurance and the social assistance/support systems require that workers be registered at the Employment Office (i.e., Unemployment Registry) in order to qualify for benefit payments. But workers can also search more actively for a job, making use of other channels other than the Employment Office (e.g., private job agencies, placing/reading advertisements, etc.). We define these types of activities as "active search" and assume they are more likely to help the recipient find a job. When we correlate this new variable with unemployment insurance recipiency, we find that workers entitled to benefits seem to be more active in their search than those who are not, but also that their behavior varies substantially depending on whether they are actually receiving the benefits or not. In particular, 41 percent of those receiving unemployment insurance are searching actively, while only 32 percent of those with no benefits are searching Table 3.13). However, the highest rates of search are found among those who once received benefits but have exhausted them: 65 percent of them are actively searching for a job. The group least likely to search actively is that of non-registered workers (with only 13 percent). Thus, at first glance it seems that receiving benefits does negatively affect the search activity of unemployed workers; although on average those receiving benefits search more than those who do not receive them.

Box 3.1 Educational Levels, Unemployment and Re-Employment

We have already pointed out that unemployment is highest among those with low educational levels, and lowest among college graduates. In addition, the number of unemployed workers per vacancy is much larger for those with low education than for workers with secondary or college studies. Such imbalances are the product of a skill mismatch between labor supply and labor demand.

Table B3.1.1 Number of Unemployed Workers per Vacancy, by Education Groups

	1993	1994	1995	1996	1997	1998
Total	50	28	22	23	18	39
None	152	73	77	162	28	80
Basic	146	137	120	95	51	131
Apprent. low	20	10	11	12	11	23
Vocational low	87	73	48	23	35	29
Apprent. com.	75	29	27	19	26	45
Vocational com.	42	24	19	29	17	61
Grammar	56	363	10	27	19	28
University (+)	11	7	5	6	4	10

Source: National Labor Office.

All this implies that workers with low levels of education are hard to re-employ in the present economic context. In other words, their probability of exit to employment is really low, as can be seen in the following graph:

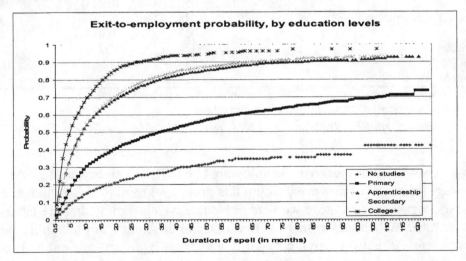

These results, together with the evidence we have presented in this section, constitute a strong case in favor of reforms of the education system (i.e., revision of curriculum, etc.), as well as in favor of retraining programs that take into account employers' needs in terms of skills.

Source: Sanchez-Paramo (2001) in Volume II of this study.

Table 3.13 Fraction of Workers Actively Searching for a Job, by UI Recipiency

	Active search
Registered and present UI	40.61**
Registered and past UI	65.07**
Registered and never UI	32.18**
Not registered	13.48**

(*) Significantly different from closest value (from above/below) in the same column at 5 percent (10 percent) level.
Source: Labor Force Survey, 1996.1-1996.4, 1999.1-1999.4, and 2000.1-2000.4.

To explore this issue while controlling for other factors, we estimate a probit model for the probability of active search (Table 3.14). As before, in addition to the benefit-related variables we also include demographic controls. According to the estimation results, women and married workers are less likely to search actively than male workers and single workers. In terms of education, the relationship is complex, and follows an inverted-U: for low levels of education both variables are positively related, while the opposite is true for high levels (i.e., college and beyond). Interestingly, social assistance/support does not have a significant effect on active search, and neither do age (except for workers over 45 searching less actively) or registration with the Employment Office (see Sanchez-Paramo, 2001).

Table 3.14: Determinants of Active Job Search

	I All years	II. 1996/99	III 2000
Registered (=1)	-0.046	-0.238**	0.320**
	(0.094)	(0.086)	(0.128)
No unemployment insurance (UI)	-0.208**	-0.163**	-0.394**
	(0.091)	(0.073)	(0.125)
Reg * No UI	0.163	0.166**	0.319**
	(0.113)	(0.098)	(0.108)
Past UI	0.114**	0.013	0.139*
	(0.050)	(0.045)	(0.082)
Receives social assistance/support	0.048	0.070**	0.054
	(0.033)	(0.034)	(0.068)
Other variables	YES	YES	YES
Number of ind	2,494	1,331	1,163
Number of obs	5,033	3,395	1,638

Notes: Robust standard errors in parenthesis. **(*) Significantly different from closest value
(from above/below) in the same column at 5 percent (10 percent) level.

Source: Labor Force Survey 1996.1-1996.4, 1999.1-1999.4, and 2000.1-2000.4. See Sanchez-Paramo (2001) for details.

Workers who do not receive unemployment benefits search less than workers than do, on average (column I). However, within this group, we need to differentiate between those who are registered and those who are not, since we also know that the latter group searches the least. When we do this we find that the difference in probability between workers who are currently receiving benefits and those who are not entitled, but are registered, is 8 percentage points, while the difference between those with unemployment insurance and those who are not entitled *and* are not registered is 20 percentage points. In contrast, those entitled to benefits and having exhausted them are the ones searching the most. These results confirm the prima facie evidence presented in Table 3.13 above.

However, due to changes regarding the phrasing of the question on search channels between 1999 and 2000, we need to be cautious when interpreting these results. In particular, in 1996 and 1999, workers asked about searching methods were given a list of search alternatives, including the registration at Employment Office, out of which they were allowed to choose *only* one. As a result, most registered workers tended to pick the Employment Office as the answer, even though it is possible that they were using other— active-channels as well. In 2000, the question "State *the* way in which you are looking for a job" was replaced with "State *all* the ways in which you are looking for a job", hence allowing for multiple answers.

In order to check the extent to which these changes may be driving our results, we re-estimate the previous model for 1996/99 and 2000 separately (see columns II and III). Not surprisingly, being registered at the Employment Office if negatively correlated with active search for 1996/99. As discussed above, this negative correlation is most likely due to the wording of the search question, and thus spurious. In fact, the result is exactly the opposite for 2000: registration with the Employment Office seems to be a good predictor for active search. It is reassuring to find that the behavioral differences between those who receive unemployment insurance (social assistance/support) and those who do not remain after splitting the sample. The same is true about the effect of demographic variables.

Having shown then that unemployment insurance recipients search more than non-recipients, we turn now to the issue of their willingness to accept (any) job offers while under the benefit system. For this purpose, we use the information on preferences for future jobs available in the Labor Force Survey. We find that individuals currently receiving unemployment insurance exhibit a slightly stronger inclination for salaried jobs than other workers, while those not entitled to benefits or not registered appear to be somewhat more entrepreneurial (Table 3.15). Registered workers with no unemployment insurance also seem to be more flexible, given the larger percentage of them who are willing to accept a part-time job, even though full-time employment is preferable. Moreover, it is interesting to notice the differences between those who are currently receiving unemployment insurance and those who did so in the past. The latter are the group with the largest share of 'any job/no preference' responses. All these pieces together (weakly) suggest the existence of a negative relationship between flexibility (interpreted as 'willingness to accept any job') and unemployment insurance recipiency.

Table 3.15 Preference on Future Job by Unemployment Insurance (UI) Recipiency

A. Salaried versus Other

	Total[A]	Salaried	Productive coop.	Entrepr.	Any job	Not decided yet
Registered and present UI	1,919	87.65	0.57	0.47	10.01	1.30
Registered and past UI	232	81.90	0.43	0.00	16.38	1.29
Registered and never UI	795	84.03	0.50	0.75	12.83	1.89
Not registered	253	76.28	0.00	5.53	15.02	3.16

B. Full versus Part-Time

	Full time	Part time		No preference
		Accept PT?		
Registered and present UI	87.04	19.82	2.30	10.66
Registered and past UI	82.76	15.10	1.72	15.52
Registered and never UI	87.67	26.96	2.89	9.43
Not registered	87.80	19.44	4.88	7.32

^A This information is available only for those workers who are looking for a job.

Source: Labor Force Survey 1996.1-1996.4, 1999.1-1999.4, and 2000.1-2000.4.

We are also interested in examining the outcome of the search process, meaning the quality of the job workers move into. As we argued earlier, it is possible that one positive effect of unemployment benefit recipiency is to allow workers to search more selectively for a better job or "match". The standard strategy for this kind of problem is to study wage differences between recipients and non-recipients after re-employment, where higher wages are associated with better matches, but in this case individual-level wage data is not available. Instead, among all other job-related variables, we choose the duration of the job as the second-best indicator for quality.[52]

We find that, on average, jobs found by workers with unemployment insurance are 10.71 months long, compared to 8.78 months for those with no benefits, and the difference between both numbers is significant at the 1 percent level. Figure 4 presents both distributions. Not only they are visually different, with the one corresponding to workers with no benefits containing a much larger number of very short spells, but the equality of both distributions can be rejected using a Kolmogorov-Smirnov test.

Figure 3.4 Duration of Job for UI Recipients (left) and Non-Recipients (right)

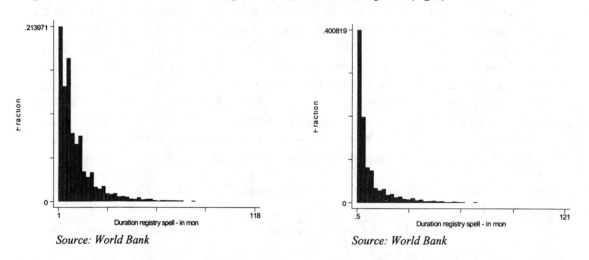

Source: World Bank   *Source: World Bank*

In sum, workers who receive unemployment insurance search actively for jobs more frequently than those who do not, and appear to be slightly pickier regarding the kind of employment offers they are willing to accept, to the extent that they exhibit a stronger preference for salaried work and less flexibility regarding their work schedule.

---

[52] We have also looked at industry and occupation of re-employment, as well as reason for job termination, and found no significant differences across groups. Unfortunately we have no data on contract type (i.e., temporary, open-ended), or work schedule (full/part-time).

They also seem to obtain better matches, or at least matches that last longer. Whereas this is really the product of their more intense search, or whether the same would be true were unemployment insurance payments reduced or eliminated is something that, unfortunately, we cannot determine.

Box 3.2 The Social Safety Net and Household Behavior

We turn here to the issue of interactions among household members, and the role that UI and, especially, SA play in shaping labor-market related decisions at the household level. We have already discussed the potential disincentive effects associated with both systems, and how these can be particularly pervasive in the case of families with young children. For this reason, we have selected for this part of the analysis only those households where both parents are between the ages of 20 and 40, and where children are present. Under this selection rule, the sample includes a total of 5,701 such families.

Employment rates are high among adults in these households: approximately half the families have both adults working. However, if we look only at those households that receive SA/SS, most families contain at least one unemployed adult, or an adult who is out of the labor force (typically the spouse). In addition, most SA is given to spouses, and spouses are also the group with the largest share of recipients, followed by household heads. Also, while 88 percent of all households heads receiving SA are unemployed, only 63 percent of the spouses are (67 percent if we exclude maternity allowances). This implies that, most likely, the majority of household heads receive SA once their UI benefits are exhausted, whereas, in the case of spouses, recipiency seems to respond to a broader set of reasons (e.g., household-level variables). These figures suggest that SA (and UI), received by both the individual and other household members, may have and effects on labor force participation and job search decisions. To explore this issue more rigorously, we estimate two different probit models for the probability of participation and the probability of (active) search. The sample for the first model contains all non-employed individuals, while the sample for the second model contains all unemployed individuals in 2000 (following our previous discussion on the accuracy of the search questions in 1996 and 1999). We estimate both models separately for household heads and spouses, since we believe that the sensitivity of each group to potential disincentives is very different (Table B3.2.1).

Table B3.2.1 Effect of Unemployment Insurance and Social Assistance on Labor Force Participation and Active Search of Household Head and Spouse

	Heads		Spouses	
	LFP	Act search	LFP	Act search
Receives SA	0.376**	0.372**	0.441**	0.045
	(0.035)	(0.075)	(0.049)	(0.065)
Receives UI	0.198**	0.325**	0.477**	0.311**
	(0.020)	(0.044)	(0.027)	(0.086)
Spouse receives SA	0.023	0.151*		
	(0.042)	(0.078)		
Spouse receives UI	0.066	0.060		
	(0.049)	(0.146)		
Head receives SA			0.004	0.054
			(0.089)	(0.125)
Head receives UI			-0.012	-0.109
			(0.067)	(0140)
Demographic controls	YES	YES	YES	YES
Number of obs.	1,804	359	4,081	659

Source: LFS 1996.1-1996.4, 1999.1-1999.4, and 2000.-2000.4. See Sanchez-Paramo (2001).

In the case of male household heads, individual recipiency of either UI or SA is, if anything, positively correlated with labor-market participation and active search. In contrast, *SA has a very strong negative effect on the participation and search decisions of female household heads.* On the other hand, spousal recipiency of any type of benefits does not seem to have a significant effect on either decision. This is not surprising, given that most household heads are also considered to be the main earner in the family, increasing their attachment to the labor force. When we re-estimate these models on the sample of spouses, generally perceived to be less attached to the labor force and, thus, more susceptible to potential disincentive effects, we obtain very similar results: a positive effect of individual recipiency on both participation and search, and no effect of 'partner's' recipiency. In fact, the only difference between both sets of regressions is that, in the case of spouses, the presence of small children does have a strong negative effect on the participation and search decisions.

Given this evidence, we must conclude that there is no apparent disincentive effect associated with SA and UI at the *household* level, neither in terms of labor force participation nor in terms of active job search. These results, however, need to be taken with a pinch of salt, as there are numerous confounding factors concerning benefits and behavior in the labor market. Moreover, the sample size is relatively small.

Source: Sanchez-Paramo (2001).

DISCUSSION AND POLICY IMPLICATIONS

What It All Means, In a Nutshell

We have shown that workers who receive unemployment insurance and/or social assistance and social support tend to spend *more time unemployed* than workers who are not untitled to these benefits. In particular, the average spell for recipients is about two months longer than the average spell for non-recipients, and benefit entitlement explains most of this difference. We view this relationship between recipiency and unemployment duration as evidence of the disincentive effects associated with these programs.

However, workers who receive unemployment insurance/social assistance/support also *look for employment more actively* than their counterparts, and have more demanding preferences regarding their future jobs. This seems to suggest that benefit payments, by reducing the opportunity cost of unemployment, act as a subsidy for these workers' search time and allow them to be 'choosier'. In addition, and maybe as a consequence of the above, benefit recipients *find jobs in the private sector more often*, and these jobs turn out to be *better matches* than the ones obtained by non-recipients (where match quality is measured as duration of the match)—the average employment spell for those who received unemployment insurance/social assistance/support is almost 11 months long, compared to 9 months for workers with no benefits.

We need to be cautious when interpreting these results. Given the demographic differences that exist between recipients and non-recipients, it is difficult to draw any causal conclusions from the analysis. In particular, we cannot dismiss completely the idea that benefit recipients constitute a pool of better workers, younger and more educated, who search more actively and find jobs more often anyway, regardless of their entitlement status. To get at this point, it is interesting to complement our comparison of recipients and non-recipients, with a discussion of the behavioral differences that arise within the former group.

As we have emphasized again and again in the previous section, unemployment insurance and social assistance/support recipients cannot be treated as a single, homogenous group, since their behavior varies tremendously depending on whether they are actually receiving benefits or not. In particular, they exit the registry at a higher rate, search more actively, and move into private-sector jobs more often, once benefits are exhausted. So when we use these workers as their own control group, performing a within-group comparison rather than a between-group comparison, we *do* find strong evidence that both unemployment insurance and social assistance/support have important disincentive effects, not only on unemployment duration, but also on search behavior and on exit-to-employment.

However, before concluding from this last set of results that these programs should be drastically reformed, we need to think about their function in a broader context.

What Good are Unemployment Insurance and Social Assistance/Support Buying Us?

All safety net programs can be thought of as income support programs, regardless of whether they are insurance-based, like unemployment insurance, or means-tested, like social assistance or social support. This particular dimension is likely to be important in situations of economic change and transformation, expected to affect a substantial fraction of the labor force or, in general, the population. The Slovak Republic has experienced such a period during the last decade or so, as part of the process of economic transition, hence it is only logical to expand the scope of our analysis to account for the effect that unemployment insurance and social assistance/support may have had on poverty.

Unfortunately, we can only present figures for 1996, a snapshot rather than a story in evolution. We use four different measures of poverty to check for the robustness of the results and, although the poverty numbers vary substantially according to the measure used, the qualitative effects of the programs are very similar across all four. To illustrate such effects, we perform the following exercise: we calculate poverty incidence based on total income (TI), and then we compare this number with incidence figures based on total income minus unemployment insurance, total income minus social assistance/support, and total income minus *all* social income.[53] The marginal effect of each program(s) can then be understood as the change in the poverty rate.

Not surprisingly, when we consider the total population as the group of reference, it can be seen that the effect of social assistance/support on poverty is much stronger than that of unemployment insurance (Table 3.16). After all, the eligibility rules for social assistance/support/SS are based on income, thus targeting the poor, and the number of recipients is much larger.

Table 3.16 Poverty Rates for the Entire Population

Income definition	Minimum Subsistence Level	Less than $2PPP/day (per capita)	Less than $4PPP/day (per capita)	Less than 50% of median equiv. income
Total income (TI)	10.1	2.6	8.6	5.8
TI – UI[A]	12.0	4.0	10.4	7.1
TI – SA/SS[B]	17.2	4.9	15.2	9.2
TI – all social income	18.7	6.2	16.6	10.7

[A] Unemployment Insurance. [B] Social Assistance/Support.
Note that pensions are <u>always</u> included in total income.
Source: Microcensus, 1996. See Chapter 1, and Steele (2001).

---

[53] Notice that in all cases pensions are included in total income.

If instead we concentrate on a smaller segment of the population, namely active and unemployed individuals, and distinguish between these two groups, the results differ from the ones discussed above (Table 3.17). In particular, unemployment insurance plays a very important role preventing poverty among the unemployed, while social assistance/support are most likely mechanisms of last resort for this group. In contrast, among active workers, social assistance/support/SS represent a more important source of support.

Table 3.17 Poverty Rates for Active and Unemployed Individuals

Income definition	Minimum Subsistence Level		Less than $2PPP/day (per capita)		Less than $4PPP/day (per capita)		Less than 50% of median equiv. income	
	Active	Une	Active	Une	Active	Une	Active	Une
Total income (TI)	9.0	44.7	2.9	5.6	7.7	38.2	5.1	23.4
TI – UI [A]	10.0	63.2	3.2	26.9	8.6	57.9	5.4	42.9
TI – SA/SS [B]	12.5	42.2	3.3	15.8	10.8	37.5	6.4	25.6
TI – all social income	17.3	79.7	4.6	49.4	15.4	76.8	8.3	65.3

[A] Unemployment Insurance. [B] Social Assistance/Support.
Note that pensions are <u>always</u> included in total income.
Source: Microcensus, 1996.

What To Do Next

We have argued above that there are significant disincentive effects associated with benefit recipiency under the unemployment insurance, social assistance and social support systems. However, we have also shown that these programs play a crucial role in preventing individuals from falling into poverty. Hence, any attempt by the Slovak government to reform the safety net system will have to face up to an important question: how can disincentives effects be eliminated without jeopardizing the protection dimension of the system?

In the presence of strong disincentive effects, some individuals find it more advantageous to remain unemployed and receive benefits than to work. Therefore, one of the main objectives of any reform should be to make employment relatively more attractive than unemployment. The government could try to do this by simply decreasing the quantity and/or duration of the benefits or tightening the eligibility criteria (as indeed, has been done in the past). However, these measures would, most likely, also have a significant negative impact on poverty, especially since job availability is an issue for certain types of workers (e.g., those with low education and skill levels).

Moreover, such restrictive measures may not significantly affect job search incentives at the margin—that is, for those workers whose only job opportunities are at a wage very close to the benefit level. For these workers, the choice between entering employment and remaining on social assistance may still balance in favor of the latter. As we discussed earlier, it is possible for the net income contribution of a household member to be negative when she becomes employed if: (i) her salary is close to the amount of benefits she receives or, as a consequence of the change in her status, the family loses any child/parental allowances they may have been entitled to; and/or (ii) there are significant costs associated with employment.

Thus, it may make more economic (and social sense) to explore other, more creative, reform options that focus on 'making employment pay' rather than on penalizing unemployment, as well as options that actually help individuals find jobs. Paradoxically, improving incentives for people to move into jobs may require making the safety net more generous at the margin, rather than more restrictive—e.g., to "ease" the transition from welfare to work.

Benefit programs that allow recipients to keep a share of their benefits after going to work could address some of the incentive problems. Implementing such programs would imply adopting a benefit phasing-out scheme with a softer profile than the one currently in place, so that employed workers earning low wages would still be entitled to a (smaller) fraction of their benefits. This would undoubtedly improve work incentives for those at the margin and would also increase income among low-income working families.

To the extent that employment involves child care and other work expenses (e.g., transportation), improvements in labor income may seriously overstate improvements in *disposable* income. Hence, in addition to alternative benefit programs, the government may want to consider allocating a larger share of public assistance expenditure to **work-related programs**, such as child care and transportation subsidies for employed individuals in low-income families, rather than to cash benefits.

Financial programs offering government assistance to prevent poverty without also reducing work incentives are not, however, the only answer to our original question. The government could put more emphasis on the **role of social assistance offices as re-employment facilitators**. In such a world, registered workers should receive from these office the information, but also the incentives, necessary to look for and find a job, and those unresponsive to these incentives should be penalized. For instance, in Spain public officers match registered workers with potential employers, according to the characteristics of the vacancy, and help them arrange job interviews. Benefit recipiency is then conditional on the workers showing proof of attendance to such interviews.

Similarly, **training** offered in coordination with private sector firms could prove an effective way of getting unemployed workers in contact with potential employers, at the same time that they acquire skills for which there is a demand. To make this scheme appealing to employers, the government could consider partially subsidizing the trainees' cost for a limited period of time, or even allowing them to use a fraction of their benefit payments to do so.

Although in the short run some of these proposals may seem very demanding from a fiscal point of view, since they really provide workers with more benefits rather than less, it is important to keep in mind their beneficial long run effects: more successful transitions to employment would translate into a **permanent** decrease in the unemployment/welfare caseload, and hence ultimately into lower spending over the long term. Moreover, fiscal stress could be minimized by combining these reforms with the recommendations contemplated in the Social Benefits Reform Administration Project. The Project urges the government to substantially simplify the rules of the different programs, especially social assistance/support, and to create better data linkages and faster information flows between different agencies and programs. This measures would create a higher degree of harmonization and coordination across different programs, therefore reducing administrative costs, and preventing potential fraud.

REFERENCES

Atkinson, A. and Micklewright, J. 1991 "Unemployment Compensation and Labor Market Transitions: A critical Review". *Journal of Economic Literature,* vol. XXIX, December, pp. 1679-1727.

Boeri, T. and Edwards, S. 1998 "Long-Term Unemployment and Short-Term Benefits: The Changing Nature of Non-Employment Subsidies in Central and Eastern Europe". *Empirical Economics,* 23, pp. 31-54.

Boeri, T. 1997 "Learning from Transition Economies: Assessing Labor Market policies across Central and eastern Europe". *Journal of Comparative Economics* 25, pp. 366-384.

Boeri, T 1997 "Labor-Market reforms in Transition Economies". *Oxford Review of Economic Policy,* vol. 13, No. 2, pp. 126-140.

Bover, O., Arellano, M. and Bentolila, S. 1998 "Unemployment Duration, Benefit Duration and the Business Cycle" CEPR Working Paper No. 1840.

Cebrián, I. *et alia* 1996 "The Influence of Unemployment Benefits on Unemployment Duration: Evidence from Spain". *Labour,* 10 (2), pp. 239-267.

Erbenova, M., Sorm, V. and Terell K. 1998 "Work Incentive and other effects of Social Assistance and Unemployment Benefits in the Czech Republic". *Empirical economics,* 23, pp. 87-120.

Ham, J.C., Svejnar, J. and Terrell K. 1998 "Unemployment and the Social Safety Net during Transition to a Market Economy: Evidence from the Czech and Slovak Republics". *American Economic Review,* December, pp. 1117-1142.

Lubyova, M. 2000 "Overview of the Evolution of the Slovak Labor Market" in *Economic Policy in Slovak Republic, 1990-1999.* A. Marcincin and M. Beblorvy, editors.

Lubyova, M. and van Ours, J.C. 1999 "Effects of active Labor Market Programs on the Transition Rate from Unemployment into Regular Jobs in the Slovak republic".

Lubyova, M. and van Ours, J.C. 1999 "Work Incentives and Other Effects of the Transition to Social Assistance: Evidence from the Slovak Republic". *Empirical Economics,* 23, pp. 121-153.

Lubyova, M. and van Ours, J.C. 1997 "Unemployment Dynamics and the Restructuring of the Slovak Unemployment Benefit System". *European Economic Review* 41, pp. 925-934.

Meyer, B.D. 1990 "Unemployment Insurance and Unemployment Spells". *Econometrica,* vol. 58, No. 4, July, pp. 757-782.

World Bank, The 2001a "Social Benefits Reform Administration Project. Project Appraisal Document. » Internal document. Washington, DC.

World Bank, The 2001b "Country Assistance Strategy for the Slovak Republic." Report No. 20232-SK. Washington, DC.

World Bank, The 2001c "Slovak Republic: Poverty, Employment and Labor Markets Study." Internal document. Washington, DC.

POVERTY AND WELFARE OF ROMA IN THE SLOVAK REPUBLIC[54]

BACKGROUND

For many reasons, Roma in Slovak Republic have been hardest hit by the process of transition from plan to market. As a whole, Roma are poorer than other population groups and are worse off in terms of nearly all basic social indicators, including education and health status, housing conditions and access to opportunities in the labor market and within civil society. Despite these developments, quantitative evidence on the conditions of Roma is sparse and often fraught with methodological problems (see discussion in Chapter 1). This chapter draws upon the existing data, as well as qualitative research of Roma settlements which was commissioned for this report (Box 4.1).

Roma are the second largest ethnic minority in Slovak Republic after Hungarians. Informal estimates suggest that there are between 420,000 and 500,000 Roma in Slovak Republic, or between 8-10 percent of the population, one of the highest in the region (Figure 4.1). This share is growing as a result of higher birth rates among Roma than the rest of the population.

Figure 4.1 Estimated Roma Populations in Europe

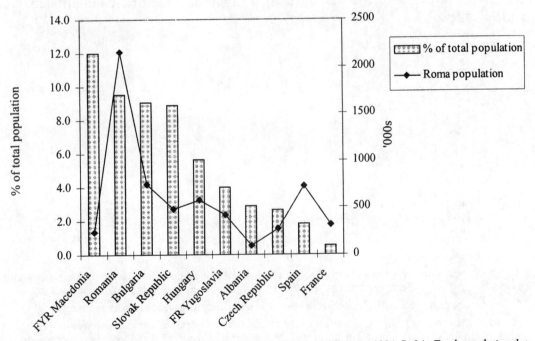

Sources: Liegeois, J-P., Roma, Gypsies, Travellers Strasbourg, Council of Europe, 1994. P. 34. Total population data: World Bank Atlas, 1995. Latest possible year; pop`ulation data are 1997; Roma data are midpoints of ranges.

---

[54] This chapter is a synthesis of a longer, forthcoming World Bank report prepared by Dena Ringold and Helen Shahriari, jointly with a team of Slovak sociologists led by Iveta Radicova. See Poverty and Welfare of Roma in the Slovak Republic: A Qualitative Study, forthcoming—referred throughout as World Bank, 2001a.

Roma Settlements. More Roma in Slovak Republic live in settlements, on the outskirts of villages and towns, than Roma in other countries in the region. An estimated one-fourth of Roma in Slovak Republic live in settlements, many of which are in the poorer Eastern regions of the country, although the actual number is difficult to gauge because of methodological difficulties in measuring the Roma population and defining what is a 'settlement.'[55] Living conditions for Roma in settlements are generally worse than for the rest of the Roma population. Some settlements have their roots in policies adopted during the Second World War and early socialist period, which required Roma to move outside of towns. Settlements vary significantly based upon geographic location and ethnic composition.

A survey of district officials estimated that there were 591 Roma settlements in 1998, a significant increase from 278 in 1988.[56] The total number of people living in Roma settlements also has grown dramatically. In 1988 there were approximately 14,988 inhabitants, and by 1997 this figure had grown to 123,034.[57] In the past decade many Roma have returned to settlements because of the availability of cheaper housing. This, in addition to the high birth rate among Roma living in settlements, partially explains this increase.[58]

Because settlements are often geographically remote, and may not be officially registered because of unclear property ownership, they are not covered in most official registries and household surveys.[59] The qualitative work commissioned for this report was designed to address this gap by focusing on conditions in settlements. The discussion in this chapter centers on the unique circumstances of Roma in different types of settlements (Box 4.1).

---

[55] In this report 'settlement' refers to a group of people living together in an distinct geographic area, either within or outside of a town or village. Settlements can be segregated (only Roma) or integrated (mixed) populations.

[56] This figure is based on a loose definition of settlements, including integrated areas in towns and villages.

[57] The database provides only a rough estimate of the number of settlements and their conditions. The fieldwork conducted for this study found significant errors in the database regarding the number and location of settlements.

[58] The database provides only a rough estimate of the number of settlements and their conditions. The fieldwork conducted for this study found significant errors in the database regarding the number and location of settlements.

[59] Although officially, the sample of the 1996 Microcensus includes Roma settlements, the analysis of the raw data suggests that this is not the case. By all indications, the sample under-represents households with typical Roma characteristics, such as a large number of children or many people living under the same household. For example, very few households in the sample report having more than 3 children; while the *average* number of children for Roma families in settlements is 4.2 per woman.

Box 4.1 Qualitative Study of Roma Settlements in Slovak Republic[60]

In order to gain a better understanding of living conditions in Roma settlements, a qualitative study was undertaken in a subset of sites in 3 contrasting districts. In each district, fieldwork was conducted in 9 settlements. As much as possible the sites were divided between integrated, separated and segregated communities.

The research involved in depth interviews with 270 individuals and households and 120 key informants, including teachers, doctors, social assistance workers and local government officials. The study examined the characteristics and correlates of poverty, conditions in the settlements, and the experience of Roma living in these areas. The districts included in the study were:

Malacky: An above average district in terms of unemployment (13.5 percent in 1999) and the share of the population receiving social assistance benefits. Malacky is in the Bratislava Region near the capital city. There are very few segregated settlements in the district.

Stará Lubovna: An average region in terms of unemployment, social assistance beneficiaries and the composition of Roma settlements. The district is located in Eastern Slovakia in the Presov Region where the concentration of Roma is high.

Rimavská Sobota: A relatively poor district in the Banska Bystrica Region, with a high level of unemployment (35 in 1999) and a high share of the population receiving social assistance.

"Poverty" in the study was defined based upon qualitative indicators and the perceptions and experience of Roma themselves. Absolute, or material poverty, refers to the absence of appropriate housing, clothing, food and access to basic infrastructure and utilities (e.g., roads, running water, electricity and sewage).

In addition, the study looks at poverty in its broader sense among Roma, including the lack of access to education and employment, insecurity, social exclusion, and the lack of opportunities for participation in civil society. The interviewers' assessments of poverty did not always coincide with those of the households being interviewed. These discrepancies highlight the highly subjective nature of the concept.

Source: World Bank, 2001a.

The Roma population is unevenly distributed throughout the country. Nearly two-thirds of the population live in the east of the country, around Kosice and in the southern districts of central Slovak Republic, such as Rimavská Sobota. According to the 1980 census, Roma constituted more than 10 percent of the population in many districts in Eastern Slovakia.

The demographic profile of Roma in Slovak Republic is considerably different than that of the rest of the population (Figure 4.2). The Roma population is significantly younger and has been growing more rapidly than other ethnic groups, due to higher birth rates. The national birth rate for Slovak Republic has declined steadily during the transition period from 15.2 live births per 1,000 population in 1990 to 10.7 in 1998 (UNICEF, 2000). In contrast, birth rates among Roma appear to be increasing, especially in the most isolated, segregated settlements. Life expectancy of Roma is considerably lower than the national average although recent data are not available. Estimates derived from the 1970 and 1980 censuses put life expectancy for Roma at 55 for men and 59 for women, in comparison with 67 for men in the total population and 74 for women (ECOHOST, 2000).

---

[60] Fieldwork was conducted by a team of Slovak sociologists led by Iveta Radicova.

Data from 1988 on family structure found that, of families living in segregated settlements, 25 percent had three children or fewer and 77 percent had four or more children. Of these, 41 percent had six or more children (Vasescka, 2000). In contrast, less than 10 percent of Roma families in integrated towns had six or more children. In the qualitative study, in the village of Lomnicka in Stara Lubovna, a settlement of approximately 1,200 inhabitants, the population has reportedly grown by 70-80 persons annually during the 1990s. Demographic patterns of Roma in more integrated areas appeared closer those of the non-Roma population.

Figure 4.2: Age Structure of Roma and the Total Population in Slovak Republic, 1991

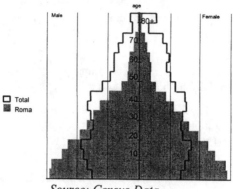

Source: Census Data

Life expectancy of Roma is also considerably lower than the national average although recent data are not available. Estimates derived from the 1970 and 1980 censuses put life expectancy for Roma at 55 for men and 59 for women, in comparison with 67 for men in the total population and 74 for women (ECOHOST, 2000). Due to low life expectancy and high birth rates, the Roma population is significantly younger than the population at large (Figure 4.2). In the qualitative study, the average age of the Roma interviewed was 34. Roma living in settlements tended to be younger and have more children than integrated Roma. There are very few older Roma living in settlements. For example, in the study in a segregated settlement of 670 people in Stara Lubovna there were only seven people over the age of 60.

POVERTY IN ROMA SETTLEMENTS

Poverty in Roma settlements is closely linked to three factors: (i) regional economic conditions; (ii) the proximity of the settlement to a neighboring town or village; and (iii) the degree of ethnic integration or segregation of the settlement. Education was also found to be a close correlate of poverty. Roma who had graduated from regular vocational secondary schools, or above, were more likely to live in integrated areas and have a higher standard of living.

The situation of Roma in more economically developed regions is generally more favorable. For example, living conditions of Roma in Malacky, a district with a lower unemployment rate—13.5 percent in 1999—than the national average of 17.1 percent, were better than Roma in Rimavská Sobota, a district with 34.8 percent unemployment in

1999. Roma houses in most of the segregated settlements in Malacky resembled those of the majority population. They were generally made of solid materials such as bricks, and had access to electricity. In contrast, housing conditions in settlements in Rimavská Sobota were poorer and health and education status was reported to be worse.

However, within regions, there is some evidence that the level of poverty in areas with higher Roma population is higher than in areas with majority non-Roma population. As discussed in Chapter 1, poverty rates in districts where at least 5 percent of the population was "officially" classified as Roma (a likely underestimate of true Roma population), where consistently higher than those for the region as a whole.

The level of poverty in a Roma settlement also appears to be closely connected to the level of ethnic integration and segregation. In general, there are three types of settlements based upon living arrangements between Roma and non-Roma. First are completely integrated towns and villages, this was the case of Nova Lubovna in the district of Stara Lubovna, an average developed district in the east of the country. Second are separated areas, in which Roma live together within a town or village, either on the outskirts, or within a particular street or neighborhood, as in Studienka in Malacky. Finally, there are completely segregated settlements outside of the village or town, such as Kyjatice in the district of Rimavská Sobota, a settlement 3 km from the nearest town.

Box 4.2 Integration and Segregation

The study found significant differences between Roma living in segregated and integrated areas, and especially between Roma who had been living with non-Roma for more than one generation, and those who in segregated areas. Although it is difficult to generalize, it was possible to document patterns. The main reasons observed for better living conditions were: (i) living in a town or village where non-Roma constituted the majority for a long period of time; (ii) higher education levels; and (iii) exposure to better living conditions (parents and grandparents of most Roma in integrated areas had been employed under socialism).

Two types of integrated Roma were interviewed. First were Roma who had been settled in areas with non-Roma, as a result of the forced assimilation polices of the 1970s. Second were Roma whose parents and/or grandparents had moved out of settlements in search of a better life for themselves and their children. In general, the education attainment and employment situation of the latter group was higher. However, the first group also had higher living standards than those living in segregated settlements. Those Roma who moved from settlements were generally followed by other members of the family, such as brothers and sisters with their families. Some had contacts with non-Roma before moving from settlements.

An issue shared among Roma living in integrated areas shared was the social distance they felt with Roma from settlements. They would refer to themselves as different from a different caste. Some were proud that they had not been allowed to speak the Roma language at home when they were growing up.

Source: World Bank, 2001a.

The most segregated and geographically isolated settlements are the most economically and socially disadvantaged. In almost all of the segregated settlements formal unemployment was close to 100 percent, and almost none of the inhabitants had graduated from secondary school. None of the Roma living in segregated settlements who were interviewed for this study had permanent employment. A number of people worked seasonally, mainly in agriculture or construction, or participated in public works, but formal employment was nearly zero. The health and education status of Roma in geographically isolated settlements was similarly worse than that of Roma in other areas.

Box 4.3 Living Conditions in Letanovce

Letanovce is a settlement in Stara Lubovna district, located 6 km from the nearest village. It is a completely segregated settlement, the deceased are even buried separately from the main village. There are 650 inhabitants in the village, of which only 7 are older than 60 years old.

Houses are made of scrap materials, or tree branches, and inhabitants have no access to electricity, running water, or sewage. Students study by candlelight, which is very expensive for many families. Of the 156 school age children in the settlement, 150 attend special schools for the mentally and physically disabled. Formal unemployment is 100 percent and only a couple of residents participate in public works jobs.

Source: World Bank. 2001a.

Perceptions of Poverty

Roma in urban and rural areas define poverty in relative and absolute terms. They describe their living conditions mainly in relation to the past.[61] For most Roma poverty is a recent phenomenon. Although none of those interviewed described themselves as well off before 1989, most felt that they had lived well relative to prevailing living standards. A minority said that they had always been 'poor.' The most salient comparison with communism for older Roma was that they had all had jobs. A respondent noted: "*During communism we were better off because everyone had to work even if it was pointless or unskilled work.*"

In addition to comparing their situation to the past, for many Roma respondents poverty also was based on their concrete experiences at the present. Roma living in segregated as well as many living in separated areas told us that for them, the worst aspects of their in the present situation were: poor housing condition, lack of infrastructure, poor health, lack of adequate clothing, lack of social network that they could rely on, unemployment and discrimination. According to one Roma respondent: "*We are poor because we don't have a proper house, we don't have any money and no one to borrow from*". This evaluation of poverty worsened by the degree of segregation.

Poverty has important social and psychological components. Respondents living in segregated settlements describe poverty as associated with feelings of defenselessness, and exclusion from the larger community. Poverty for many is also associated with shame. Even those respondents who appeared extremely poor to the interviewers often preferred to define themselves as "close to" but not completely "poor." For the very poorest, however, "not completely poor" means little more than "not dying of hunger". This has its roots in communism which defined and understood poverty as a consequence of personal failure and laziness.

---

[61] This sentiment is common to many poor in the transition countries. See, for example, *Bulgaria: Consultations with the Poor, 2000.*

Although young Roma are less likely to compare their situation to the past than their parents, the experience and interpretation of "poverty", surprisingly, does not vary much across generations. Most young people identify the same problems and constraints in their lives as their parents: lack of jobs, proper education and a sense of exclusion.

Material Dimensions of Poverty

The poorest respondents identified common elements of poverty, including: inadequate nutrition, poor housing conditions and ill health. Ability to provide a good education for their children and lead a better life—for example, having opportunities to travel—were also identified as important, but took second place to the more immediate issues of hunger and cold.

Nutrition. In the poorest settlements, child nutrition was observed to be a frequent problem. Researchers observed evidence of stunting among some children. Some teachers reported that Roma children do not attend school lunches because their parents are unable to pay the lunch fees. The director of a school in Stara Lubovna noted that *"in the entire primary school only one [Roma] child goes to lunch at school."*

Roma in integrated and segregated communities have contrasting consumption strategies, which have an impact on the nutritional status of the entire family, especially children, and not necessarily a reflection of being better off. Roma in more integrated areas, prefer to plan ahead and economize in order to secure enough food for the rest of the month. Those living in rural areas who own land are able to grow vegetables during the summer months for home consumption. The wife of an unemployed respondent in a relatively integrated community in Stara Lubovna reported that they tend to buy many things which last, such as potatoes and beans in bulk. As much as possible, she makes sure that her children have sufficient food, despite the fact that her husband is unemployed and they live mainly on social assistance, *"sometimes I buy on credit, but usually I make sure that we have enough to feed our family during the month"*.

In contrast, Roma in segregated settlements focus more on immediate survival and are less able to plan ahead. Consumption tended to increase after social assistance payments were made. A resident of Lipovec in Rimavska Sobota noted *"why not eat now that we have money, it doesn't matter what comes tomorrow."* A doctor in the town of Pobilinec in Stara Lubovna who sees patients from a number of nearby settlements reported that she sometimes encounters dehydrated babies . Mothers report that they have no money to buy milk after they have spent all of their social assistance benefits. Very few residents in segregated settlements had access to land to grow for own consumption. In some segregated settlements, such as Lomnicka, where the majority did own land, Roma did not plant anything and claimed that if they did, the crops would be stolen by the poorer landless residents of the settlement. Some Roma pick mushrooms or berries from the forests, and many non-Roma living in nearby villages accused Roma of stealing potatoes and other food items from their fields.

In general, Roma diets deteriorate as the month comes to close. Many Roma from marginalized regions, including some integrated ones but mostly separated, admitted that during the week before the day of disbursing welfare benefits their families often had one simple meal (for instance, beans) for the entire week. Many also said that they had to buy cheap food items to make it through the month.

> *"We have to buy the cheapest food and prepare it in such a way that the whole family will not feel hungry. I am using fatty meat and potatoes to feed my family"*—one woman respondent.

Housing Conditions. Housing conditions are also the poorest in the most isolated and segregated settlements (Box 4.4). The homes of Roma living in more integrated areas and those separated within a village are similar, and it is not possible to identify the ethnicity of the owner from the outside of a house. In segregated settlements, Roma houses are typically made of wood or scrap metal, plaster, tin and tree branches. However, the construction type varies within regions depending on the availability of building materials as well.

Box 4.4 Housing Conditions in a Village in Stara Lubovna

Kolačkov is a segregated settlement of 220 inhabitants in the Stara Lubovna district. Unemployment is nearly 100 percent. In the village, a family of 7 people (the parents, their oldest daughter of 17, newly wed and pregnant, her husband, and 3 other children) lives in a two-room shack constructed from wood and tin. The house lacks access to water, sewage and there is no garbage collection in the settlement. The family has a wood burning stove which is used for heating and cooking.

Source: World Bank. 2001.

The extent of overcrowding within Roma houses was found to be closely related to the degree of segregation and geographic isolation of the community. In general, in both Roma and non-Roma houses in integrated areas there were about 1.5 people per room, while in segregated settlements there were an average of 2.5 to 3.5 persons per room. Estimates by district officials put the number of people per dwelling in Roma settlements at 8.6 in 1997.

Access to utilities and public services is nonexistent, or limited, in most marginalized settlements. The most serious problems include lack of access to electricity, water, sewage and garbage collection. Integrated settlements, and separated settlements within a town or village had greater access to services. In the better-off district of Malacky all settlements, with few exceptions, had access to electricity and roads. The situation differed in the other districts, where more isolated settlements did not have access to utilities.

Many settlements lack access to running water. Five of the seven segregated settlements in the study, and four out of 10 separated settlements had no access to running water. Even in a better off district such as Malacky, some settlements (for example, the one in Jabolonnova and the totally segregated settlement in Plavecky) did not have access to running water. In the former case, the mayor deliver water to them by tanks, whereas in the latter case there is a common fountain in the middle of the settlement. The situation is more difficult in the poorer districts of Stara Lubovna and Rimavská Sobota. Running water is rather an exception, and is not available in many communities in these districts. In four of the settlements included in the study, Roma use the same stream for both drinking water and sewage.

In some areas, residents linked the inadequacy of the water supply to poor health conditions. Residents of Rimavská Píla in Rimavska Sobota complained that their drinking water was contaminated and caused diarrhea, parasites, and trachoma among their children. In other areas, parents blamed epidemics of scabies and lice on the lack of running and hot water for washing.

In some of the most isolated settlements electricity was unavailable. In Stara Lubovna, two settlements lacked coverage and in four of the settlements households were receiving electricity through illegal connections. The situation was similar in Rimavska Sobota, where seven of the thirteen settlements either lacked electricity, or relied on illegal sources. Residents of Rimavská Sobota explained that the lack of electricity was particularly problematic in the winter, as it is difficult for them to afford candles or fuel.

Lack of garbage collection services also seriously affects living conditions and creates health problems for residents as a result of contamination. In the majority of segregated settlements garbage collection was either non-existent or sporadic because residents were unable to afford the service. This is despite the fact that the amount for collection of garbage is nominal.[62] In some cases, local authorities attempted to finance waste removal. Roma also complained that garbage dumps were too close to their settlements, leading to contamination of land and water, and in some cases, attracted rats and stray dogs and cats.

Health Status. Doctors in the study areas noted that the health status of their Roma patients was generally worse than that of non-Roma. They attributed this to unhealthy lifestyle factors including poor diets and smoking and poor housing conditions. The prevalence of communicable diseases, associated with poor living conditions, was found to be higher in more isolated and segregated settlements. Doctors reported epidemics of hepatitis, trachoma, tuberculosis and skin diseases, including scabies in settlements in Stará Lubovna and Rimavská Sobota. Four settlements in Stara Lubovna which were included in this study have had outbreaks of hepatitis A, as well as skin diseases. Even in the better off district of Malacky there was an outbreak of hepatitis A in a segregated settlement. Many of these conditions have been eliminated in the majority population. These developments are likely linked to problems of overcrowding, unsafe water, lack of waste disposal and proximity to environmentally contaminated areas.

Non-communicable diseases, including disabilities, were also found to be more frequent among Roma in both segregated and separated areas. A large number of those interviewed were receiving disability benefits. Conditions ranged from chronic illnesses, to back pain and injuries. Others were considered disabled due to heart conditions and related cardiovascular disorders. Among social security officials, there is a perception that a sizeable fraction of these disability claims are fraudulent, but there is no concrete evidence to help ascertain whether this is true or false. The most frequently cited reasons for the high incidence of non-communicable diseases among Roma include lifestyle factors, such as smoking and diet, and untreated injuries. Information on congenital disorders is scant.

---

[62] The amount differs from one municipality to another, depending on the wealth of the municipality. For instance, in a better off neighborhood close to Bratislava the annual collection fee is 1000 Slovak crowns (about US$ 21). In other areas it is much less.

These findings are consistent with the existing body of evidence on epidemiological developments in Roma communities. Gaps in health status between Roma and non-Roma were observed during the socialist period (ECOHOST, 2000). More recently, epidemics have been documented of hepatitis and measles in Roma communities. In 1997, a measles outbreak was documented near Kosice, affecting 10 Roma and 9 Slovaks and was partially attributed to lapses in vaccination coverage.

The isolation and poverty of many settlements may have limited the problem of drug abuse. The remoteness of settlements, the poverty of their inhabitants and the absence of social contacts do not provide a conducive environment for distribution of drugs. In contrast, more integrated settlements in closer proximity to urban centers are more vulnerable to drug trafficking. Two cases of heroin abuse among Roma were noted in the village of Zohor in Malacky. Inhaling of glue and paint thinner was also reported in some areas. Alcoholism was found to be significantly more prevalent in settlements.

Educational Attainment. According to the 1991 census, 77 percent of Roma included in the sample had completed primary education, 8 percent had completed vocational training, and less than two percent had completed academic secondary education or university. An earlier survey from 1990 found that 56 percent of Roma men and 59 percent of Roma women had not completed basic education (grades 1-8) (Vasecka, 2000). Education patterns of Roma in the settlements confirm this pattern. The majority of adult Roma who were interviewed had some primary education, although not all of them had completed all eight grades. The findings presented in Chapter 1 on the risk factors associated with poverty would suggest that such low educational attainment would, on its own, put many Roma families at risk of poverty.

Almost all Roma from segregated, as well as some from separated areas, had not completed secondary school. In many cases, students completed 10 years of compulsory education and then dropped out. After 9 years of primary education, Slovak students have three options. First are regular vocational schools, which mainly, but not exclusively, cater to graduates of special primary schools. These schools have the lowest academic standards and graduates have limited labor market opportunities. Most Roma from segregated, as well as some from separated settlements, attend this type of school. The second type of school is special secondary schools which are a type of vocational school. These schools train workers in specific fields and there are special universities which graduates of these schools can continue their education. Many integrated Roma, and some better off Roma from separated areas, attend such schools. Most of the respondents who had graduated from these schools had regular jobs. The last category is gymnasiums which provide general academic training and prepare students to continue on to university. None of the students included in this study had attended gymnasium.[63]

School Attendance. Teachers and school directors in the study districts reported that the attendance of Roma children had been declining since the transition. Particularly in the poorest settlements, many children were observed playing in the streets during the school day. Some doctors complained that Roma children came to them to ask to be excused from school. One doctor said that at least 10 healthy Roma students from nearby

---

[63] In 2001 in Slovak Republic there were 157 Gymnasiums with 67,487 students, 309 special schools with 84, 553, and 363 vocational schools with 104, 039 students. The Ministry of Education.

settlements came each day to ask for a release form. Very few Roma children in the areas visited for the study continue their education beyond compulsory education. A number of children from segregated and separated areas had completed one or two years of secondary education, but had subsequently dropped out.[64] Constraints to participation in education are discussed further below.

THE LABOR MARKET AND COPING STRATEGIES

The labor market status of Roma has changed dramatically during the transition period, with huge increases in unemployment and inactivity. Under socialism, many Roma held formal public sector jobs, most commonly in agricultural cooperatives, factories, public construction enterprises and mines. Many of these enterprises have closed or have been substantially restructured over the last decade. Roma were often among those first laid off in the early transition period, because they commonly held low or unskilled jobs. Because of low education levels and discrimination, Roma have faced substantial barriers to reentering the labor force.

While official unemployment data by ethnicity are lacking, a 1997 survey by the Ministry of Labor, Social Affairs and Family, estimated that Roma comprised between 17 to18 percent of the total unemployed in 1996, with this figure as high as 40 to 42 percent in Eastern districts with large Roma populations (e.g., Kosice, Spisská Nová Ves). Similarly, the registries from the National Labor Office (which contained information on ethnicity until 1997) suggest that, for the country as a whole, the Roma represented between 15 and 20 percent of all the registered unemployed in the Slovak Republic up through 1997 (Table 4.1).[65] Furthermore, the share of the Roma receiving unemployment benefits was lower than the average share. This was mostly due to the long duration of unemployment for Roma, who had therefore largely exhausted their eligibility for insurance-based benefits.

Many Roma have been unable to find work because their skills and level of education are not in demand, leading many to rely on social assistance. Others have turned to sporadic informal employment, or even illegal activities. Many Roma do not see a direct relationship between the kind of education they received and employment. The majority of Roma in separated and segregated communities have only primary or unfinished secondary education, categories which comprise the highest share of the unemployed in Slovak Republic. In general, unskilled workers have found it increasingly difficult to assert themselves in the labor market. Part of this may reflect the lack of demand for labor with low skills; part of it may be due to the fact that high payroll taxes and other non-wage costs make hiring unskilled labor relatively more costly than hiring workers with higher skills, given the differences in their productivity (see Chapter 2).

---

[64] This may be linked to the fact that compulsory education is 10 years in Slovak Republic.

[65] The practice of collecting information based on ethnicity was discontinued in 1998 after protest from the Roma and Hungarian minorities. One reason for these criticisms was that ethnicity was being determined by labor office staff, which was inconsistent with Slovak legislation aimed at protecting basic individual rights.

Table 4.1 Share of Roma in Total Registered Unemployment, 1991-98

	1991	1992	1993	1994	1995	1996	1997	1998
Number of registered unemployed and share of Roma:								
Total	301,951	260,274	368,095	371,481	333,291	329,749	347,753	428,209
Roma (%)	15.5	15.5	14.0	13.5	16.6	19.0	19.2	--
Eligibility for unemployment benefits:								
Total (%)	82.0	33.6	33.4	22.9	27.0	28.4	26.7	28.0
Roma (%)	--	15.2	10.7	4.7	5.3	--	--	--

"--" = not available

Source: National Labor Office, as reported in Lubyova (2000).

The re-integration of unemployed Roma workers into the labor force may also be made more difficult by the perverse incentives arising from the design of the social safety net. As we saw in Chapter 3, the design of the social safety net is such that, for a family where the adults have low education and where there are many children, there are strong incentives for the adults to remain at home or unemployed. The ratio of what the family can receive in benefits to what they would make were one (or both) of the adults to find employment at the minimum wage is well over 100 percent: In other words, the family is worse off if one of the adults finds a job that pays only the minimum wage. Given the lack of well paid jobs for workers of low skills, it is not surprising that many workers would choose to remain at home—in this, they are making a rational decision of what is best for their family income.

Because social benefits are not allowed to taper off gradually as workers become employed so as to build pro-work incentives, the system penalizes those who may go out and find a job; thus setting up a dependency trap, much like that documented in many OECD countries during the 1960s and 1970s. The relationship between design of the safety net and these perverse work incentives is not in any sense unique to Roma families, but the demographic characteristics of the Roma, with relatively low levels of educational attainment among the adults, and a large number of children, makes them particularly vulnerable to falling into this dependency trap.

Unemployment. Long-term unemployment among Roma is particularly high. Many of the Roma interviewed had been unemployed for more than two years. Even though unemployment is a problem that all Roma in Slovak Republic face—as well as the majority population—its extent, to a large degree, is linked to regional economic conditions, educational attainment and the level of integration of the settlement. In Malacky, where the overall district unemployment rate was 13.5 percent in 1999, formal sector unemployment among Roma ranged from approximately 60 percent in integrated and separated areas, to nearly 100 percent in the most isolated settlements. In Stara Lubovna and Rimavská Sobota, unemployment among Roma was between 80 to 100 percent, while district-wide the total unemployment rate was 35 percent.

Many Roma identified on-going unemployment and insecurity as the most demoralizing aspect of their lives. A resident of Klenovec, in Rimavska Sobota explained: *"we were happy that we found a meaningful way of spending a day. In two or three years a man gets used to doing nothing and then it gets really tough."* Roma also expressed discouragement with the lack of employment opportunities. Roma in segregated settlements are particularly disadvantaged, as job prospects are generally limited to seasonal employment in neighboring towns and villages. A 35 year old father of five in a marginalized settlement in Stara Lubovna explained: *"Who is going to give me a job? I have no education, no skills and am Roma, even in my neighboring village nobody wants to give us any work."*

Unemployment among young people in settlements, and especially women, is high. Most young Roma under the age of 25 interviewed in these areas had never been formally employed. Young women do not generally enter the labor force, because of early pregnancies. Many get married and begin having children soon after completing primary school. The majority of girls, age 18 and above, who were interviewed were already married with children, or pregnant. The situation was different among integrated Roma, and even some living in separated neighborhoods. Some of these women worked, as teachers, music teachers, or cleaning ladies, and some held jobs in the public administration.

Of Roma living in non-integrated areas who are employed, most are engaged in unskilled labor, frequently in seasonal agricultural work or construction activities. Some Roma are employed in various public works programs including jobs as street cleaners and working in the forest as guards. In many settlements, public works are the only source of employment. Some Roma are employed in more skilled labor, including construction and stone masonry. Some of the Roma who were engaged in more skilled labor had some vocational training. However, not all Roma with vocational education, had jobs. Therefore, even though vocational training could help some living in areas with more job opportunities, it did not automatically guarantee employment.

Many Roma cited ethnic discrimination as a significant barrier to employment, and as a rationale for not searching for work outside of their communities and villages. Although Slovak Republic has adopted anti-discrimination legislation, including ILO conventions, Roma in the study described experiences of discrimination. A number of Roma noted that they had applied for a job, and although they were accepted over the phone, they were subsequently rejected as soon as the employer realized that they were Roma. Respondents also explained that they were denied employment because of low education levels: *"Even trained people have not chance to find a job, so how could I find one?"* Women noted this problem even more than men: *"Men are allowed to take jobs for which they are not trained, but from a woman, they always require that she be trained."*

In a recent study on the impact of active labor market policies in the Slovak Republic, Lubyova and Van Ours (1999) found that Roma had a lower exit rate to jobs than any other group. The other sizeable minority, Hungarians, were not different in their exit behavior from the majority population, and both had higher exit rates than the Roma.

As among the majority population (see Chapter 2), labor mobility among Roma is low. Of those Roma in the study areas who were employed, most had jobs in the immediate surroundings of their settlements. High transportation costs were cited as the most significant deterrent to seeking work elsewhere. Costs were perceived to be too high in relation to the wages paid for unskilled workers. Very few Roma sought employment in neighboring districts or countries, such as Hungary and the Czech Republic, those that did still commute to the Czech Republic complained that their wages were too low to make it worthwhile, that employers were often late with payments, and that sometimes they were not paid at all. Roma were more likely to work abroad if someone else in their family or settlement had gone first and had a successful experience.

Because of the extent of long-term unemployment, many Roma have become discouraged and have stopped looking for work. Job search strategies among the Roma include labor offices and municipalities for public works. But overall, the Roma appear to be much more limited (less active) in their job search strategies than other parts of the population. In general, more unemployed Slovaks find new jobs through informal personal connections and other search avenues (private job agencies, placing/reading advertisements, etc.) than through labor offices, even though most (some 90 percent) are also registered with the labor office (see Chapter 3). According to the Ministry of Labor, Social Affairs and Family in 2000, 28 percent of the unemployed who found jobs did so through labor offices, while 38 percent found jobs through social contacts or other means. However, very few Roma said that they use informal channels such as personal connections for finding work. Roma mainly rely on local labor offices for information on formal employment. Many, though, noted that the offices were not helpful, as their activities focused on distribution of passive unemployment benefits, and did not provide much in the form of job counseling, training or placement services.

Public Works Programs. Many Roma participate in public works programs run by the Ministry of Labor, Social Affairs, and Family through local municipalities. This program was initiated in 2000 to provide employment through local public works. Jobs generally last three months and most commonly include unskilled work, such as cleaning of streets and parks, and garbage collection. None of the jobs offered provided training or prepared participants for future employment opportunities. A significant share of Roma, especially those in separated settlements in all of the three districts, participated in these projects. However, these programs may not always be effective in reaching Roma. In two localities, Roma explained that they were denied participation in the local public works program because the mayor preferred to hire non-Roma.

Local officials expressed concerns about the incentive effects of the public works programs. An amendment to the Social Assistance Act which took effect on July 1, 2000, halved social assistance benefits for individuals who had been unemployed for two consecutive years or longer. Full benefits are reinstated only once the individual has been officially employed again for at least three months, providing a strong incentive for beneficiaries to seek short term employment in the public works program. Mayors noted:

> *"Finally somebody pressed them against the wall and cut their [welfare] benefits. Do you really believe that they would [apply for the program] if the government did not cut their benefits?"*

> *"When the government introduced a similar program back in 1995, nobody [of the Roma] wanted to apply. They said 'why should I go to work if I don't have to.' Now they will do anything in order to receive benefits."*

Some Roma respondents found the quality of work provided in the program poor and observed that in some cases was focused almost exclusively on cleaning around non-Roma houses, and ignored Roma quarters and settlements. On the other hand, many

Roma interviewed explained that the public works program was a beneficial alternative to unemployment: *"When a man has a job, it is easier to live, he is healthier, he has more energy and life is more fun."*

Informal Employment. Due to limited formal employment opportunities, many Roma are involved in the informal sector. Activities include playing music, salvaging and selling scrap metal, petty trade, and part-time work in agriculture and construction. Some of them have small workshops where they produce tools for construction workers (such as in Kaloša in Rimavská Sobota district). A number of Roma also admitted to resorting to theft as a coping strategy, including stealing potatoes, firewood and construction materials. Informal sector activities are fueled by incentives for employers to hire labor while evading taxes and insurance contributions. Roma in geographically isolated and segregated areas have fewer opportunities for involvement in the informal sector, because communities are more closed and have limited connections outside of the settlement to find work.

Box 4.5 Public Works in Stara Lubovna

A number of respondents from Letanovce, a poor segregated settlement in Stara Lubovna were involved in an unusual public work activity. The settlement borders on a national forest. The forest rangers asked the mayor to pay for six of the Roma in the settlement to work as forest rangers, and for another six to collect wood from the forest, transport it and sell it to other Roma. The objective was to reduce the number of people who were going to the forest and cutting down trees themselves.

The Roma involved in the program were pleased to have the chance to work. A middle aged man reported, *"this is the first time I am working after a couple of years and I am very happy."* All of those who were interviewed were concerned that the work would end after six months. One said *"I do not know what to do after this, this was one of the best things happened to us in a long time"*. The workers asked the interviewers to intervene with the mayor to have the work extended. The forestry officials reported that the workers were doing an excellent job.

Source: World Bank. 2001.

The most widespread informal economic activity was in the field of entertainment, mostly playing music (especially in Jesenské, Hodejov, or in the urban ghetto of Dúžavská cesta in Rimavská Sobota). Another prevalent activity, especially among Roma from segregated localities, was to salvage scrap material, especially iron scrap. For instance, in the Southern Slovakia village of Sirk-Šrobárka, where according to the mayor, Roma managed to salvage most of the equipment from an old mine and sold it as scrap. Other occasional and informal employment includes working as domestic help.

Household Assets. Ownership and cultivation of land did not appear to be an important coping strategy for Roma. While Roma in some integrated and separated areas own at least a small amount of land, not all of them made use of it for home consumption or commercial use. With few exceptions, the majority of Roma in segregated settlements do not own land. For instance, in two settlements in Stara Lubovna, families owned their homes and land, and have been involved in agricultural activities for three generations.

Roma explained that they did not make use of their land for a number of reasons. In some cases the plot of land was too small, in other cases the soil was poor, there was no convenient source of water, or the household could not afford the necessary inputs. Others explained that cultivation of land was not traditionally a Roma occupation. In Studienka and Malé Levare in Malacky, all of the households owned land, but only half of them grew crops. Those who did not use their land explained that they were unprepared: *"How can I farm the land if I don't have a tractor or a horse."* Another noted, *"farming is a job for gadjos"*.[66]

Cultivation was more common among Roma in integrated areas. Some of those interviewed for this study, especially those from better off villages or towns, did grow crops if they owned land. Two integrated families in Pobilinec had land which was not attached to their home. In both cases they grew wheat and potatoes. This could be partly because they had better access to water, and did not fear the crops would be stolen.

More Roma were involved in raising animals than in agricultural activities. Even in some separated and segregated settlements where almost no families own land, about half of those visited breed small animals such as chicken and pigs. Very few families— only five of those interviewed—both cultivate land and raise animals. Some non-Roma explained that breeding of animals for home use had declined during the transition period. Prior to 1989 it was common for agricultural cooperatives to give employees animals for domestic use, however now, according to a key informant, *"they do not breed them since no one hands out small pigs for free anymore."*

Access to Credit. Roma lack opportunities to borrow money, and therefore have limited capacity to establish small businesses. As noted in Chapter 2, credit is scarce and costly for all small borrowers in the Slovak Republic; but the Roma may face additional difficulties in accessing credit. Procedures for borrowing are complex, and in many cases Roma lack collateral to borrow, because of unclear property ownership. Some Roma do borrow small sums from neighbors, friends, and relatives, and shop on credit. However, access to loans from commercial institutions is virtually zero. Besides, the small amount that some may want to borrow is not available through commercial channels. Some Roma do borrow through local Roma moneylenders—in some communities the Roma leader, or vajda, lends money. However, in many cases interest rates are extortionary.[67]

ACCESS TO PUBLIC SERVICES

Education

Roma children often face stiffer challenges in accessing education than other ethnic groups. In addition to issues common to other poor households, such as economic constraints, limited access to quality education and parents' education levels, Roma children face additional barriers including low demand for education, geographic isolation, discrimination and low language proficiency. Roma children are also more

---

[66] Gadjo is a Roma term for non-Roma.

[67] Rates were reported as high as 40 percent, when the going interest rates on consumer credit are on the order of 14 percent.

likely to end up in special schools for the mentally and physically disabled which limit their future education and labor market prospects.

Children from the most segregated and isolated settlements face the greatest challenges in accessing education. Geographic isolation is an issue in some areas. Roma mothers from Kyjov, a settlement in Stara Lubovna asked school officials not to pass their children on to the fifth grade, because they were unable to pay for their children to commute to the new school.[68]

Poverty and lack of basic infrastructure are notable barriers. The absence of electricity in isolated settlements makes it difficult for children to study and do homework. Economic constraints are considerable. Some Roma children need to stay home to help with housework and take care of siblings. As a result, they have difficulty keeping up with the curriculum. Some teachers also noted that children were frequently absent on the day after social assistance benefits were paid, because families would use the funds to go shopping or visit relatives.

Preschool Attendance. Few Roma children from segregated settlements attend preschool. Most segregated settlements lack preschool facilities. Moreover, many parents interviewed did not recognize the value of preschool, and felt that mothers could adequately prepare their children. A Roma mother explained, *"all of my children are at home, together with me, I am at home, so why send them to the kindergarten?"* Parents also cited costs related to attending kindergarten such fees and clothing as a deterrent. *"Kindergarten is not free of charge, we would need to pay and we cannot afford that."*

Lack of preschool education is a significant constraint to Roma education. Without this preparation, children are at a disadvantage because they lack exposure to basic knowledge and skills, socialization and communication with other children. Perhaps most importantly, Roma children who do not speak Slovak at home miss out on an opportunity to acquire essential language skills. Without preschool, Roma begin primary school at a further disadvantage. A teacher from Rimavska Sobota noted:

"In the first grade, we spend our energy teaching [Roma children] what they should have mastered long ago: telling colors, the basics of hygiene, and physical activities. The reason is that these children do not acquire this basic knowledge in their families and they do not attend kindergartens that could partially substitute for parents."

Because Roma children begin primary school unprepared, they have additional difficulties in adapting to the school environment. These circumstances exacerbate preconceptions of non-Roma students and teachers and leads to further exclusion. In many cases Roma are placed in separate classes or special schools because of their lack of preparation.

---

[68] In the districts of Malacky and Stara Lubovna, in the study sample, all separated settlements either had primary schools or there was a school close by. For segregated settlements in Stara Lubovna access was more difficult, but still the majority lived in close proximity to a village with schools. In Rimavska Sobota there was no primary schools in 7 settlements, five of them with less than 500 inhabitants.

Language. Experts estimate that about 70 percent of Roma in Slovak Republic speak some Roma language. It is not known how many Roma only speak the Roma language at home. Roma from isolated and segregated settlements are at a particular disadvantage in this regard, as they lack the exposure with non-Roma that children have in more integrated areas, and may be introduced to the Slovak language only once they enter primary school. Teachers are poorly equipped to handle this gap in the children's knowledge, and in some cases may send Roma children to separate classrooms or special schools if they cannot keep up with the rest of the students. A school director noted, *"Children from segregated [Roma] settlements do not master the Slovak language and do not understand their teachers. The teachers do not speak the Roma language, so they communicate by using gestures."*

The issue is even more complex in ethnically diverse areas, such as Slovak-Hungarian areas in the south. In the district of Rimavská Sobota some children speak Hungarian in addition to the Roma language, but are not proficient in Slovak. The situation is similar in some villages in Stará Lubovna where most non-Roma speak Ruthenian.

Demand for Education. Low demand for education among some Roma families discourages children from attending school. In particular, the dismal labor market situation leads parents to undervalue the importance of education. Particularly in isolated settlements where the majority of adults are long-term unemployed, parents do not have examples of education paying off, and as a result may not encourage their children to go to school. A Roma parent noted, *"my daughter completed secondary school, now she is sitting at home without work"*. Another asked, *"why force our children to study when there aren't jobs for the educated ones?"*

Demand for education among Roma in isolated and segregated communities was particularly low. Because of poverty constraints and the low premium placed on education, Roma parents also poorly positioned to help their children with school work at home because of their own limited educational background. There were exceptions, particularly among Roma in integrated settlements. A parent in Malacky said: *"I help my children learn every day, if I miss out one day of reading with my son, the very next day he has a problem. Therefore I help them learn every day."* Another parent from an integrated area in Malacky was proud that her children were going to vocational secondary schools, specializing in economics and chemistry. Most integrated Roma viewed education as a tool for upward mobility and were pleased that their children were receiving better education that they had.

A significant share of Roma view education as a system representative of majority society which is of limited relevance for them. Parents explained: *"From the beginning, since the first grade our children have difficulties understanding what is going on: other children are singing the songs we do not know."* And, *"all poetry, literature, history is not about and from our life."*

Under socialism penalties for truancy were more stringent and frequently enforced through various mechanisms including interrogation by the police, placement of children in institutions and reduction of social benefits. Some examples of these types of penalties were reported in the study sites. In Rimavska Sobota teachers reported absent students to the police and cut the families welfare benefits to motivate attendance.

Box 4.6 Zero Grade Classes

"Zero grade classes" were first implemented in 1992 in order to prepare children for basic school through provision of basic social, cultural and hygiene skills. Children attend zero grade class after preliminary psychological tests at the age of compulsory primary school attendance. These classes are located at primary schools. The zero grade program is designed to prepare children to attend regular compulsory first class after one year. Together with socialization, language preparation is emphasized along with basic skills such as reading and writing.

Source: World Bank. 2001.

Special Schools and Classes. Roma are at a higher risk of receiving lower quality education because of institutional factors and incentives which lead to separate education for Roma and non-Roma. Special schools are a legacy from the socialist era, and were designed to provide special education for children with mental and physical disabilities. A disproportionate share of Roma are enrolled in special schools. In the Czech Republic, which inherited a similar system, a survey from 1997 indicated that 64 percent of Roma children in primary school were in special schools, in comparison with 4.2 percent of the total population (ERRC, 1999). Although data are not available for Slovak Republic, the situation may be similar. A majority of Roma students from the segregated settlements in the qualitative study attend special schools.

Students enrolled in special schools are at a dual disadvantage, first because the curriculum is less rigorous and expectations of teachers are lower than in mainstream schools, and second because opportunities for graduates of special schools are limited. Even if children are able to overcome the low expectations of teachers in these schools, they are not prepared for secondary school exams and are disadvantaged on the labor market, as employers look unfavorably on graduates of special schools.

Even when Roma children are educated within the mainstream Slovak school system, they may be placed in separate Roma classes. According to teachers, non-Roma parents favor this separation by arguing that Roma students slow down the educational process. Non-Roma prefer to enroll their children in schools that provide separate classes for Roma students. These dynamics create an environment that can be hostile. A Roma mother in a village in Stara Lubovna observed that *"children are not racist, it is their parents that tell them to keep separate, and that is why they tease our kids and call them names"*.

Despite the disadvantages of special schools and classes, some parents interviewed supported them, believing that their children would receive more attention at special schools. The director of a special school noted, *"approximately 30-40 percent of children attend special grammar school on the basis of their parents decision. Sometimes, the parents do not want to put their first child here, but as they have more children they find out that here the children achieve better results than in a "normal" grammar school.* Roma parents also indicated that they preferred special schools because there are more Roma children and their children are "protected" from discrimination and hostility from non-Roma students. In some cases special schools provide housing, making them more financially attractive to parents.

Teachers. Teachers are central to the quality of education and play an important role in motivating student attendance and performance. In many of the settlements, teachers were poorly prepared to work with Roma children. Very few teachers had any knowledge of Roma history, language or culture. Educational advisors played an important positive role in some schools. In Sarisské Jastrabie, educational advisors worked with Roma parents to encourage them to send their children to school and continue on to secondary education.

The study also found a number of examples in which teachers and school directors took the initiative to reach out to Roma communities and support Roma children at school, but these examples were sporadic and stemmed from individual initiative. In some communities, such as Jarovnice, Teplý Vrch and Jablonové in Malacky and Rimavaská Sobota, teachers and school officials maintain close relations with Roma parents and children. They make frequent visits to the Roma settlement and work to mitigate conflicts between children. Roma parents in these areas expressed satisfaction with the schools and children were happy to attend school.

Health Services

Access to health care among Roma in the settlements was influenced negatively by the geographic distance of settlements from urban areas and by poor communication between Roma and health providers, as well as by discrimination. . In most settlements, access to health services was not cited as an issue by inhabitants, but some – especially from better off separated settlements – complained about the quality of health care available to them.

Because of poor road conditions, ambulances are often unable to reach geographically isolated areas at the time of emergency. A young man in a segregated settlement in Stara Lubovna noted, *"in the winter we have to carry our pregnant women who are about to give birth about a kilometer to the ambulance since it refuses to come to our settlements"*. In many cases communication and understanding between Roma and health professionals was poor. Some health officials believed that Roma in settlements abuse ambulance services, by calling for doctors in non-emergency situations, while Roma complain that ambulances refuse to come or take too long to reach the settlement. Roma report instances in which the local hospital would not send an ambulance. In other cases Roma expressed satisfaction with the level of care in their settlement. Nurses regularly visit some of the settlements, as do doctors, if there is a school in the settlement.

Roma gave numerous examples of discrimination within the health system. A number of Roma mothers complained that maternity wards in some hospitals placed them in separate rooms. Some of the hospitals admitted they had introduced such a practice because of the behavior of some Roma women—smoking was cited as an example.

Social Assistance

Because of high levels of unemployment and poverty, social assistance benefits provide an important source of income for many Roma households. Nearly all of the long-term unemployed Roma interviewed for this study, and especially those living in poorer segregated settlements, are dependent upon social assistance benefits for income support. Many noted that these benefits were indispensable, but felt that they were not adequate to secure basic living conditions. Non-Roma local officials and priests described the high level of dependency on benefits in Roma settlements and noted that consumption patterns changed visibly on days when benefits were paid. For many outsiders, the dependency of Roma on benefits reinforced stereotypes of Roma as social parasites who would rather receive income support than work.

As noted earlier, the design of the social assistance and support mechanisms may in fact encourage such a dependency, but penalizing those who can find low-paying work. According to the calculations carried out in Chapter 3, a family of two adults—of whom at least one must stay at home to receive child allowances—and five children can earn on average SK 16,490 per month through the combination of social assistance and child allowances, which is at least as much as they would make if one of the adults were to get a job. The possible perverse incentives of the social assistance scheme are reinforced by the fact that: (i) what an unskilled adult can earn via wages is likely to be something very close to the minimum wage, which is very low; and (ii) the system is designed so that if both adults get work, the family immediately loses its child allowances. Faced with these incentives, households may be simply making a rationale choice of maximizing family income by staying at home. In this context, incentives to work can be improved not only by cutting benefits and restricting eligibility (as was done in the past) but also by thinking of introducing tapering mechanisms, and more innovative ways to encourage benefit recipients to engage in paid work. Recent efforts to reform welfare in the United States may provide some useful lessons for how to do this (Box 4.7).

Many Roma complained that the reforms to the Act on Social Assistance, which cut benefits for those who had been unemployed for two years or more, made it unable for them to survive on social assistance. Although this change was intended to promote work incentives, Roma in isolated settlements were particularly disadvantaged because of the absence of employment opportunities. Non-Roma social workers and local government officials also felt that the current system of child allowances provided incentives for Roma to have large families. While there is no rigorous evidence to confirm this, the perception breeds resentment and contributes to the impression among non-Roma that Roma are overly dependent on the state.

Box 4.7 Lessons From US Welfare Reform

During the 1990s, as concerns grew about the increasing number of welfare caseloads, the US government introduced substantial legislative changes in programs design to assist low income families. In particular, the federal government granted a growing number of waivers early in the decade, allowing states to experiment with alternative rules for the Aid to Families with Dependent Children (AFDC) and food stamps programs. In addition, these changes were followed in 1996 by the approval of the Personal Responsibility and Work Opportunity Act, which fundamentally changed the public assistance system in the United States. The Act abolished AFDC, which required states to match federal welfare funds, and replaced it with the Temporary Assistance to Needy Families (TANF), which granted unconditional, fixed amounts of funding to states and allowed them to set their own rules for eligibility and benefits.

In the light of these changes, several states started using "diversion" (one-time assistance rather than enrollment in ongoing TANF-funded programs), and benefit programs which allowed recipients to keep a higher level of public assistance benefits after going to work, thus increasing both work incentives and income among low-income families. They also worked to transform public assistance offices into employment assistance offices, where applicants are given constant incentives to seek and find work, and they did more sanctioning, imposing penalties on those who did not respond to these work incentives. Finally, they spent more money on work-related programs relative to cash benefits.

These changes were followed by a reduction in the use of public assistance (i.e., the AFDC/TANF caseload was cut by half between 1994 and 1999, from 5 to 2.5 millions), and noticeable increases in labor market involvement among recipients. Poverty rates also declined steadily, although at a more gradual pace than the caseload. The question then arises as to what extent the reform of the welfare system was responsible for such trends.

The US economy enjoyed a decade of tremendous prosperity during the 1990s. As a consequence, employment growth was high, unemployment was low and, since 1996, wages grew significantly among workers of all skill levels. All these factors disproportionately benefited less skilled workers and are therefore important in explaining the trends described above. In fact, between one-third and two-thirds of the caseload change can be attributed to the overall performance of the economy[69].

Unfortunately, a strong economy not only affects poverty but also economic policy, which makes it difficult to measure the magnitude of the effect of welfare policy changes independently of the business cycle effect[70]. However, while the overall effect of welfare reform is difficult to pin down, one should not dismay since there have been a few places that experimented with particularly innovative types of programs in ways that allow for some form of evaluation. These programs combined financial incentives with work mandates. In particular, the Minnesota Family Investment Program (MFIP) substantially decreased the benefit reduction rate for public assistance recipients, thus allowing them to keep more public assistance income when they went to work, but mandated participation in work/welfare programs. Similarly, the Self-Sufficient Program (SSP) in Canada provided substantial financial support to long-term public assistance recipients who went to work 30 hours or more. The evidence concerning these two programs shows that employment, earnings and family income increased for program participants while poverty fell.

Although these programs are not money savers in the short run—they actually provide more assistance to low-income families than did traditional welfare programs—, it is important to consider their long-run effects, since studies of people leaving welfare tend to suggest that the majority of them (55 to 85 percent) are employed at a future date, and about one-half to two-thirds report higher incomes post-welfare (Brauner and Loprest, 1999).

Moreover, the probability of success of such programs can be increased through good design. For instance, it is important to consider that employment is associated with extra expenses in the form of child care, transportation and others. Hence in some states public support for those items was included, together with provision of health insurance coverage by the Medicaid system[71], as part of their welfare policy. At the federal level, the Earned-Income Tax Credit program served a similar function.

In sum, it seems that in the US case a conflux of events came together at the same time (a strong expanding economy, substantial revisions of public assistance programs that emphasized work and reduced benefit eligibility, and major policy changes that increased the returns to work and the subsidies to support work, particularly among vulnerable groups), and created the right environment for the decline in poverty rates and welfare caseload that is observed in the data. Moreover, because a large number of the programs described above rely strongly on the availability of jobs, it is then not clear how sustainable these welfare policy changes are in the long run or how dependent their success has been on the strong economy. However, the fact that SSP managed to succeed despite the fact that the Canadian economy did not do as well as the US in the 1990s, shows that programs can work in less favorable environment with high unemployment if designed correctly.

Sources: Blank 2000, Peterson 2000, Schoeni, R.F. and Blank 2000

Relations between social workers and Roma were found to more contentious than relations with other public service providers. Roma view social workers as representatives of the state, and are frequently their only contact with government authorities. Social workers are responsible for conveying 'bad news' on eligibility for benefits, and as a result, are often the target of frustration with decisions that are not

---

[69] Different studies provide different measures. See Wallace and Blank (1999), Figlio and Ziliak (1999) and Schoeni and Blank (2000).

[70] There is some crude evidence that such changes had a substantial effect on *caseloads*, but there has been significantly less research relating TANF changes to work behavior or poverty rates. In this respect, the best evidence comes from the fact that participation rates are increasing among vulnerable groups (e.g., single mothers with young children).

[71] Most low-skilled jobs do not offer health insurance and this could act as a deterrent for employment.

necessarily under their control. On the other hand, social workers are poorly prepared to work with Roma communities. This lack of preparation is linked to systemic problems within the welfare system itself. Social workers in Slovak Republic rarely do field visits and are not trained to work directly with clients. Instead, their jobs are largely administrative, focused on disbursing cash benefits and social workers explained that they had no time left for field visits. Only two of the social workers interviewed for the study actually visited Roma settlements.

Many Roma complained that social workers were not responsive to their needs, explaining: *"They come to our settlement only when they want to screen us."* It appeared that social workers were not effective at communicating with Roma, as many Roma lacked basic information on social assistance programs and eligibility criteria. Many Roma asked the interviewers for information on various benefits. Social workers, for their part, complained about the administrative burden of their work: *"Every time the law is amended, we have to check and review all files; we often work late in the evening and do not have time for fieldwork."* The lack of contact between Roma and social workers contributes to poor communication on both sides.

Housing

Most Roma in segregated settlements do not own their homes or land. In some settlements, property ownership has not been clarified. This prevents the improvement of housing conditions—as individuals and local governments are unable to maintain or invest in buildings or local infrastructure when ownership is unclear. Roma were more likely to have been left out of property and land privatization processes that took place during the early 1990s than non-Roma. During the communist period, houses and apartments were mostly privately held, however the land belonged to the state. The "tenants" would rent their house or flat for 99 years from the state. After 1989, the government privatized the land, or gave it municipal governments. The land was given to the tenants for free if two basic conditions were met: (i) the house had a valid building permit, or had the appropriate legal status; and (ii) the property was registered in the land-registry office and there was no pending application for restitution. If these conditions were met, the tenant could apply for the transfer of property to his or her name.

Public communication regarding the process was limited, and many people were unaware of their options and the steps needed to initiate the transfer of land. In theory, the mayor was responsible for informing residents of their rights. However, in practice, few mayors did so. None of the mayors in the settlements included in this study, with the exception of one in Stara Lubovna, provided information to their constituents unless explicitly asked. Roma in integrated areas were more likely to learn about the process from their neighbors, while Roma in segregated areas had more limited access to information. As a result, a larger share of integrated Roma were able to gain property ownership. This has limited the ability of many to make necessary improvements to their homes. A man from Kyjov explained: *"We built our house with a building permit, but there are still problems with the site, though it was officially given us during socialism. But today the land is not ours, therefore we can not install any water, gas, or sewage pipes"*.

Roma in segregated areas have also faced substantial challenges with legalization of their homes. The vast majority of houses in segregated settlements have been built illegally, mostly on land with unclear ownership. In some of these settlements, such as the village of Jablonove in Malacky, Roma moved into the village in the early 1990s and began to build houses on municipal land at the edge of the village. As a result, they do not have legal access to electricity and water. In the case of electricity they tap into the house of a neighbor who has a legal connection, and they pay him. In many cases, houses in settlements constructed with makeshift materials do not comply with basic construction standards, and were built without the necessary construction and building permits. Some Roma explained that the only way that they could afford to build a shelter for themselves was to use materials they found around their settlements, in the forest or in garbage dumps. One explained, *"we can never have legalized housing and obtain a permit, so why ask"*. This creates a vicious circle in which buildings do not have legal status, and as a result, municipalities cannot provide funds for investment in infrastructure (e.g., roads) and public services.

Roma are also poorly positioned to borrow money, because of their economic status and lack of access to information on processes and procedures. The criteria for receiving loans have become more demanding since 1989. In addition, the process for getting a building permit has become extremely complex. Current requirements include 32 individual permits and approvals from different government bodies. The research team encountered many unfinished houses that consisted of one or two rooms and a kitchen. Many of the occupants began building them before 1989 and were unable to finish construction because of lack of financial resources and/or building permits. A Roma in Stara Lubovna explained, *"I started to build this house before 1989, but could not finish it because I have no chance to put together enough money and cannot get a loan."*

SOCIAL EXCLUSION

Social exclusion and discrimination of Roma within civil society is an important factor which affects access to opportunities in the labor market and education, and other public services. Exclusion of Roma in Slovak Republic stems from a combination of historical, cultural, sociological and geographic factors and varies extensively across communities. Identifying the extent of the issue and its roots is extremely complex and a full discussion of these issues lies outside the scope of this report.

A number of sociological surveys conducted since 1989 have confirmed a high degree of social distance between the Roma and non-Roma populations in the country (Vasecka, 2000). A 1995 survey found higher negative impressions of Roma by non-Roma in Slovak Republic than in the Czech Republic. The survey also found that these impressions were largely based on stereotypes—rather than direct experience. Fifty percent of respondents had never had a negative personal experience with Roma. Another survey from 1995 found that as much as 66 percent of those surveyed believed that Roma should live separately from non-Roma (e.g., in settlements).

There are indications that negative perceptions of Roma are worsening for a number of reasons, including their declining social status, growing unemployment and increasing dependency on social benefits. Negative stereotypes are also reinforced by geographic separation, and the limited contact between Roma and non-Roma. Contacts between Roma and non-Roma were extremely limited in the segregated settlements visited for this study. Roma are separated geographically, in schools, and in some cases even in churches. In one settlement in Stara Lubovna, Roma were reportedly not allowed to enter the local pub. The village store was identified as the most important center for social contact between Roma and non-Roma.

In integrated communities, the level of contacts and interactions between Roma and non-Roma was naturally higher and relationships were reportedly smoother. Many respondents noted that they have regular contacts, and some said that if they have to borrow money, they prefer to borrow from non-Roma, than from other Roma. *"If I borrow the money from my non-Roma neighbors I trust them and they know I will return the money on time. Usually they do not ask me for any interest."* In segregated and some separated settlements, Roma mainly borrow from professional money lenders since there is no one else to provide them with cash when they need that and pay up to 40 percent interest.

Local authorities in some of the integrated settlements noted that personal conflicts involving Roma are usually not between Roma and non-Roma, but rather between local Roma and other Roma from outside settlements. A mayor from a town in Stara Lubovna explained, *"If a strange Roma is causing disturbance in the village, it is the local Roma who come running to file a complaint with the police or local council."* Some of these tensions may be based on intra-ethnic divisions. The interviews indicated strained relations between Slovak-speaking Rumungres and Hungarian speaking Vlachika Roma in some settlements in Rimavska Sobota. Roma also identified tensions between different Roma communities. Roma living in integrated areas, especially those who had been living with non-Roma neighbors for more than one generation, do not associate with or relate to Roma living in settlements.

Relations with Local Governments

Relations between Roma and mayors and local council members are particularly complicated. In some cases, leaders of municipalities with segregated settlements under their jurisdiction did not hide their strong views on Roma from the interviewers. These were largely due to their own frustration and lack of understanding and knowledge of how to address the needs of Roma communities. The chairman of a local council in Malacky refused to acknowledge the presence of Roma in his municipality, explaining: *"Officially they declare Slovak nationality, so I don't have any Roma here. I see nothing to comment on."* Other mayors expressed typical negative stereotypes about Roma. From their side, Roma criticized local officials of corruption in assigning people to public works programs, and for their unwillingness to make necessary investments in their settlements (e.g., for roads).

Most mayors contend that they do visit Roma settlements, that they know their Roma neighbors, are aware of their problems, and that they are trying to solve them. Roma claim that their experience is quite different and point out the inability of municipal authorities to dispose garbage from their settlement, build access roads, or allow them register for permanent residence in the village. One exception was documented in the study, of a mayor in Malacky who regularly visits the Roma settlement and informs the residents about ongoing initiatives of the municipal council. There were no examples of collaboration between Roma and non-Roma leaders (e.g., mayor, teachers, priest), to address the needs of settlements.

Participation and Political Representation

There has been considerable political activity among Roma groups in Slovak Republic. However, because of fragmentation the aggregate impact has been limited. After the collapse of the socialist regime in 1989, a national Roma political party, the Roma Civic Initiative (ROI), was established in Czechoslovakia. ROI received 4 seats in the Federal Assembly in the first democratic parliamentary elections in 1990. Since then, Roma politics has become increasingly splintered with the emergence of nearly 15 national and local Roma political parties. Currently there are no Roma representatives in the Slovak parliament. Activity has increased at the local level. In the municipal elections in December 1998, 56 Roma were elected to local councils and 6 as mayors.

At the national level, the most significant development in Roma political involvement was the establishment of the Office of the Plenipotentiary for Roma Affairs, which was established in 1998. The Office is under the jurisdiction of the Deputy Prime Minister for Regional and Ethnic Affairs, and has been headed by a Roma since its establishment.

In the three districts, Roma participation in civic affairs was low. This was largely due to a lack of trust of public officials and limited information about local politicians and their roles and responsibilities. Many Roma expressed apathy and a sense of hopelessness about the potential of politicians to make a difference in their lives: *"Nobody from political parties, also those called Roma parties has visited us. What are they doing for us?"*

Some Roma did identify themselves as members of political parties, both Roma and majority. Very few Roma in the study sites were involved in politics themselves. An exception was Lomicka in Stara Lubovna, where the mayor is Roma. In some cases Roma were working as advisors to local councils.

Roma were more informed about mayors than other politicians, as mayoral candidates were most likely to campaign in Roma settlements. There were some indications that candidates took advantage of Roma's lack of knowledge and access to information about electoral choices. One Roma noted: *"I don't know [which ballot] I threw in [at the polling station], I can't write or read, but they gave me a hundred crowns for it."*

POLICY IMPLICATIONS

Addressing poverty among Roma in Slovak Republic is a complex challenge which will take time and collaboration among many partners, Roma and non-Roma alike. Over the past decade there has been considerable project activity by the government and NGOs. In September 1999, the government adopted a comprehensive strategy to address the needs of the Roma minority and established the office of the Plenipotentiary for Roma Affairs to oversee policy toward Roma across the government. A recent review by the European Union and the Open Society Foundation in Bratislava identified 700 projects, implemented by NGOs, which had been targeted to Roma.[72] Despite this level of activity little is known about the impact of these initiatives and the lessons from their experience. In its most recent pre-accession evaluation report, the European Union noted that the government's strategy on Roma remained vague, lacking specifics on objectives, measures and allocation of resources.[73]

The analysis of conditions in Roma settlements raises difficult policy issues. A central question raised by the study is how to develop an effective strategy for addressing the needs of Roma in settlements. The most segregated and geographically isolated settlements face the greatest challenges on all fronts, including access to employment opportunities and public services, while conditions in integrated communities are more favorable. Although it is important to adopt measures to meet the immediate needs of residents of the poorest settlements in the short run, over the longer-term investing in settlements may lead to further institutionalization of segregation and, consequently, on-going marginalization.

There are no easy answers to this dilemma. The failure of socialist era policies which aimed at forced assimilation of Roma indicate that encouraging Roma to leave settlements is not a viable solution. On the other hand, lessons from existing projects in Slovak Republic and Hungary illustrate the importance of community involvement and participation in policies and projects. In this regard, a balanced package of measures which aim at: (i) improving living conditions for Roma in settlements; and (ii) expanding possibilities for Roma to take advantage of economic opportunities outside of settlements and access public services should be considered.

A related trade-off is whether programs and policies should be targeted to Roma, directed more broadly at poor communities, or the population at large. Targeted programs can be tailored to meet specific needs of Roma, but may create divisions among the community and resentment that some groups are receiving special treatment. Broad based programs may be easier to administer and may be more politically popular and facilitate integration and cohesion among communities. On the other hand, untargeted programs may be ill suited to reaching the poorest and most isolated Roma settlements.

A number of the themes identified in the study relate to systemic policy issues which need to be addressed at the national level. A priority issue is generating more employment opportunities, for Roma and non-Roma alike. As discussed in Chapter 2, to

---

[72] This project database can be found at: www.osf.sk

[73] The full report can be found at: http://europa.eu.int/comm/enlargement/slovakia/index.htm.

a large extent this hinges on creating a more favorable environment for job creation, including through measures aimed at supporting micro, small and medium enterprises, and at improving the access to credit of small entrepreneurs. Many of these measures, moreover, can have a very positive impact on Roma households as well as non-Roma ones by encouraging self-employment and entrepreneurship, which historically have engaged Roma populations in much of Central and Southern Europe. Another national-level issue, with positive benefits for unskilled Roma workers, is lowering the non-wage costs of labor. High payroll taxes and non-wage labor costs in effect discourage employers from hiring unskilled labor, as it makes them proportionately more expensive than workers with higher skills. Studies in numerous OECD countries have documented that often it is the unskilled who are most hurt by such non-wage labor costs (Blanchard et al, 1995).

Education reform is another systemic issue of particular relevance for the Roma community. Comprehensive reforms of both general and vocational education are needed to prepare workers for the labor market more effectively. Improved vocational education hold potential for attracting young Roma's and helping them secure skills that the market demands. Similarly, secondary school programs and curricula need to be reviewed to ensure that they provide adequate preparation for the labor market. Opportunities for training and retraining of adults should also be explored.

A final, but crucial, systemic issue is the reform of social assistance, to improve work incentives and reduce the risk of falling into a dependency trap. The role, capacities and training of social workers is another area that deserves attention, not only as regards the Roma but also the rest of the population.

Improving Living Conditions

Housing. Measures can be undertaken to alleviate poor conditions in some of the most disadvantaged Roma settlements. A priority in housing policy is creating conditions to enable communities and local governments to make necessary improvements in housing and basic local infrastructure, such as roads and water supply. Policy measures can include:

- Clarifying property rights and resolving questions regarding ownership of buildings which prohibit residents and local governments from investing in and maintaining properties;

- Reviewing and simplifying procedures for obtaining building permits to allow residents to upgrade their property;

- Providing clear information to the public on procedures for applying for permits and acquiring property; and

- Expanding access to credit for renovation and improvement of living conditions.

Utilities. Mechanisms for expanding coverage of utilities and public services to settlements should also be identified. A possible mechanism is:

- Introducing incentives for local governments and communities to provide services in settlements, possibly through a central fund.

Increasing Opportunities

Employment. Expanded income generating opportunities are key to moving Roma out of poverty on a sustained basis.

- Enforcing anti-discrimination legislation, and provisions for appeals;
- Reducing non-wage costs and other biases working against hiring of unskilled labor;
- Improving training/re-training of both unemployed workers and new entrants;
- Supporting employment and income-generating programs (social fund-type mechanisms, such the Autonomia Foundation in Hungary (Box 4.8); and
- Strengthening work incentives in social assistance.

Education. Increasing the educational attainment of Roma is central to their ability to take advantage of opportunities in the economy and labor market.

- Reducing barriers that keep children from starting school. Programs could include scholarships, provision of school lunches and materials and linking eligibility for social benefits to school attendance;
- Addressing the language constraint. Initiatives should be implemented to help Roma children make the transition to Slovak schools;
- Teacher training, including training of Roma teachers and teacher's assistants;
- Outreach, involving families in education;
- Increasing preschool attendance;
- Facilitating secondary school attendance by reducing economic costs (e.g. through scholarship programs) and by providing support to prevent students from dropping out (e.g., through Roma assistant teachers and mentoring programs);
- Reforming special education to focus on real disabilities; and
- Limiting the use of separate classrooms.

> **Box 4.8 Promoting Employment among the Roma**
>
> Programs in both Eastern and Western Europe have been adopted to promote employment income generating opportunities for Roma. One of the most established is the Autonomia Foundation in Hungary which provides grants and interest-free loans to develop employment programs for Roma. Small-income generating initiatives include livestock breeding, agricultural programs, and small enterprise development.
>
> The success of Autonomia's projects, as measured by the repayment rate of its loans, has increased greatly since it was established in 1990. In 1998 repayment rates reached nearly 80 percent, in comparison with 10 percent during the first year. Autonomia attributes this improvement to the involvement of trained monitors, some of whom are Roma, who work closely with project teams throughout the implementation of the project. Autonomia is now in the process of expanding its programs to other countries in the region. In 2000, the first group of Roma began training in preparation to start small grant and loan programs for Roma in four CEE countries, including Slovak Republic.
>
> A different type of employment program is the Acceder Programme run by the Asociación General Gitano in Madrid, Spain. The program provides individualized support to participants in identifying and preparing for employment. While the program is open to all interested applicants, 79 percent were Roma in 1999. Roma mediators work closely with job-seekers and employers to identify their skills, training needs and employment opportunities. The mediators provide support to applicants throughout the training and job search process.
>
> In 1999 there were 304 active job seekers enrolled in Acceder and 63 percent found employment. However, the job retention rate is not known, and rigorous cost-benefit analysis of the program is not available. Staff of the Asociación and participants noted that the strengths of the program are its individualized approach in assessing and matching skills and jobs and the use of mediators who can bridge the gap between gitanos (Roma) and non-Roma. Challenges include the difficulty of providing adequate and appropriate training for individuals with low education levels, persistent discrimination on the labor market and incentives. Participants may be reluctant to accept low paying jobs and risk losing access to social assistance benefits.
>
> *Sources: Ringold, 2000; Martin, 2000.*

Addressing Exclusion

Discrimination

- Ensuring anti-discrimination legislation is in place and is enforced;
- Providing training for public officials, particularly mayors;
- Public information campaigns; and
- Multi-cultural education.

Health Care

- Improving access in remote areas—local infrastructure (roads);
- Outreach activities (health professionals visiting settlements); and
- Improving public health awareness, particularly reproductive health and contraception.

Improving Information

- Coordinating better between governments, NGOs and donors. Need to share lessons from project experience. The Office of the Plenipotentiary for Roma Affairs can serve as an important resource and referral service;

- Monitoring of programs and policies, especially outcomes; and

- On-going monitoring of the situation of Roma through surveys, beneficiary assessments.

Box 4.9 Desegregation of Roma Schools in Bulgaria: The Vidin Model

In Bulgaria many schools have been designated by the Ministry of Education as "Roma schools." These schools are located in Roma neighborhoods and have a disproportionately high share of Roma pupils – as much as 80 percent in some cases. The overrepresentation of Roma in these schools is due to geographic reasons and the high concentration of Roma in certain areas, as well as discrimination by non-Roma parents and teachers who encourage the separation of non-Roma students into different schools. The quality of teaching and school infrastructure in Roma schools has been found to be significantly worse than in mainstream schools. In Vidin, the Open Society Institute and the Roma NGO, DROM, have been collaborating on a successful program to integrate Roma students into the mainstream school system. Vidin is a town of 85,000 in north-west Bulgaria, 6 percent of the population identified as Roma in the 1992 census. In the 2000/2001 school year 460 students, or 50 percent of school-age students, were integrated into the mainstream school system, more are expected to follow in the next school year. Under the project, students are bussed from the settlement to school, and back. In addition to transportation, the project involves Roma monitors who interact with parents and the school to encourage attendance. Low income students also receive shoes and school lunches – students are given lunch on the bus to reduce the stigma of receiving it at school.

Last summer, DROM went door-to-door in the Roma settlement explaining the project to Roma families. DROM also sought the support of the schools, the mayor and the media. The project eventually gained support of all stakeholders, excluding the mayor. However, he did not try to block the project. With the agreement of a number of Roma parents, DROM invited the 6 mainstream schools in Vidin to participate in a TV program at which each school presented its program, philosophy, and teachers. Roma parents selected the school they wanted their children to attend. This lessened their concerns and was the first time, that their views had been solicited by the authorities.

Project success at the end of the first semester of the project was measured by 100 percent attendance; first term final grade averages were identical to the level of the non-Roma pupils; parental and teacher satisfaction; no known anti-Roma racism in the schools; full support from the Regional Directorate of the Ministry of Education and encouragement to scale up in other cities. In addition, 35 Roma parents of the bussed children have returned to school in adult education programs; 3 teenagers who had dropped out in the third grade asked to join the program and teachers agreed to work extra hours with them and others. On the negative side, 24 pupils received failing grades in one or more subjects and three have left the program. One returned to the Roma school and two 8th graders who were functionally illiterate dropped out.

The success to date of the program is attributable to three major factors. First, the parents feel (a) that their children are protected from racial humiliation because of being bused to and from school and monitored throughout the day by adult Roma and (b) that they can meet the higher scholastic standards. Second, the schools have accepted young adult Roma monitors in the schools who assure the children aren't mistreated. The monitors also monitor the engagement of the parents in overseeing homework, the participation of the pupils in extra-curricula activities and the cleanliness, feeding and appropriate attire of the children. The monitors help the teachers with teaching aides and understanding cultural differences. Working through the monitors and the local Roma NGO which employs them, grades and progress are monitored every day; problems are addressed on the spot. Third, the children are happy to be in schools where learning takes place.

This approach may be applicable in Slovak Republic. However, it is important to note that many Bulgarian Roma children speak Bulgarian. This clearly contributed to the early success of the project. In countries such as Slovak Republic, where Roma children in eastern Slovakia do not speak Slovak, pre-school programs for national language acquisition and social integration will be critical preconditions.

Source: World Bank

REFERENCES

Blanchard, O., et al., 1995. *Spanish Unemployment: Is There a Solution?*. London: CEPR,

Blank, R. M. 2000 "Fighting Poverty: Lessons from Recent US History". Journal of Economic Perspectives, vol. 12, No. 2, Spring 2000.

Bulgaria: Consultations with the Poor, 2000.

European Centre on Health of Societies in Transition (ECOHOST). 2000. "Health Needs of the Roma Population in the Czech and the Slovak Republics: Literature Review." Draft.

ERRC (European Roma Rights Center), 1999. "A Special Remedy: Roma and Schools for the Mentally Handicapped in the Czech Republic." Country Reports Series No. 8.

Lubyova, M. and J. Van Ours, 1999. "Jobs from Active Labor Market Policies and their Effects on Slovak Unemployment", *Journal of Comparative Economics*, 27, 90-112.

Lubyova, M. "Labor Market", 2000 in Marcincin A. and M. Beblavy (eds.), *Economic Policy in Slovakia 1990-1999*, pp. 165-206. Bratislava: Center for Social and Media Analysis (and others).

Martin, F. A. 2000. "Roma in Spain," Background paper prepared for the World Bank. Draft. Washington, DC.

Peterson, J. 2000 "Welfare Reform and Inequality: The TANF and UI Programs". Journal of Economic Issues, vol. 34, No. 2, June 2000.

Ringold, D. 2000. "Roma and the Transition in Central and Eastern Europe: Trends and Challenges, The World Bank: Washington, D.C.

Schoeni, R. F. and Blank, R. M. 2000 "What Has Welfare Reform Accomplished? Impacts on Welfare Participation, Employment, Income, Poverty and Family Structure". NBER Working Paper, No. 7627.

Vasecka, M. 2000. "Analysis of the Situation of Roma in Slovakia," draft prepared for the World Bank. Washington, DC.

Wallace and Blank 1999, Figlio and Ziliak 1999) and Schoeni and Blank 2000.

World Bank, 2001a. "Poverty and Welfare of the Roma in the Slovak Republic: A Qualitative Study", forthcoming. Washington, DC.

REGIONAL DISPARITIES IN THE SLOVAK REPUBLIC[74]

A COUNTRY OF WIDE DISPARITIES

The Slovak Republic is a country with large and persistent regional disparities. Parts of the Slovak Republic, in particular the Eastern and Southern regions and old industrial areas are increasingly lagging behind the more dynamic Western part of the country.

These large regional inequalities are largely related to the location of industries under the socialist planned economy. During that period, in response to political and strategic considerations, heavy engineering plants and armaments industries were located in agricultural regions in the East, far from the Western border and less exposed to attacks. These plants produced for export and were barely integrated with the rest of the economy. As a result, the surrounding areas failed to develop a local industrial base. These initial disparities persisted and were aggravated by weakness in transport infrastructure and by the sharp increase in transportation costs that followed the liberalization of energy and transport prices.

One clear measure of economic and social disparities across regions is the fraction of the population living in poverty. In 1996, the poorest region, Kosice, had 14.3 percent of its population living in poverty, compared to 9.4 percent in richer Bratislava and 10.1 percent for the country as a whole. These differences in poverty outcomes mirror those observed for other social and economic indicators, such as income per capita or unemployment. Regardless of the indicator used, the country can be divided into two very different parts: a more prosperous, dynamic and modern Slovak Republic, centered around Bratislava and a much poorer, more rural, Eastern and Southern Slovakia.

Data from Eurostat on regional per capita GDP serve to highlight these differences (Table 5.1). The table shows that the Bratislava region of the Slovak Republic has a GDP per capita that is equal to the EU average, and is the second richest region in all of the CEEC countries, after Prague. In contrast, Eastern Slovakia has a per capita income that is only 39 percent the EU average. In terms of business activities, Bratislava, with 13 percent of the economically active population of the country, concentrates 31 percent of business entities and 20 percent of individual tradesmen. Moreover, more than 60 percent of total inflows of equity capital were directed to Bratislava, and business entities in the Bratislava region absorbed almost two-thirds of total foreign direct investment in 1997, while firms in Presov, that has around the same population, have absorbed under 4 percent (Table 5.2).

---

[74] This chapter draws heavily on the background paper by Lucia Haulikova and Vladimir Benc, "Regional Disparities in the Slovak Republic", Background Paper 5, Volume II of this study. The chapter also makes use of materials presented in De La Rocha (2001), Sanchez-Paramo (2001), and Steele (2001).

Table 5.1 Regional GDP per Capita in Several CEEC Countries, 1998

REGION	Per capita GDP 1998 (PPS[1])	Per capita GDP 1998 EU15=100	Per capita GDP 1995-98 EU15=100	Rank
EU – 15	20213	100	100	2
CZECH REP.	12186	60	63	6
Praha (richest)	23187	115	118	1
Strední Čehy (poorest)	9484	47	49	18
HUNGARY	9899	49	48	15
Kozép Magyarország (richest)	14633	72	70	4
Észak Alfold (poorest)	6700	33	33	33
POLAND	7287	36	34	28
Mazowieckie (richest)	10648	53	50	13
Podkarpackie (poorest)	5530	27	26	48
SLOVAK REPUBLIC	9828	49	47	16
Bratislava	20092	99	95	3
Western Slovakia	8962	44	43	19
Central Slovakia	8503	42	40	20
Eastern Slovakia	7931	39	37	23

Notes: For methodology, see "Regional Accounts Methods: Gross value added and gross fixed capital formation by activity", Eurostat, 1995, ISBN 92-827-0159-X.
1/The comparisons are carried out in purchasing power parities.

Source: Eurostat, Statistics in Focus, General Statistics, No 4/2001 "Regional Gross Domestic Product in Central European Candidate Countries 1998".

Large disparities in terms of investments and business creation are reflected in very different employment and unemployment outcomes across regions. Thus, while in 1998 the region of Bratislava recorded the lowest unemployment rate in the country, at 5.8 percent; in Kosice it was 18.3 percent and in Presov 16.4 percent. By 2001, these differences had only increased: unemployment in Bratislava had risen up to 6.6 percent, but unemployment had jumped to 27 percent in Kosice, and to 25.4 percent in Presov. These differences mirror differences in job creation, as well. For example, the likelihood of getting a job for an unemployed individual in Bratislava is 10 times higher than in Kosice: in Bratislava, there are 26 unemployed per vacancy posting; in Kosice, there are 266 (see Chapter 2).

Table 5.2 Slovak Republic: Selected Economic Indicators by Region, 1999-2000

	% of total population	% of business entities (2000)	% of economically active population	Unemployment rate (%)	% of foreign capital	% of inflow of FDI[1]	% of gross output	% of value added
Bratislava	11.5	31.2	13.1	6.8	51.9	60.5	22.9	23.6
Trnava	10.2	7.2	10.2	15.7	8.0	10.0	10.1	10.4
Trencin	11.3	9.6	11.6	13.5	8.3	6.4	10.2	9.7
Nitra	13.3	8.7	13.0	22.7	6.3	3.8	10.5	11.5
Zilina	12.8	10.0	13.0	17.7	7.5	3.1	10.8	10.7
Banska Bys.	12.3	11.2	12.2	22.8	6.6	4.9	11.8	10.9
Presov	14.5	9.5	13.5	23.2	3.6	3.6	9.7	9.1
Kosice	14.2	12.7	13.4	25.5	7.9	7.7	13.9	14.1

[1] Accumulated as of March 2000.
Source: Statistical Office of the Slovak Republic.

There is evidence that these outcomes tend to go together: regions with lower income per capita are, not surprisingly, those with higher poverty rates, but also those with the highest unemployment (see Figure 5.1). Similarly, regions with highest unemployment are those with lowest vacancy and job creation rates. Moreover, although trend data are not abundant, all indications suggest that differences between regions are getting larger, not smaller, over time. Poor regions were poorer at the start of transition, and have seen the differentials only increase since then.

Present and past Governments have been well-aware of the problem of regional disparities, and have made regional development one of their main priorities, implementing a whole range of programs especially directed towards the lagging regions. However, judging by the evolution of these disparities, results to date have not been too encouraging.

Figure 5.1 Unemployment and Income per Capita, by Region

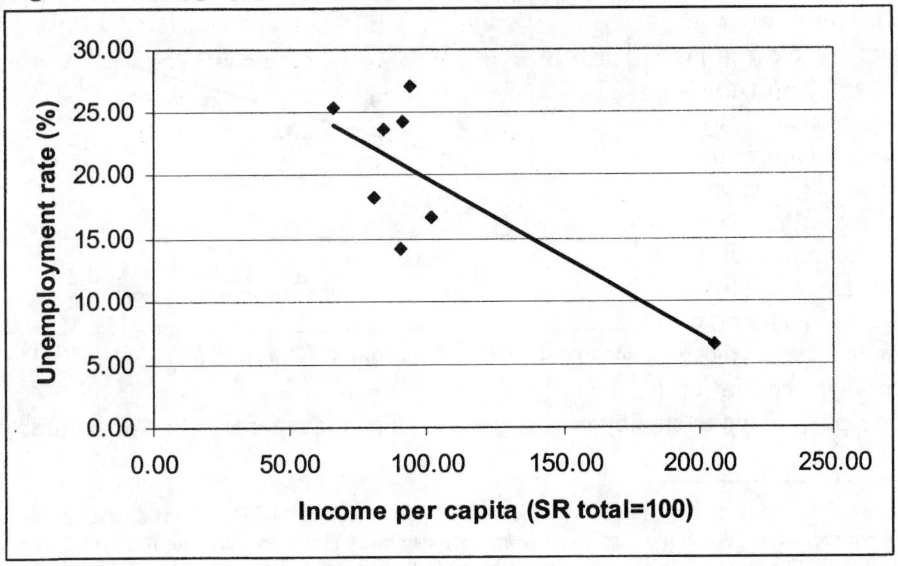

Source: Haulikova and Benc, 2001

WHAT LIES BEHIND THESE DIFFERENCES

The existence of large regional disparities is not the sole result of the transition. At the root of these large regional differences lie very different endowments, production structures, and economic/policy environments, all of which have greatly affected the evolution of regional performance over the past decade. The difficulties of Southern and Eastern Slovakia have their origin, in part, in the structure of production inherited from the socialist system, which concentrated heavy industry, engineering, and armament industries in those regions of the country. But the burden of an unfavorable production structure has been aggravated by a number of other factors, such as poor transportation networks and infrastructure, a less-educated workforce, more unfavorable demographic patterns, a poor business environment, and weak public administration.

We can divide the underlying determinants of regional disparities intro three broad groupings: (i) endowments, comprising the stock of human and physical capital (including supporting infrastructure); (ii) the business and economic environment, which is affected by the inherited production structure but also by economic policies; and (iii) the institutional and political frameworks, which condition both policies and their outcomes. In some regions we may observe better initial conditions along with a concentration of these positive factors, which strengthens their economic potential and growth. On the contrary, in poor, lagging regions, we will tend to observe worse initial conditions and a concentration of negative factors.

The importance of some of these underlying factors can be gleaned from some simple correlations. Take for example, regional unemployment as an important regional outcome variable that we want to explain.[75] It is clear from Figures 5.2 and 5.3 that it is highly correlated with endowments of both human and physical capital. Regions with lower educational attainment of the labor force are also those with higher rates of unemployment (and those with lower wages and lower income per capita). High-unemployment regions are also the regions with worse infrastructure.

Figure 5.2 Regional Unemployment and Education

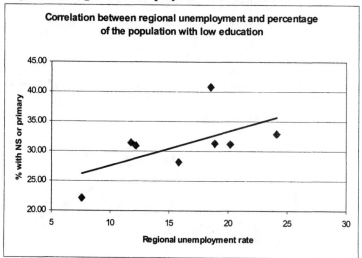

Source: LFS data; Haulikova and Benc (2001)

---

[75] We could use the regional poverty rate as our measure of outcomes but the lack of trend data on poverty makes it less useful as an indicator. We could also use income per capita as the main outcome indicator, with very similar results. We chose to use regional unemployment as the main "outcome" indicator in the chapter for several reasons. First because of its importance as a determinant of poverty outcomes. Second, because we have access to good quality trend data on unemployment, both for registered unemployment and for figures computed from the LFS. Third, because of the huge variance in outcomes across regions, and because it is a good "summary statistic" that captures what is happening on many fronts.

The quality of infrastructure and of the human capital stock influence the mobility of labor and goods, the allocation of production and attractiveness of any location to FDI inflows. This, in turn, affects job creation and employment performance. On the other hand, endowments by themselves are not enough to attract investors and create jobs. Even superior infrastructure and a highly-skilled labor force in some

Figure 5.3 Regional Unemployment and Infrastructure

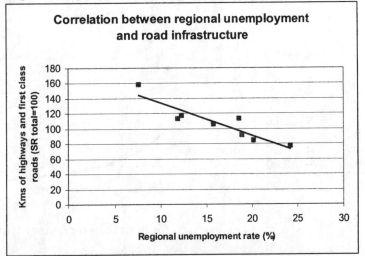

Source: LFS data; Haulikova and Benc (2001).

of the more backward regions would not be sufficient to attract domestic or foreign investors, in the absence of an adequate business environment. Availability of credit and investment resources, allocated in a transparent manner; predictable and clearly enforced legislation, regulations and taxation; well-functioning market-supporting institutions and public administration—these are equally important factors in determining whether a locality will have a favorable business environment, whether it will attract investors, and hence whether it will grow and create jobs.

Measuring the "attractiveness" of the business environment is somewhat difficult given the lack of detailed region-level data on availability of credit, enforcement of regulations and taxation, etc. However, much anecdotal evidence suggests that in these respects, regions are far from uniform. Indeed, lack of predictability of how regulations (and corporate taxation) will be enforced is an often-heard complaint among foreign investors.[76] Let us take, however, FDI flows as one measure which somehow may "synthesize" the attractiveness of a region to investors (in this case foreign). If we plot the share of FDI flows going to each region against the unemployment rate, we find that clearly regions with high unemployment are also those that seem to be less attractive to foreign investors (Figure 5.4). Obviously the constraint in these regions is not scarcity of labor—it must be scarcity of skills, of supporting infrastructure, or an inadequate business environment.

---

[76] See, for example, de la Rocha (2001)

Figure 5.4 Regional Unemployment and the Share of FDI

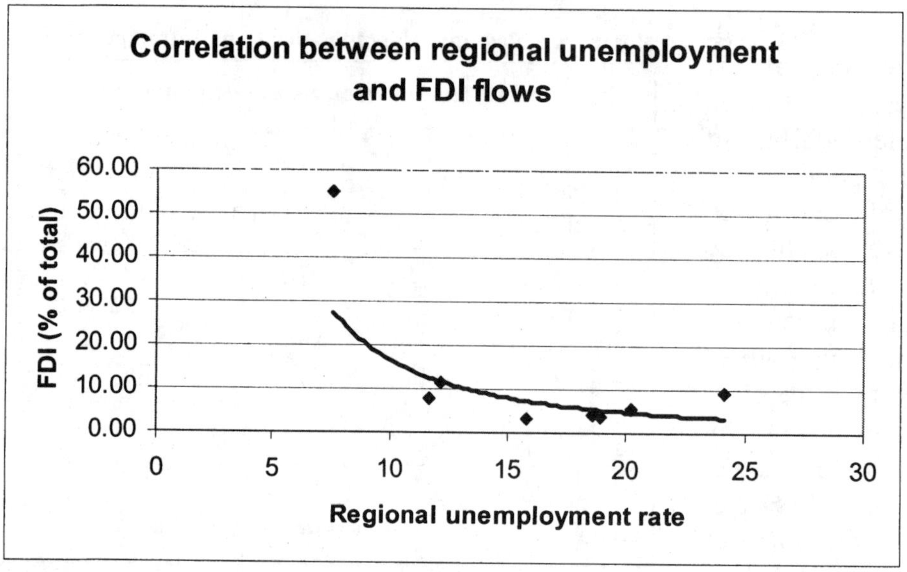

Correlation between regional unemployment and FDI flows

Source: LFS data; Haulikova and Benc (2001).

Thus, at first glance, it seems that the combination of endowments (human and physical) and business environment can go a long way in explaining why regional outcomes vary as much as they do. In the rest of the chapter, we move on to analyze the evolution and role of each of these main underlying factors in more detail. We then examine what policy can do facilitate growth and employment creation in lagging regions. Our analysis necessarily remains partial and incomplete, as it is hampered by lack of comparable data series at the region level over time. For many variables we have information only at a single point in time, or for a few years. Certainly not enough to underpin an analysis of whether (and why) Slovak regions may be diverging in their economic and social conditions. Moreover, for some very important dimensions –such as the quality and effectiveness of local administrations—we simply lack any data at all. This chapter thus offers a preliminary analysis, which may hopefully serve to orient and motivate further work on regional disparities.

THE ROLE OF ENDOWMENTS

Human Capital Stock

Demographic factors. Unlike in other European economies, the population structure of the Slovak Republic is such that the fraction of the population in their prime "productive age" is growing fast (by 4.2 percent per annum). This is mainly the result of secularly declining birth rates, in combination with an aging but still relatively young population (by European standards). This demographic development presents both opportunities and challenges. On the one hand, growth of the productive age population can provide a strong spurt to overall GDP growth, if these cohorts are able to find employment. Yet, at the same time, large cohorts of new labor market entrants place additional pressures on the labor market to create jobs.

Although these trends are observed nationwide, the age structure of the population actually varies significantly across regions, and even across neighboring districts. The age structure of the local population is influenced by factors such as job opportunities, new housing construction, migration due to work and studies, but also health status, life styles and ethnic structure. Birth rates, for example, are much higher in Eastern Slovakia than in the western part of the country, where they have been declining much more rapidly. As a result, the age composition of the population in parts of Eastern Slovakia is younger, and the population is growing more quickly (Table 5.3).[77]

Table 5.3 Natural Increase/Decrease (-) of the Population per 1,000 Inhabitants

Region	1995	1996	1997	1998	1999	1-3Q2000	Population 3Q 2000
SR Total	1.6	1.7	1.3	0.8	0.7	0.8	5,403,101
Bratislava	-0.5	-1.0	-1.0	-1.4	-1.5	0.4	617,238
Trnava	0.5	0.3	-0.1	-0.5	-0.7	0.5	551,553
Trenčin	1.0	0.6	0.1	-0.5	-0.2	-0.3	609,096
Nitria	-1.3	-0.8	-1.5	-2.1	-2.1	-1.1	715,071
Žilina	3.6	3.6	3.0	2.8	2.1	1.8	693,864
Banska Bystricka	-0.5	-0.2	-0.4	-1.3	-0.9	-0.8	662,390
Prešov	6.4	6.2	5.7	5.2	5.0	3.2	787,003
Košice	2.7	3.2	3.3	3.0	2.8	2.1	766,886

Source: Statistical Office of the Slovak Republic (Haulikova and Benc, 2001).

Experts suggest that the regional distribution of the Roma population is an important factor in explaining these differences in population structure. The shares of the Roma minority in the overall population in every district of Eastern Slovakia are fairly high (exceeding 10 percent in some districts as early as 1980). And the demographic characteristics of the Roma are quite distinct from those of the majority population. They have much higher birth rates, larger families, and a much younger population structure. The average number of 4.2 children per Roma mother is more than twice the average 1.51 children per non-Roma population (see Chapter 4).

With its reproductive behavior, the Roma population fills an important demographic vacuum. Many regions of Slovak Republic would be unable to sustain their population without the contribution of Roma families. However, fast population growth also adds pressure to the need to generate employment, and has implications in terms of public spending given very different needs for public services (greater need for schools, primary care facilities, and social services).

Health Status. Despite moderate growth in life expectancy indicators over the last several years, life expectancy in Slovak Republic remains in the lower part of the European ranking. Although there are no systematic calculations of life expectancy in Slovak districts, data gathered through reliable research reveal considerable disparities between regions (as much as 6 years in male life expectancy). The highest male life expectancy is recorded in Bratislava and Trencin, while females tend to live longest in

---

[77] According to projections of further demographic trends, a decline in the population after 2005 is expected mainly in the Bratislava and Nitra regions. The highest total growth is expected for the Presov region.

the Trencin, Zilina, and Bratislava regions.[78]   In general, people in urban areas tend to enjoy higher life expectancy than people in rural areas.

Figure 5.5 Life Expectancy and Unemployment by Districts, 1996

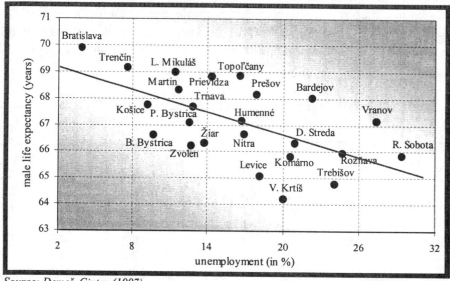

Source: Demeš, Ginter (1997).

Figure 5.5 shows a significant indirect relation between the unemployment rate and life expectancy.   Districts with highest unemployment figures are mainly those reporting the lowest life expectancy numbers.   These districts are disproportionately concentrated in Eastern and Southern Slovakia.   However, it is impossible to draw an unequivocal conclusion about the relation between higher unemployment and worsened health conditions.   Shorter life expectancy had been recorded in the same districts even during the communist regime, which was known for reporting virtually zero unemployment rate.   Surprisingly, high levels of environmental pollution were not always correlated with decreased life expectancy.   Although the emission of pollutants is highest in Bratislava and Kosice, the country's two largest urban centers, these cities also have higher proportions of inhabitants with higher education, which appears to be positively correlated with life expectancy.   As a result, overall life expectancy in Bratislava in the highest in the country.

An important omitted variable which may be correlated with both unemployment and male life expectancy, and which may underlie the apparent correlation in Figure 5.5, is ethnicity. Districts with some of the lowest life expectancy figures—such as Rimavská Sobota—are also those with some of the highest concentrations of Roma population. As discussed earlier in this Report, the Roma do suffer from worse health status and lower life expectancy, on average, than the non-Roma population (Chapter 4). The prevalence of communicable diseases, associated with poor living conditions, is much higher among Roma living in segregated settlements than among the rest of the population.

---

[78] Based on 1991-1993 data on weighted averages for selected districts.

142

The lowest male life expectancy is found in districts with a high ratio of males with only elementary education (see Haulikova and Benc, 2001 for details). Again, these tend to be concentrated in Eastern and Southern Slovakia. It seems that negative behavioral habits (such as smoking, high alcohol consumption, improper diet, and more risky jobs) are more widespread among individuals with lower levels of education. There is an important link between the life expectancy of both sexes and their level of education: educated men and women tend to live significantly longer than those who are less educated. As with unemployment, there may also be an omitted ethnic factor that is simultaneously correlated with both low education and lower life expectancy.

Educational Attainment. Regional indicators of the educational level of the total population may only be estimated, as accurate numbers are collected only in the national census (and the latest census dates from 1991). Based on partial data from the Statistical Office, we can conclude that Bratislava ranks the highest in terms of educational achievement (Table 5.4). It has the highest proportion of university graduates, and the lowest levels with primary and vocational education. Generally, larger cities with better access to educational and R&D facilities have larger proportions of population with higher levels of education (Bratislava, Kosice, Banska Bystrica, Zilina, Nitra). However, the link between higher education and labor market outcomes is not linear. For example the cities of Kosice and Nitra, both of which have universities, also report high unemployment rates, particularly among youth.

Table 5.4 Completed Education Level by Region (% of population aged 16 years and over)

Region	Without education	Primary	Vocational	Secondary	University
Bratislavsky	1.05	21.63	18.68	39.99	18.64
Trnavsky	1.01	29.18	34.71	29.57	5.53
Trenciansky	0.70	28.50	35.55	29.27	5.98
Nitriansky	0.88	36.25	29.68	28.67	4.52
Zilinsky	1.06	27.53	32.22	32.81	6.39
Banskobystricky	1.42	30.85	27.66	33.45	6.61
Presovsky	0.91	30.08	35.18	28.10	5.72
Kosicky	1.71	32.18	28.13	33.12	4.87

Source: Labor Force Survey 2000:1.

Table 5.4 refers to all inhabitants aged 16 and over. However, a better measure of the "human capital" stock of a region may be derived from the educational composition of those who are actually employed. Table 5.5 shows that also on this dimension Bratislava outperforms other regions, with over a quarter of all employees in Bratislava having a completed university education (more than twice the national average). The lowest educational levels among the employed are recorded in the Nitra region. The structure of production in this region, more agricultural, demands less highly qualified labor.

Table 5.5 Employed by Level of Education

Region	Total number of employed (1,000s)	Structure by education (in %)			
		Primary or no education	Lower secondary	Upper secondary	Tertiary
SR in total	2 132.1	8.0	40.3	39.9	11.9
Bratislavský	309.2	6.0	25.1	43.0	25.9
Trnavský	229.8	10.4	47.0	33.3	9.2
Trenčiansky	252.4	7.9	43.3	38.9	9.9
Nitriansky	266.9	11.7	46.0	34.8	7.5
Žilinský	275.1	8.8	41.9	40.0	9.4
Banskobystrický	246.2	6.9	36.9	44.6	11.7
Prešovský	285.9	5.4	44.1	40.7	9.8
Košický	266.9	7.3	40.7	43.0	9.1

Source: Regional Comparisons in the Slovak Republic 1999. Statistical Office of the Slovak Republic

Slovak Republic had a total of 3,314 kindergartens and 2,482 primary schools in 1999/2000.   Primary enrolment ratios are among the highest in transition countries. There were 1,340 secondary schools (of which 209 are grammar schools, 348 vocational schools, 371 apprenticeships, and 381 special schools), with a total number of 309,364 students. The highest number of secondary schools is in the Kosice and Presov regions, corresponding to a higher number of children of school age; the lowest number of secondary schools is in the Trnava region. In 1999/2000, Slovak Republic had a total of 18 universities with 118,848 students. Most students are concentrated in Bratislava (41.8 percent of the total number in 1998) and in Kosice (16.7 percent).

Figure 5.6 Government Education Expenditures by Region, 1999 ('000s SKK)

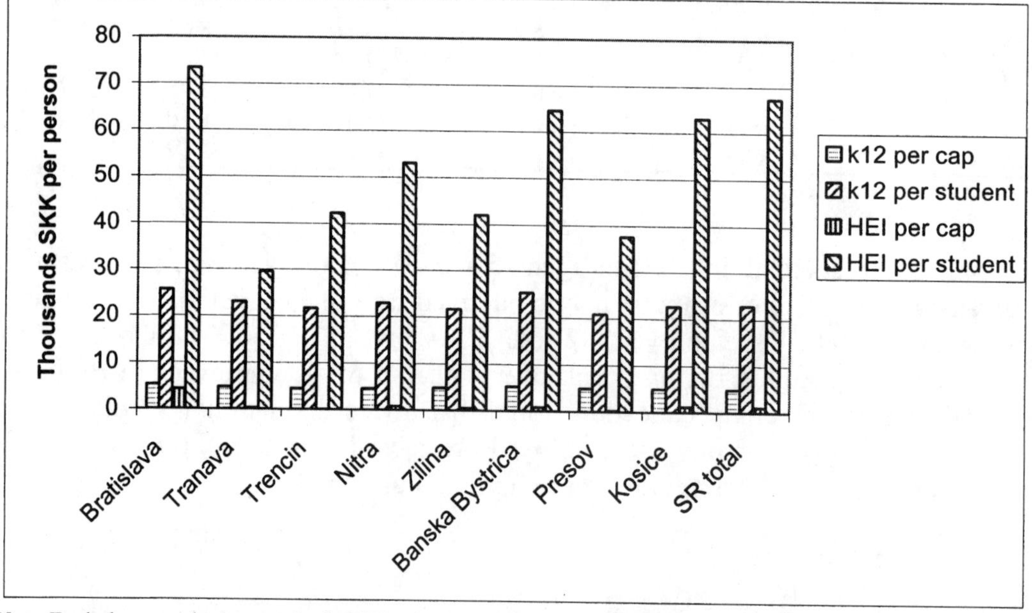

Note: Excludes extra-budgetary funds. HEI = higher education institutions; k12= kindergarten through 12th grade. *Source: Statistical Office of SR, as reported in Haulikova and Benc (2001).*

144

In terms of education expenditures per student, Bratislava ranks the highest for higher education institutions (HEI), and the second highest along with Banska Bystrica for expenditures in grades kindergarten through 12th (K12). Although on a per capita basis expenditures are fairly evenly distributed, there still seems to be a slight pro-Bratislava bias in the allocation of spending in education, especially at the tertiary level. These figures are summarized in Figure 5.6.

Crime and violence. The region of Bratislava, mainly the capital districts, achieves highest values concerning negative social aspects, such as crime. Bratislava leads the ranking in criminal offences, as a result of the high concentration of human, material and financial resources in the region. Additionally, the geographical location of the capital strengthens its position as the traffic and destination point of drug-related criminality (based on recorded drug crime evidence, approximately 70 percent of all drugs are consumed in the capital).

Housing

The latest exact data on the housing structure in Slovak Republic was collected in the 1991 population and housing census. According to the 1991 census, the total housing stock consisted of 1.77 million dwellings, of which 1.62 million were permanently occupied. Experts estimate the current number of total dwellings at 1.8 million, of which about 1.65 million are occupied. Quantitative comparisons rank Slovak Republic among the average of the transition countries (Haulikova and Benc, 2001).

The Slovak housing stock is relatively new—in average 36 years old—and of seemingly high quality. More than 75 percent of the dwellings have central heating and more than a half of units are connected to the state gas network. More than 82 percent of the population is supplied from water systems and 55 percent connected to public sewage systems. However, there are significant regional differences. While in Bratislava 95 of dwellings are connected to water systems and 83 percent to public sewage, in some rural districts the share of population connected to public water and sewage networks is rather low (e.g., public water system is available for 75 percent of the Presov region; population connected to public sewage in Trnava counts only 45 percent). Moreover, a large portion of the housing stock, mainly the block-of-flats houses, requires renovation and modernization of construction and equipment elements.[79] The majority of these buildings can be found in urban districts.

About 60 percent of the housing stock is in private ownership, consisting primarily of houses located in smaller towns and villages. Dwellings (apartments) in municipal and cooperative ownership, as well as dwellings in private ownership are situated predominantly in urban areas. Of the two major forms of housing occupation—ownership and rental (including cooperative)—the former is far more dominant accounting for more than 70 percent of housing. New housing construction is also dominated by home ownership.

---

[79] Modernization costs are estimated at more than hundred billion crowns. However, studies indicate a 30-40 percent saving in energy costs due to technical improvements.

High ratios of home ownership may be one factor contributing to low labor mobility across regions. Recent work by Vagac (1997) finds an association between the fraction of home owners and labor mobility across countries, and there is evidence that a similar relationship could hold across regions. Areas with higher levels of owner-occupation (and hence a small rental sector) do report higher unemployment rates. But outwards mobility from these areas seems to be limited by lack of housing options in the destination regions, and by large price differentials in the price of rentals (see Chapter 2).

Estimates suggest that Slovak Republic does suffer from a housing shortage, especially in those regions with higher employment growth and better job creation performance. A rough estimate based on the average size of households, the number of dwellings and inhabitants, suggests that there is a shortage of some 200,000-300,000 dwellings in Slovak Republic.[80] As argued above, such shortages may be hampering labor mobility, and preventing the internal migration of the population. Labor mobility is not only critical for lowering unemployment in depressed regions, but is also an important tool for reducing economic and social disparities across regions., Hence, a lack of mobility associated with deficiencies in the housing market could be an important explanatory factors behind the persistence of wide regional differences in incomes and opportunities.

New housing construction seems to be mainly concentrated in Bratislava, which is also the area of greatest shortages (Figure 5.7). However, the pace of construction is relatively slow. The main barriers to housing construction include legislative, institutional, procedural and financial matters, including: a complicated system of land exemption from the agricultural fund; often unsettled ownership of grounds/land; ineffective operation of cadastral offices; unclear division of public funds between the state budget and local/municipal budgets; non-transparent financing and ownership of infrastructure (water and sewage, gas, electricity); delayed rent liberalization in many areas; lack of long-term capital; and limited public resources for housing support.

Figure 5.7 New Housing Construction by Region (completed dwellings by 1000 population)

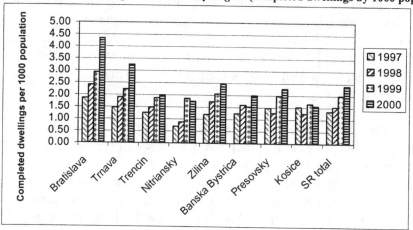

Source: Haulikova and Benc (2001).

---

[80] Based on the internationally accepted rule that the housing market of a given country is saturated with 102 dwellings per 100 households. Available statistical data from 1991 show that there is 1.12 households per 1 dwelling in Slovak Republic at an average of 3.26 persons per household.

Very different conditions in local housing markets have resulted in sizeable price differentials in housing (and real estate in general) across the regions—although overall price differentials remain modest when compared to what is observed in more mature market economies. Available information on prices of dwellings suggests that newly constructed dwellings are some 15-30 percent more expensive than existing units. Prices in Bratislava city are approximately 25 percent higher than in other regional centers with more than 30,000 inhabitants (Table 5.6). It is not clear, however, whether price differentials alone would explain low inter-regional labor mobility since differences in average wages between Bratislava and other regions are roughly of a very similar magnitude, on the order of 20 to 25 percent (30 percent in the case of Zilina, but only 10 percent for Kosice). Enough in principle to allow workers to move to regions with more expensive housing without suffering large drops in real incomes.[81]

Table 5.6 Prices of Dwellings (1997, SKK per m^2)

Location of dwelling	New housing construction	Existing dwellings
Bratislava – standard quality	19,000 – 26,000	15,000 – 20,000
Bratislava – high quality	30,000 – 35,000	--
Towns within 30 km from Bratislava	14,000 – 18,000	12,000 – 15,000
Regional and district towns (more than 30,000 inhabitants)	16,000 – 22,000	12,000 – 15,000

Source: Profiles of Countries in the Housing Sector: Slovak Republic (1999).

Infrastructure

As discussed above, a first glance there appears to be a strong correlation between lower-quality infrastructure (especially road networks) and higher regional unemployment and poverty (Figure 5.3). Poorer regions have a lower proportion of good quality roads than richer regions, and a higher fraction of "third-class roads" (Table 5.8). The situation with the railway system roughly mirrors that of the road network: only some 17.9 percent of the railway network is appropriate for track speeds of at least 100km/hr, and only 8.4 percent for the speed of 120 km/h. All of these higher-speed portions are located in Western Slovakia. As a result of these deficiencies, average transport times (and consequently transport costs) for getting products produced in Eastern Slovakia to Western markets are high. There are also significant regional differences in access to water supply and public sewage systems, with the poorer regions having significantly lower access to both water and public sewage (Table 5.7).

---

[81] The problem may be, however, the difficulties of securing financing and meeting down-payments on home purchases. The mortgage market is barely emerging in the Slovak Republic, and opportunities for obtaining financing are scarce.

Table 5.7 Selected Infrastructure by Region, 1999

Region	Total Roads (km)	Share of highways and 1st class (%)	Population connected to water supply (%)	Population connected to public sewage (%)
Bratislava	799.5	29.11	94.5	82.2
Trnava	1,946.7	17.90	82.2	44.6
Trencin	1,856.7	19.63	84.4	52.7
Nitria	2,552.6	20.14	81.9	45.2
Zilina	1,967.3	26.21	84.1	48.7
Banska B.	3,158.7	18.18	82.3	56.8
Presov	3,079.6	19.25	75.0	51.5
Kosice	2,372.8	15.71	77.0	57.3

Source: Statistical Office of the SR, as reported in Haulikova and Benc (2001).

In principle, telecommunication services are provided uniformly across the Slovak Republic. However, access does seem to vary by region (Table 5.8). There has been very rapid growth in the number of mobile telephones and internet connections. In 1999, 14.6 percent of all households in Slovak Republic owned a mobile phone, by 2000 the share had grown to 21.4 percent. Access to both internet and mobile communication services seems highly concentrated in more prosperous and urban areas. According to a recent survey[82], there is a strong correlation between household income levels and the ownership of a computer or mobile phone. Only 5.4 percent of households with income of 8 to 9 thousands SKK own a PC. In higher income groups, the proportion of owners of these appliances is increasing. More than 63 percent of households with an monthly income higher than SKK 35,000 has a mobile phone and 44.3 percent have a computer. The survey also shows that the with a higher urbanization degree of the location the number of people using phones, mobiles, PCs etc. grows.

Table 5.8 Households Equipped with Phone, Mobile Phone and PC, by Region (%)

Region	Phone station	Mobile phones	PC
Bratislava	74.9	33.8	20.0
Trnava	53.5	18.5	12.3
Trencian	55.8	21.6	11.4
Nitria	55.5	20.0	9.4
Zilina	62.3	16.7	14.0
Banska. B.	57.1	17.3	8.9
Presov	63.4	15.8	10.1
Kosice	67.1	18.4	13.1

Source: Cenzus 2001, GfK Slovakia, in Haulikova and Benc (2001).

THE BUSINESS AND ECONOMIC ENVIRONMENT

Structure of Production

In the past decade, the structure of the Slovak economy has been influenced by a combination of several overlapping, and in many cases, intertwining developments: the socio-economic transformation associated with transition; catching up and adjusting to the EU; and the *stop and go* nature of economic reform, as influenced by political changes and the political process. The different regions inherited very different

---

[82] Survey conducted by agency GfK Slovak Republic in 2001. Source: *SME* daily, April 25, 2001.

production structures from the previous regime, which greatly conditioned their ability to adapt to these three developments. The more industrialized regions have had to undergo much more adjustment—most of it taking place early on during the first phase of reforms in the 1990s. This has placed a heavy burden on these regions in terms of creating a large stock of unemployment. Many of the regions are still struggling to adapt to the new market conditions.

The economic weight of the capital, Bratislava, is evident from Table 5.2. Bratislava region alone, with about one-seventh of the population of the Slovak Republic, accounts for almost a quarter of the country's total GDP. Presov, with roughly the same population, accounts for less than 10 percent. Between 1997 (the first year for which regional GDP on a national accounts basis is available) and 1999 all regions experienced some growth, but of varying magnitudes. The fastest growing region was (surprisingly) agricultural Nitria, followed by Kosice, Presov and Bratislava. Trnava (also fairly agricultural), Trencin and Zilina (both heavily invested in manufacturing) turned in the worst performances.

Employment Structure

The structure of employment across regions largely parallels differences in the production structure. Thus, Bratislava has a very low share of agricultural workers (less than 2 percent of total employees) and a relatively low number of industrial occupations (17 percent). In contrast, it has a very high proportion of public administration officials and high employment in trade, hotels and restaurants, and the banking sector (particularly the city districts of Bratislava I and II). The Nitra, Banska Bystrica and Trnava regions have the highest proportion of workers engaged in agriculture (more than 10 percent). Indeed, the southern lowland districts of these regions have traditionally been the agro-food reservoir of Slovak Republic. Trencin and Zilina have above-average proportions of industrial workers due to the traditional location of heavy industry (machinery, chemicals), but also light industry (mainly textiles). The composition of employment, however, can vary significantly across districts within a single region. Thus, Bratislava does have a couple of very small, rural (and surprisingly poor) districts. Similarly, more rural regions like Nitria or Trnava do have an important share of their workforces engaged in manufacturing activities. Moreover, there are still a large number of districts (mainly small rural ones) that depend on a single enterprise, sometimes not even located in that very district.

As suggested by wide disparities in regional unemployment rates, declines in employment during the 1990s have not been evenly distributed across regions. The most dramatic decreases in employment were recorded in the Kosice, Banska Bystrica, Zilina, and Presov regions. The agricultural sector was the most affected by the drop in employment, and every region lost agricultural jobs. This was felt the most in rural regions like Nitra, Trnava and those of eastern Slovakia. Employment declines in Zilina and Banska Bystrica were mainly concentrated in industry. A number of companies in these two regions were closed or went bankrupt, because of insufficient restructuring, non-transparent ownership structure , and so-called "tunneling" of companies by the owners.

149

Labor Productivity and Labor Costs

Differences in the skill composition of the work force, capital intensity and technology are reflected in widely different labor productivity levels and trends across regions, even within the same sectors. Productivity per employee in industry, for example, is three times higher in Bratislava than in Presov, and over four times higher than in Trencin (Table 5.9). Such productivity differentials are visible (although smaller) even in a relatively low-skilled sector such as construction. Differences in productivity are a key explanatory factor behind differences in both income levels and employment opportunities. They also help explain why investors (domestic or foreign) may be much more attracted to better-off regions such as Bratislava.

Table 5.9 Labor Productivity per Employee ('000s SKK)

| Region | Industry | Labor productivity per employee in 1999 | | |
		SR = 100	Construction	SR = 100
SR Total	1 250.4	100	563.0	100
Bratislava	2 700.6	216	838.8	149
Trnava	1 204.2	96	489.4	87
Trencin	708.1	57	463.3	82
Nitria	972.3	78	486.4	86
Zilina	869.3	70	511.4	91
Banska B	914.1	73	499.9	89
Presov	780.3	62	440.1	78
Kosice	1 494.3	120	523.5	93

Source: Haulikova and Benc, 2001.

If we compare regional differences in labor productivity to differences in labor costs, we see that differences in labor productivity greatly exceed those in labor cost, making workers in some of the poorer areas actually more expensive in relative terms (Table 5.10). For example, monthly labor costs in Presov are almost 90 percent of the SR average; but labor productivity for workers in industry in Presov is only 62 percent of the average (and only 78 percent of the average in construction). The labor productivity differential between Bratislava and Presov is huge, with productivity in Bratislava more than double that in Presov. In contrast, the differential in labor costs is much smaller, on the order of about 30 percent. This may be a critical reason why job creation performance is so different across regions, and why unemployment differentials remain so persistent. Relative to its productivity, labor is simply more expensive in the poorer regions.

Part of this may be due to high indirect labor costs, and other restrictions on wage setting (such as nation-wide agreements on wages that do not sufficiently account for differences in labor productivity across firms and areas). We argued earlier in this Report that high indirect costs may actually be hurting less-skilled labor the most. Table 5.10 gives some evidence that suggests that they may be hurting labor in the poorer regions more than those in richer regions as well, due to the large differences in labor productivity.

Table 5.10 Monthly Labor Costs and Productivity by Region

Region	Monthly labor costs (SKK)	Of which (%): direct costs	indirect costs	Index (SR=100)	Labor productivity in industry (SR=100)
SR Total	15,780	69.78	30.23	100.0	100
Bratislava	18,862	70.06	29.95	119.5	216
Trnava	15,567	70.16	29.84	98.7	96
Trencin	14,764	70.06	29.95	93.6	57
Nitria	14,955	68.94	31.07	94.8	78
Zilina	13,218	70.61	29.44	83.8	70
Banska B	15,104	68.83	31.19	95.7	73
Presov	14,008	67.26	32.74	88.8	62
Kosice	17,168	71.06	28.94	108.8	120

Source: Statistical Yearbook, Statistical Office of the SR, as reported in Haulikova and Benc (2001).

Several studies have shown a negative correlation between the level of wages and unemployment at the district level (as would be expected), with higher unemployment rates districts paying lower wages.[83] However, this relationship does not seem to hold too strongly at the regional level. The correlation between the level of unemployment at the regional level and the growth in real monthly wages is negative but very close to zero (Figure 5.8). The same weak correlation emerges if we look at changes in unemployment versus changes in real wages. This lack of correlation is somewhat puzzling, and could point to the existence of some downward wage rigidities in poorer regions, or to that of an emerging "disconnect" between wage setting and unemployment outcomes. One possible explanation for this is that wage levels at the sector level are negotiated on a nation and sector—wide basis, and then applied to all firms in the sector regardless of location or specific circumstances. Firms in poorer regions, facing worse market conditions, may thus be forced to set wages too high for their productivity levels. This would also tend to break the link between local unemployment conditions and local wages.

---

[83] Renčko (1995)

Figure 5.8 Regional Unemployment and Change in Real Wages, 1997-99

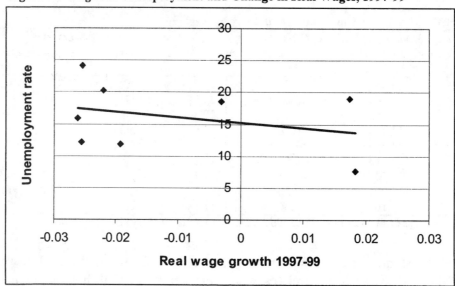

Source: Own calculations from LFS. Statistical Office of the SR.

It is interesting to look at how the wage structure by education and by age cohorts varies across regions, because it can tell us much about workings of labor market. Often, wages of new entrants, for example, are more sensitive to market conditions than those of older workers who have been employed for some time at a firm, and whose wages may be set more by internal labor ladder considerations. Figure 5.9 presents the ratio of wages in Bratislava to those of several other regions (the two poorest regions, Presov and Kosice, plus the most agricultural region, Nitria). Clearly, workers of all ages receive a wage premium for working in Bratislava, but this premium is actually lowest for young workers (reflecting perhaps their abundant supply in the Bratislava area), increases quite sharply with age for those in their prime productive years (30-54), and then declines to form an inverted u-shape pattern. Interestingly, the wage structure by age in Kosice— dominated by the country's second largest city—is very similar to that observed in Bratislava, and the premium in favor of Bratislava is very close to zero at all age groups (despite Kosice's much higher unemployment).

Figure 5.9 Ratio of Wages in Bratislava to other Regions, by Age Cohort (1999)

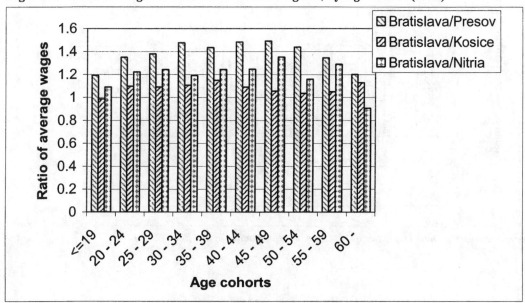

Source: Statistical Office of SR, as reported din Haulikova and Benc (2001).

Figure 5.10 presents a similar graph for wages by education, for all region. The figure plots the ratio of the average wage of vocational education graduates, and university graduates relative to those of someone with only basic education, by region. It shows that the premium for a university education (relative to basic education) varies from a low of 112 percent in Nitria to 188 percent in Kosice. Presumably this reflects the different degrees to which higher education skills are in demand across regions (and how interacts with the existing supply).

In contrast to what happens with the university premium, the premium for a vocational education is basically the same across all regions. It is hard to know whether this is because demand for those skills is essentially uniform across regions, or because —as discussed earlier with respect to the link between unemployment and wages across regions—mechanisms that negotiate wages for occupations/sectors where vocational education is prevalent, tend to impose "uniformity" in wages across regions, irrespective of differences in local conditions and productivity. The fact that such uniformity of the wage premium by education is not evident for higher education (or for general secondary schooling) lends some credibility to this second explanation.

Figure 5.10 Wage Ratios by Education, by Region (1999)

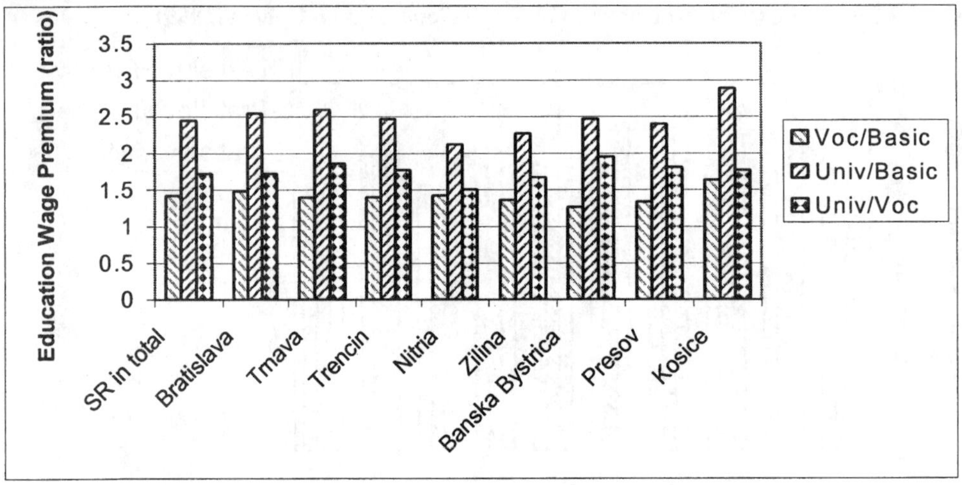

Source: Source: Statistical Office of SR, as reported in Haulikova and Benc (2001).

FDI Flows and the Investment Climate

As documented earlier in this Report (see Chapter 2), FDI flows have mainly gone to Bratislava and the better-off regions. Bratislava alone has received close to two-thirds of all cumulative foreign investment flows (excluding FDI in the banking sector, all of which has been directed into Bratislava, as the financial center). The region's more advantageous location, better qualified workforce, and proximity to Government institutions have all been cited as major factors influencing the regional allocation of FDI. However, there have been a few major recent investments in the poorer regions—such as American textile firm Molex, which has invested in Kosice; Matsushita in the Spissky district, Whirlpool in Poprad and Volkswagen in the central district of Martin—which give some reason for optimism. The share of FDI flowing to poorer Kosice and Presov has, in fact, increased very significantly starting in 1998 when U.S. Steel made some major investments into the metallurgy sector. There is a widespread perception throughout Slovak Republic, and among policymakers that such FDI flows can be critical to reducing regional differentials—by bringing in new technology and know-how, helping create jobs, and contributing over the long run to raising labor productivity and incomes in these lagging areas.

Table 5.11 Regional Allocation of FDI (excl. banking)

Corporations	Dec. 1996	Dec. 1997	Dec. 1998	Dec. 1999	Sep. 2000
Total SR (mil. SKK)	*38,424*	*44,606*	*62,249*	*77,845*	*128,553*
of which in %					
Bratislava	59.5	60.0	53.2	54.0	66.4
Trnava, Trenčín, Nitria	21.9	22.2	21.8	22.9	15.3
Žilina, Banska Bystrica	11.7	11.5	10.5	9.3	6.4
Prešov, Košice	6.8	6.2	14.5	13.7	11.9

Source: National Bank of Slovak Republic, Monetary Survey 2000.

There appears to be a strong positive correlation between FDI flows and lower regional unemployment (see Figure 5.4), and between the regional distribution of FDI flows and the distribution of private enterprises. Bratislava, with the bulk of FDI inflows, also concentrates over 30 percent of all private firms in the country, and an even larger share of large enterprises.

Unemployment

Large and persistent regional differences in unemployment rates across regions are a major factor behind regional differences in poverty rates and incomes. Given the documented strong link between unemployment and the risk of poverty, it is not surprising that the regions with highest unemployment are also those with the largest share of the population living below the Minimum Living Standard. Evidence suggests that, if anything, regional differences in unemployment rates have gotten bigger over time.

Regions with high unemployment rates (Kosice, Presov, Banska Bystrica, and to a lesser extent Nitria) have evidenced higher inflows into unemployment (higher job destruction) but also much lower outflows from unemployment. Job creation is particularly poor in these areas (Figure 5.11), and hence, once unemployed, individuals in those regions are much less likely to find a job than workers in regions with lower unemployment. Exit rates into employment—measured using individual level data from the Unemployment Registry and the labor force survey—are especially low in Kosice, Presov and Banska Bystrica (see Sanchez-Paramo, 2001 in Volume II). Not surprisingly, long-term unemployment is a much more serious problem in those regions than elsewhere. In Kosice and Presov, for example, nearly 50 percent of the unemployed have been so for over a year; and over a quarter have been unemployed for over two years. The corresponding shares for Bratislava are 21 percent and 7,2 percent; for Trencin (another relatively low unemployment region) they are 31 percent and 12 percent.

Figure 5.11 New Job Postings and Unemployment, 2000

There are also very large differences in unemployment rates within regions, i.e., between districts of the same region. The highest levels of unemployment are recorded in some of the districts of Eastern and Southern Slovakia. Among the most affected districts, with unemployment reaching 30 percent and more, are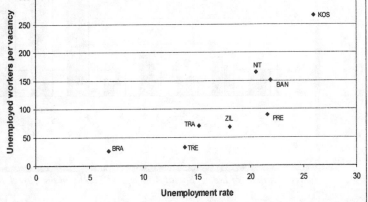

Rimavska Sobota, Velky Krtis, Revuca, Kezmarok, Stropkov, Vranov nad Toplou, Gelnica, Michalovce, Roznava, Sobrance, Trebisov. These districts also evidence the highest levels of poverty (Chapter 1). They all share certain common features: a significant deficit of industrial production, decreasing share of previously important agricultural production, low inflows of FDI, lower levels of attained education, lack of job opportunities, low incomes, weak infrastructure, and also a high share of Roma population.

That there is a connection between the share of the region's (or district's) population that is Roma and regional poverty (and unemployment) outcomes is not surprising, given the high risk of poverty observed for Roma families (see Chapters 1 and 4). Low educational status, high unemployment, a high number of children, low female labor force participation, and the impact of discrimination, all work to increase the risk of poverty for this group (Chapter 4). Of particular importance is their precarious labor market status, with unemployment rates among the non-integrated Roma population well into the double digits. Some of the most disadvantaged Roma settlements in Eastern and Southern Slovakia report unemployment rates which are as high as 100 percent (Chapter 4).

Figure 5.12 shows the share of unemployed Roma in the total number of unemployed by Region. It is clear from the table that they account for a large share of the total unemployed in all three regions with high unemployment (Kosice, Presov, and Banska Bystrica). They also comprise a very large share of all the unskilled unemployed. According to NLO data on registered unemployment data from June 1999, the Roma—who represent by the highest estimates some 10 percent of the population, and a smaller fraction of the labor force—accounted for some 41 percent of all the unemployed with only primary education; and for 83 percent of those with no completed formal education.

Figure 5.12 Shares of Unemployed Roma in the Total Number of Unemployed (%)

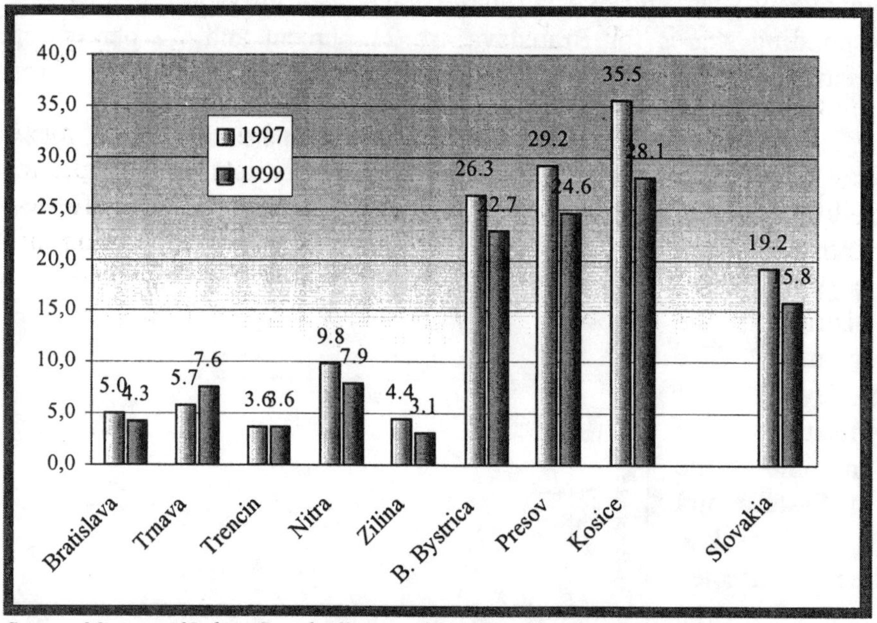

Source: Ministry of Labor, Social Affairs, and Family of the Slovak Republic.

156

Reliance on the Social Safety Net

The poorer regions of the Slovak Republic are characterized by a much higher reliance on the social support mechanisms provided by the state. As discussed earlier in this Report, such mechanisms have played a fundamental role in protecting large parts of the population from falling into poverty. However, they may have also had some negative impact on job search behavior and encouraged welfare dependency, especially among low-skilled and low-wage workers. Given higher unemployment rates, a greater incidence of long-term unemployment, less educated work forces and lower overall wages and job opportunities, these dependency problems are likely to be more acute in Eastern and Southern Slovakia than in other regions. Indeed, the analysis carried out in Sanchez-Paramo (2001), presented in Volume II of this study, shows strongly negative "regional" effects on exit from unemployment for the Kosice, Presov and Banska Bystrica regions.

The largest number of recipients of social benefit, as of December 1999, was recorded for the Kosice region. That included 17.6 percent of the region's total population and 23 percent of the total numbers of recipients of social assistance benefits in Slovak Republic.[84] The Region of Presov had corresponding numbers of 16 percent and 21 percent respectively. The Region of Bratislava recorded the lowest numbers of 2.1 percent and 2.2 percent (Table 5.12). Among the districts with proportion of social benefit recipients exceeding 20 percent we find those most affected by high unemployment rates, often combined with a significant concentration of the Roma population. (Table 5.13)

Table 5.12 Share of Social Assistance Benefits Recipients (including dependents) in Total Regional Population (%)

Region	1997	1999
Bratislavsky	1.51	2.1
Trnavsky	5.34	7.5
Trenciansky	3.61	6.8
Nitriansky	7.63	10.6
Zilinsky	5.32	9.3
Banskobystricky	9.43	13.5
Presovsky	10.57	15.9
Kosicky	12.62	17.6

Source: Report on Social Situation, MLSA (1999, 1997).

[84] Figures include dependent persons on recipients of social assistance benefits (until 1998, social care benefits).

Table 5.13 Ranking of Selected Districts by Recipients of Social Assistance Benefits (as of Dec. 1999)

Rank	District	SAB recipients in total (persons)	SAB recipients (including dependent persons)	Share of SAB recipients (incl. depend. Persons) on total district population (%)
1	R. Sobota	9 587	21 666	26.3
2	Revuca	4 666	10 414	25.5
3	Trebisov	11 364	25 179	24.6
4	Kezmarok	5 367	14 745	23.9
5	Roznava	6 763	14 547	23.6
6	Sabinov	4 419	11 714	22.2
7	Gelnica	2 670	6 524	21.6
8	Spisska N. Ves	7 644	19 116	21.0
9	V.n. Toplou	6 324	15 307	20.3
.....				
72	Trencin	2 574	3 632	3.2
73	Senec	809	1 327	2.6
74	Pezinok	865	1 275	2.4
75	Bratislava I	542	771	1.7
76	Bratislava V	1 482	2 068	1.6
77	Bratislava II	1 152	1 625	1.4
78	Bratislava III	513	837	1.3
79	Bratislava IV	795	1 108	1.1

Source: Report on Social Situation. (1999).

Political/Sociological Map

A recent sociological study on values offers some interesting insights on regional attitudes towards markets, liberal democracy and other cultural factors which may affect the local population's attitude towards economic reform and pro-market changes, as well as the attractiveness of a locality to domestic and foreign investors.[85] The author put together groups of questions, which express respondents' acceptance of authoritarian behavior, disrespect for minorities, aversion to "Western" culture, and attitudes towards paternalism and inequality. Detailed results of this survey are presented in Haulikova and Benc (2001). Here we just summarize some of the main conclusions.

- Poorer and more rural districts have a higher tolerance for authoritarian behavior, and tend to view "Western" culture—associated with markets, integration into the EU and NATO—with suspicion. The highest levels of aversion to "Western" culture and greater tolerance for authoritarianism were found in rural districts of Trencin, Zilina, Banska Bystrica and parts

---

[85] Krivý, V.: *Value Orientation in Slovakia—Group Portraits.* Bratislava: Institute for Public Affairs, 1998.

of Presov. Politically, these districts had high voter support for the HZDS party (Movement for a Democratic Slovak Republic) in the 1998 parliamentary elections. They are less likely to be open to foreign investors, and less supportive overall of economic reforms;

- The highest levels of support and tolerance for minority rights were found in districts with a large Hungarian population. The districts of Northern Slovakia, on the contrary evidenced little tolerance for minority rights and high levels of discrimination. In these districts, the dominant political force in the 1998 elections was the nationalist party (SNS). The exception was some districts in Presov, where there is very little tolerance for minorities but where the SNS won a very low proportion of votes. In general, discriminatory attitudes were widespread throughout the country;

- Throughout the country, repondents evidenced little tolerance for inequality, probably an inheritance of the previous regime. Only the two biggest cities—Bratislava and Kosice—evidenced some degree of comfort with the observed trends towards more inequality in income and wages; and

- Another interresting finding was widespread scepticism, or disrespect, for the rule of law, and widespread tolerance for non-civic behavior. These attitudes were the least prevalent in Bratislava and Kosice, but common elsewhere.

CONCLUSIONS AND POLICY RECOMMENDATIONS

The above discussion has examined regional differences in the SR along a diversity of fronts, with a special focus on differences in critical social outcomes such as poverty and unemployment at the regional level. The analysis is somewhat limited by the lack of data on many critical dimensions, including reliable data series on regional income per capita. However, the analysis does suggest several interesting conclusions:

- The poorer regions (mainly Eastern and Southern Slovakia) have overall less favorable endowments: younger populations (which could, however, be an asset if all were gainfully employed); lower levels of education of their work forces (lower human capital stock); worse health status; and lower-quality infrastructure (especially roads) which makes production in these regions relatively less attractive and more expensive;

- Poorer regions exhibit much lower labor productivity than richer regions, but the difference in productivity exceeds that in labor costs, rendering labor in the poorer parts of the country expensive in relative terms. A main cause of this problem appears to be high indirect labor costs, which disproportionately affect less-skilled and lower-paid labor;

- Poorer regions have also inherited a less favorable structure of production, with a heavier reliance on agriculture and heavy manufacturing, both of which have gone through massive adjustment. Transition has required

159

greater restructuring in these regions and been more costly in social terms than in the Western parts of the country;

- The poorer regions of Eastern and Southern Slovakia suffer much higher unemployment than the better-off regions, and especially face much more long-term unemployment. Vacancy to unemployment ratios are worse, job creation is lower, and individuals exhibit much lower probability of escaping from unemployment into jobs. Partly as a result, these regions show much greater depedency on social assistance and support payments, and may face a greater problem of disincentives to finding work and welfare dependency; and

- Poorer regions also have benefitted less from FDI, which has worked to accentuate productivity differentials between west and east parts of Slovak Republic. In addition, they seem to have overall less attractive business environments and less dynamic private sectors. The attitude of the population in some of the poorer regions (e.g., Presov) is more suspicious and less supportive of markets and economic reform, possibly less open to foreign investors, and politically more supportive of anti-reform parties.

These conclusions, in turn, point towards several important policy recommendations that can help, over time, reduce the gaps between richer and poorer regions. The key issue is clearly improving productivity growth and generating income-earning opportunities in the lagging regions. The difficult question is how to do this.

Investment in education is of primary importance in both the short and long term, as it is key to raising labor productivity and incomes. It also rends people more flexible and more adaptable to changing economic conditions. Efforts are needed on two fronts: reform of the existing education system to render future graduates more employable and productive; and facilitating the training and acquisition of skills by workers already in the labor force. However, education on its own is unlikely to be enough, unless there are accompanying measures aimed at stimulating the demand for labor. An example of education not being enough is Kosice, where a fairly highly educated and young workforce suffers from high unemployment.

Poorer regions clearly face a problem with low labor productivity relative to labor costs. Efforts to increase labor productivity should thus receive a high priority. Attracting foreign direct investment flows that can bring in new production and management techniques, as well as technology and know-how can prove crucial in this regard. But it is also important to ensure that there is good quality infrastructure—human and physical—to support production. Improving roads and transport networks has been identified as a high priority. But communications networks and ensuring access to internet and information services are also going to be important. Efficient provision of public services, and a transparent and effective local administration will also contribute to improving productivity and growth opportunities at the regional level.

Over time, investments in education, FDI and technology will all work to raise productivity, and help lagging regions catch up. However, improving labor productivity will take time. In the short term, measures have to focus on bringing down the cost of labor in the lagging regions to entice firms and investors to locate here. One way to do this is to reduce non-wage labor costs significantly (reduce the payroll tax). It is also important to look for ways to allow labor costs to differ more significantly across the country so as to reflect productivity differentials. Nationwide agreements on wages may be setting the wage floor too high for firms in some of these regions. A move towards broader negotiated wage brackets, or towards agreements that allow enterprises to adjust more easily to local conditions could do much in terms of rendering wage setting more flexible.

There may be a need to consider special programs of assistance to SMEs and new private firms in the poor regions, focusing on improving productivity and efficiency at the firm level Such programs can involve some degree of cost-sharing by the public sector in the beginning, and can focus on providing assistance by brokering training services, certification and quality control services, and export support services. A number of middle income countries, including Mexico and Colombia, have had very successful experiences with such programs.

Improving the business environment will also require greater credibility and uniformity in the application and enforcement of business legislation, regulations and corporate taxation. Nationwide measures to lower licensing and administrative requirements for SMEs, as well as measures to simplify taxation for this group of enterprises can also be especially helpful in the poorer regions.

In addition, there are a number of nationwide, systemic measures that are needed to help underpin growth and employment generation throughout the Slovak Republic, and in the poor regions most of all. These were mentioned in Chapter 2 and involve: consolidating macroeconomic stability and building credibility in economic policy and vis-à-vis foreign investors; strengthening and restructuring the financial sector to ensure that credit is available (and flows) to the more dynamic private firms; improving governance and transparency, and creating a more favorable environment for new private enterprises; reducing the tax burden on labor, especially the payroll tax (but possibly also considering reductions in direct income taxation as well); and reforming social support systems so as to reduce disincentive effects on work.

REFERENCES

De la Rocha, M. 2001. "Corporate Sector and SME Environment in the Slovak Republic". Background Paper for the World Bank, "Slovak Republic: Living Standards, Employment and Labor Market Study."

Steele, Diane. 2001. "A Snapshot of Poverty and Living Conditions in the Slovak Republic." Paper 1, Volume II, "Slovak Republic: Poverty, Employment and Labor Market Study," Report N. XXXX, World Bank. Washington DC.

ERRATA SHEET

Chile's High Growth Economy: Poverty and Income Distribution   SN15108

The Abstract on page v should be replaced with the following.

Abstract

Chile remains one of the outstanding countries in Latin America in terms of its record in reducing poverty. A combination of strong growth and well directed social programs have combined to reduce the poverty rate in half during a period of just eleven years. This study shows that previously noted trends in falling poverty, in terms of incidence, depth and severity, continued into 1998. As a result, only 17% of the population now lives in poverty (compared to 40% in 1987), while those living in extreme poverty are barely 4% of the population. In terms of social indicators, there has also been substantial progress in indicators of education, health and access to water and housing services. Few families have major social deficits.

In terms of income inequality, the report finds that the situation appears to have substantially worsened between 1994 and 1998, with most of the deterioration happening during 1994-96. Within these four years there has been an increase in the dispersion within both the top and the bottom of the income distribution; while the bottom decile increased its real income by 15%, the real income of the top decile grew by 31%.

This study develops and applies a methodology for the estimate of the imputed income transfers from government subsidies in health, education, and housing, for the years 1990, 1994, 1996 and 1998. The analysis has confirmed that adjustments for in-kind income transfers substantially reduce the Gini coefficient on income inequality. For 1998, this coefficient falls from 0.56 (unadjusted) to 0.50 (adjusted) and the ratio of the highest (richest) to the lowest (poorest) quintile falls from 20 to 11.

The analysis concludes that the impact of social policies was more significant in 1998 than in 1990. This resulted primarily from the significant increases in the budget allocation to such programs between 1990 and 1998, rather than from better targeting or lower delivery costs. Expressed in 1998 pesos, the subsidy component of social programs increased from $4,486 per capita in 1990 to $10,225 per capita in 1998.

Chile's success in reducing income disparities through social spending is linked to its system for targeting social programs, the *ficha* CAS. This system for proxy means testing provides a cheap and relatively easy mechanism for determining eligibility, which is consistent across programs. It appears that targeted programs such as family allowances, pensions, water and housing subsidies and child care programs help reduce the overall Gini concentration of household incomes. Nevertheless, the coverage of these programs among the poor is far from universal, and substantial amounts go to non-poor households. Part of the problem appears to be that poor families are often unaware of their eligibility for certain programs, although the level of awareness vary between programs.

Unemployment is a severe problem for younger and poorer workers. Overall, unemployment rates have generally averaged about 6-8% of the labor force, although in recent years there has been some acceleration in this rate. Unemployment among the poorest has been much higher. In general, women tend to have lower unemployment rates at all income quintiles.

Chileans of indigenous origin represent a special group of concern, because of their chronic high rates of poverty. Evidence shows that indigenous people are 56% more likely to be in poverty, and receive half the income of non-indigenous people, and have 2.2 years less schooling. Overtime, indigenous people have become increasingly urban, with 80% now living in urban areas. A number of Government programs have been put in place to assist indigenous people, and greater protection now exists for the land and water rights of the rural indigenous. However, tensions between indigenous groups and the Government continue. Part of the problem has been the weakness of indigenous organizations, and a lack of coordination between groups.